O
TH   ...OW PRESS, INC.

The A to Z of
Jehovah's Witnesses

George D. Chryssides

The A to Z Guide Series, No. 104

The Scarecrow Press, Inc.
Lanham • Toronto • Plymouth, UK
2009

Published by Scarecrow Press, Inc.
A wholly owned subsidiary of
The Rowman & Littlefield Publishing Group, Inc.
4501 Forbes Boulevard, Suite 200, Lanham, Maryland 20706
http://www.scarecrowpress.com

Estover Road, Plymouth PL6 7PY, United Kingdom

British Library Cataloguing in Publication Information Available

Library of Congress Cataloging-in-Publication Data

The hardback version of this book was cataloged by the Library of Congress as
follows:

Chryssides, George D., 1945–
    Historical dictionary of Jehovah's Witnesses / George D. Chryssides.
        p. cm. — (Historical dictionaries of religions, philosophies, and movements ;
    no. 85)
    Includes bibliographical references.
    1. Jehovah's Witnesses—Dictionaries. 2. Jehovah's Witnesses—History—
Dictionaries. I. Title.
    BX8526.C48 2008
    289.9'203—dc22   2008004305

ISBN 978-0-8108-6891-5 (pbk. : alk. paper)
ISBN 978-0-8108-7054-3 (ebook)

Printed in the United States of America

To Bill and June Thompstone

and their family,

who made this book possible

Contents

Editor's Foreword

How does one go about presenting the Jehovah's Witnesses? It can be done with a string of negatives, namely, that the group disagrees with all mainstream Christian religions, starting with their translation of the Bible and continuing with their understanding of much of what it says. The religion rejects smoking, gambling, and premarital sex; refuses blood transfusions; and more broadly disapproves of politics and secular government. But it is surely not the negatives that have attracted so many members—members who come not only for their own private concerns, but more universal ones, and who engage in evangelization even at a cost to their own careers and pocketbooks, so there must be more to it. And there should be a place to discover just what this is, because no other denomination has aroused as much controversy or created as many enemies, as can easily be seen by searching the Internet.

The A to Z of Jehovah's Witnesses is certainly not the last word on the topic, but it will be a useful first word since it provides a helpful background on which to base one's opinions. The chronology is a good starting point, since it traces the major events and notes the most significant leaders of a group working on a century-and-a-half of existence—not much compared to other religions but much more than its detractors would ever have expected. The introduction provides a broad survey of the denomination's history and leaders, precepts and principles, and organizations and publications and concludes with information on its present situation. The dictionary gives further details on all aspects—details that are extremely important in escaping more facile interpretations thereof. Unlike most other volumes in this series, this book starts with a sequence of numbers and dates, all of which are crucial in understanding what essentially remains a millennialist movement with hopes that lie more with the future kingdom than the present world. The bibliography includes both the official views of the Watch Tower organization and those of its critics and also some academics.

This dictionary is written by George D. Chryssides, head of religious studies at the University of Wolverhampton in England. His specialization is new and minority religious movements, which he has been studying for some two decades and on which he has lectured at several universities and written quite extensively in academic journals. He has also written and coauthored seven books, one of them *Historical Dictionary of New Religious Movements*. Among the new religious movements, he has a particular interest in Sun Myung Moon and Unificationism and now the considerably older but equally controversial Jehovah's Witnesses. It was not easy for him to gather the information included here, but he brings together a comprehensive work with material presented in an objective and straightforward manner, leaving any interpretation or conclusions to the reader.

Jon Woronoff
Series Editor

Preface

A history of the Jehovah's Witnesses, first and foremost, has to be a genuine history. While this may be to state the obvious, academic authors in the field of new religious movements find themselves under constant pressure to take on other agendas. Because of the Watch Tower organization's controversial nature, there can be expectations that one should comment substantially on incidents that have attracted negative media publicity, their alleged "failed prophecies" and revised dates, or controversial practices, like opposition to blood transfusion. In the late stages of this book's compilation, a colleague—no doubt with the best of intentions—passed me a scurrilous newspaper report about a Witness who was accused of child neglect and suggested that this was "just in time for inclusion."

One defining characteristic of a historical event is that it is something significant, in the sense of making an impact on and influencing subsequent events. In this case, the impact can be either on the Watch Tower organization itself or on society more widely. Historical events, too, are not isolated incidents but require placement in a wider context. The issue of blood, for example, must be considered in the context of the development of medical science and events during World War II, coupled with the Watch Tower Bible and Tract Society's understanding of scripture and in particular the appropriate attitude to Jewish law.

There are few independent studies of Jehovah's Witnesses, that is, studies that are not written by the Watch Tower organization itself but by former members or countercult critics. The vast bulk of existing literature consists of attempts at rebutting the organization's doctrines, targeting their understanding of the Bible, and in particular concentrating on their views on the end-times, in which they believe humanity to be living. It is difficult to see why such literature continues to proliferate, since it rarely, if ever, adds to one's understanding of Watch Tower doctrine. The frequent accusation against the Witnesses is that they have set successive dates for the world's end, only to find that their expectations were unfulfilled. This assumption is probably fuelled by the evangelical Protestant belief in Christ's Second Coming—sometimes called the Rapture—which is believed to be a single, unique, and imminent event in the future. While it is undoubtedly true that Jehovah's Witnesses have experienced failed expectations at times, their eschatology can only be truly understood in historical terms, as a development of Adventist ideas that were rife at the movement's inception. The key dates that Watch Tower leaders have referred to do not relate to one single event ("the end of the world") but to various elements of a complex end-time calendar: Christ's second presence, his entry into his heavenly kingdom, the end of a "harvesting period," the end of the Gentile times, the return of the Old Testament patriarchs, the end of the sixth millennium, and the beginning of Armageddon. Such events have sometimes been viewed as distinct and sometimes regarded as identical. At times the date of one end-time event has been reassigned to another; at other periods events get dropped from this end-time calendar. Some dates have been given prospectively, but others are retrospective and hence not "prophetic" in the popular sense of the term. It is therefore simplistic and naïve to view the Witnesses as a group that continues to set a single end-date that fails and then devise a new one, as many counter-cultists do.

Although I have attempted to address issues of doctrinal as well as organizational developments, the nature of *The A to Z of Jehovah's Witnesses* prevents detailed examination of the fascinating developments in Adventist doctrine, but readers who wish to explore these issues further can be referred to Robert Crompton's meticulous analysis in *Counting the Days to Armageddon: Jehovah's Witnesses and the Second Presence of Christ* (1996).

What to include and what to leave out is a difficult decision for a compiler of any reference work. Decisions about individuals who merit inclusion have been particularly problematic since the Watch Tower Bible and Tract Society tends to take the stance that God should be given the credit for much of its work rather than human individuals; and therefore, the society is inclined to withhold the names of those responsible for significant achievements, like the New World Translation of scripture. At times, a *Watchtower* magazine will run a feature on a well-known leader or even allow such a person to write a brief autobiography, thus providing information that is not available elsewhere. In other cases, one can discover little more than when a leader was elected to an office and the dates on which he or she was scheduled to address gatherings. Inclusion has therefore been influenced by the availability and quality of information, as well as by the contribution he or she made to the work of the society.

There is often the expectation that authors of books on controversial religious groups should adopt a viewpoint and make judgments on their teachings and practices. However, the scholar is not so much interested in religious truth but in understanding what lies behind the truth. Judgments are needed about competing claims regarding the organization's history. Critics often allege that the Jehovah's Witnesses "rewrite history," and of course care has been taken to consult as comprehensive a range of sources as possible. However, *Watchtower* source material remains invaluable; not only is it primary source material, extending from 1877 to the present day, but it meticulously documents key events and teachings. Most of the information is available electronically and is therefore searchable, thus permitting a thoroughness of research that would not have been possible even a decade ago.

This book would not have been possible, at least in its present form, without the help and cooperation of *Watchtower* staff, both in England and Brooklyn, New York. There are always those who believe that cooperation from controversial groups comes with strings attached and that they expect to be portrayed in the best possible light. On the contrary, one Brooklyn researcher, when offering to read a draft of my manuscript, explicitly stated that she did not want my writing to be compromised in any way by such an offer. The quality of a piece of writing, however, should not be judged by speculating about ulterior motives of the researcher. I have sought to produce a work that is neither anticultist nor apologetic, and its integrity stands or falls on the content itself.

Acknowledgments

The A to Z of Jehovah's Witnesses is the result of several years of research on the Jehovah's Witnesses. It started as part of an undergraduate unit of study on new religious movements. I am grateful to past students, whose questions often stimulated further research on the Watch Tower Organization, and to colleagues who have listened to numerous conference presentations on various aspects of the Watch Tower Society's beliefs and practices.

I am very grateful to have experienced the help of the Watch Tower Organization, whose cooperation has been invaluable. Thanks are due to office bearers at the British Branch for providing me with continually updated versions of the society's searchable CD-ROM, containing nearly all *Watchtower* material from 1950 to the present, and which is normally only distributed to active Jehovah's Witnesses. I am particularly grateful to Jolene Chu and James Pellechia at the Brooklyn headquarters in New York, for their advice, for their detailed scrutiny of the text, and for making many valuable suggestions. I first met Bill Thompstone, City Overseer for Walsall, England, when he came to the University of Wolverhampton and agreed to talk as an informant to my students. This marked the beginning of a long relationship, in which the Thompstone family fielded innumerable questions, both from me and from my students, and it is appropriate that the book is dedicated to Bill and his wife, June.

My wife, Margaret, has been subjected to much of the material in the form of conversation, has scrutinized various drafts of the manuscript, and has accompanied me to numerous events pertaining to the Jehovah's Witnesses.

Finally, thanks are due to Jon Woronoff, the series editor, for patiently awaiting a much-delayed manuscript and for making valuable editorial suggestions.

Acronyms and Abbreviations

B.C.E.	before the Common Era
CD	compact disc
C.E.	Common Era
D.C.	District of Columbia
GA	*Golden Age*
IBSA	International Bible Students Association
IUD	intrauterine device
KJV	King James Version
NWT	New World Translation
PBI	Pastoral Bible Institute
P.O.	presiding overseer
SA	Sturmabteilung
SS	Schutzstaffel
TMS	Theocratic Ministry School
UFO	unidentified flying object
UN	United Nations
U.S.	United States
WBBR	code name for Watchtower radio station
WT	*Watch Tower/Watchtower*
WTBTS	Watch Tower (or Watchtower) Bible and Tract Society
YMCA	Young Men's Christian Association
ZG	special edition of *Zion's Watch Tower*, published on 1 March 1918, reproducing the text of *The Finished Mystery*
ZWT	*Zion's Watch Tower*

Chronology

BIBLICAL DATES

These dates are the ones designated by the Jehovah's Witnesses. Some are contested by historians or other religious organizations.

4026 B.C.E.   Adam is created.

2370 B.C.E.   The Great Flood occurs.

1513 B.C.E.   The Israelites escape from Egypt.

607 B.C.E.   Babylonian captivity begins.

537 B.C.E.   The remnant returns from Babylonian captivity.

2 B.C.E.   Jesus is born.

29 C.E.   Jesus' ministry begins.

33 C.E.   Jesus dies.

70 C.E.   Jerusalem is destroyed.

MODERN DATES

1844   22 October: In the "Great Disappointment," William Miller's prophecies fail to materialize.

1870   Charles T. Russell begins his Bible study group in Allegheny, Pennsylvania.

1876   Charles T. Russell is elected pastor of the Bible Study Group in Allegheny, Pennsylvania.

1877 *Three Worlds and the Harvest of This World* is jointly published by C. T. Russell and Nelson Barbour.

1879 C. T. Russell and Nelson Barbour split. The first issue of *Zion's Watch Tower and Herald of Christ's Presence* is published.

1881 **16 February:** Zion's Watch Tower Tract Society is organized. Tract distribution commences.

1884 Zion's Watch Tower Tract Society becomes legally incorporated in Pennsylvania.

1886 C. T. Russell's *Divine Plan of the Ages*, volume one of *Millennial Dawn*, is published.

1889 "Bible House" is constructed as the Zion's Watch Tower Tract Society's headquarters in Allegheny, Pennsylvania.

1891 C. T. Russell undertakes a tour of Europe. The first convention is held in Allegheny, Pennsylvania.

1893 The first major convention is held in Chiacgo, with 360 attendees and 70 baptisms.

1896 Zion's Watch Tower Tract Society is legally renamed the Watch Tower Bible and Tract Society of Pennsylvania.

1900 **23 April:** The first branch office opens in London, England, which is the first foreign office to be established.

1902 First office in Germany opens in Elberfeld.

1904 C. T. Russell completes the sixth volume of *Millennial Dawn*. The first office is established in Melbourne, Australia.

1909 The Watch Tower Bible and Tract Society relocates its headquarters to Brooklyn, New York.

1912 C. T. Russell travels to Honolulu, Hawaii, and Hong Kong.

1914 *Photo-Drama of Creation* is screened for the first time. C. T. Russell announces the end of the Gentile times.

1916 The first blood depot is established by the British for wounded soldiers. **31 October:** C. T. Russell dies.

1917 The Bolshevik Revolution, led by Vladimir Ilych Lenin and Leon Trotsky, occurs. **6 January:** J. F. Rutherford is appointed as C. T. Russell's successor. **2 November:** Balfour Declaration is issued, in which the British government declares support for the return of the Jews to Palestine. *The Finished Mystery* is published. P. S. L. Johnson and his supporters split from the Watch Tower organization.

1918 **12 December:** The League of Nations is endorsed by the Federal Council of Churches of Christ in the U.S.A. **24 March:** J. F. Rutherford's gives the lecture *Millions Now Living May Never Die*. Rutherford and other Watch Tower leaders are imprisoned in Atlanta's penitentiary.

1919 The League of Nations is formed. J. F. Rutherford and other leaders are released from prison. The first issue of *The Golden Age*, a precursor of the periodical *Awake!*, is published. House-to-house work begins. Congregations register as service organizations. The Watch Tower Bible and Tract Society henceforth "theocratically" appoints a "director" to each organization. The anointed class begins to assume their places in heaven.

1920 *Zion's Watch Tower* is renamed *The Watch Tower*. All witness work begins to be recorded in weekly reports. *Millions Now Living Will Never Die!*, by J. F. Rutherford, is published. The Brooklyn Bethel opens in New York.

1922 A convention is held in Cedar Point, Ohio. J. F. Rutherford announces the "Advertise the King and the Kingdom" program.

1924 **24 February:** WBBR, the Watch Tower Bible and Tract Society's radio station, makes its first broadcast.

1925 The date given by J. F. Rutherford for the return of the ancient patriarchs.

1926 The British Red Cross establishes the world's first blood transfusion service. House-to-house ministry commences. **25 December:**

The last Christmas celebration is held at the Brooklyn Bethel in New York.

1927 Adolf Hitler's *Mein Kampf* is published.

1931 The name "Jehovah's Witnesses" is adopted at a convention in Columbus, Ohio.

1932 The system of "elective elders" is abolished.

1933 Adolf Hitler becomes chancellor of Germany. The first concentration camp is completed at Dachau. The Bible Students' Association is banned in various German states. The Berlin-Wilmersdorf Convention adopts the "Declaration of Facts."

1933–1945 Many Jehovah's Witnesses in Germany are imprisoned and sent to concentration camps.

1934 **9 January:** Anna Seifert is incarcerated in the women's concentration camp in Moringen, Germany. It is the first documented case.

1935 **May/June:** J. F. Rutherford identifies the "great crowd" at an assembly in Washington, D.C. Rutherford denounces the practice of saluting the national flag. The First Kingdom Hall is so named in Honolulu, Hawaii.

1936 **June:** The Gestapo sets up a special unit to monitor Jehovah's Witnesses. **August/September:** Mass arrests of Jehovah's Witnesses begin. **4–7 September:** The Lucerne convention of Jehovah's Witnesses is held, where a resolution is passed condemning persecution of members in Germany.

1937 **Fall:** A second wave of mass arrests takes place in Germany. The *Gobitis* case is first brought to court. **20 December:** A declaration is introduced enabling Jehovah's Witnesses to secure freedom as a consequence of apostasy.

1938 The purple triangle is introduced in concentration camps. The system of theocratic government of the Watch Tower Bible and Tract Society is completed.

1939 World War II is declared.

1940 The U.S. Supreme Court rules the flag salute mandatory.

1942 8 January: J. F. Rutherford dies. Nathan H. Knorr is appointed president of the Watch Tower Bible and Tract Society.

1943 The Watchtower Bible School of Gilead opens. The U.S. Supreme Court rules in favor of Jehovah's Witnesses in 20 out of 24 cases.

1944 6 March: In Germany, Dr. Robert Ritter proposes a plan to investigate the racial and genetic ancestry of Jehovah's Witnesses.

1945 The election of the Watch Tower Bible and Tract Society's board of directors is no longer carried out by shareholding voters. The "No blood" policy commences.

1946 *Let God Be True* is published. The periodical *Awake!* replaces *Consolation*. Congregations are grouped into circuits.

1950 2 August: The Watch Tower translation of the Bible, *New World Translation of Christian Greek Scriptures*, is launched at the New York convention.

1955 The "zone" system is introduced.

1959 9 March: The Kingdom Ministry School starts the training of congregation and traveling overseers in South Lansing, New York.

1961 The *New World Translation of the Holy Scripture* (complete Bible) is published in English.

1963 The *New World Translation of Christian Greek Scriptures* is translated in six more languages.

1965 The first Assembly Hall opens in New York.

1971 1 October: The Governing Body is enlarged, with rotating chairmen.

1972 Congregations become governed by bodies of elders, each with rotating chairmen.

1973 Jehovah's Witnesses are instructed to quit smoking.

1975 The Governing Body is reorganized, and six subservient committees are created. Some 6,000 years of human history ends. Expectations of the end of the present system are unfulfilled.

1976 *Watchtower* magazine becomes available in Grade II English Braille.

1977 Nathan H. Knorr dies. Frederick W. Franz becomes president of the Watch Tower Bible and Tract Society.

1980 Organ donations and transplantations are declared to be matters of conscience for Jehovah's Witnesses.

1981 Raymond Franz is disfellowshipped.

1983 Raymond Franz publishes *Crisis of Conscience*. Congregations are reorganized, with presiding overseers replacing rotating chairmen of the body of elders.

1987 **1 October:** Ministerial Training School begins with the first class being held in Coraopolis, Pennsylvania.

1989 Communism falls in Eastern Europe. Three conventions are held in Poland.

1990 Governmental restrictions on Jehovah's Witnesses are lifted in African and Eastern European countries.

1992 Frederick W. Franz dies. Milton G. Henschel becomes president of the Watch Tower Bible and Tract Society.

1993 *Jehovah's Witnesses: Proclaimers of God's Kingdom*, the Watch Tower Bible and Tract Society's history, is published.

1995 Teaching that the "generation" of 1914 will witness Armageddon is formally revised.

1997 The Jehovah's Witness official website goes online.

1999 The third millennium after Jesus' birth commences, but no specific expectations are mentioned.

2000 The Watch Tower Bible and Tract Society is reorganized. Milton G. Henschel stands down as president and is succeeded by Don A. Adams and Max H. Larson.

2002 *Course in Theocratic Ministry* is published.

2003 Milton G. Henschel dies. *Watchtower* magazine becomes available on video and subsequently DVD in American Sign Language.

2004 The Watch Tower printery at the Brooklyn Bethel in New York closes and relocates to Wallkill, New York, with a new production plant. *Watchtower* magazine becomes available on CD.

2006 *Awake!* magazine becomes a monthly publication.

2008 *Watchtower* magazine appears in two different editions, each monthly.

Introduction

PERCEPTIONS AND PRECONCEPTIONS

The Jehovah's Witnesses are typically perceived as "sectarian." The "sect" is typically contrasted with the religion or the Church, which, according to Ernst Troeltsch, is all-embracing and dominates society, whereas the sect is more introverted, promoting its own aims, being indifferent or even hostile to those in society, or more widely, in mainstream religion. Much of the popular literature on Jehovah's Witnesses—particularly that of Protestant evangelical Christianity—highlights their sectarian character, seeking to demonstrate important ways in which they deviate from mainstream Christianity. Most members of the public commonly associate Witnesses with such subversive practices as their refusal to accept blood transfusions or rejection of patriotism expressed by refusal to salute national flags, sing national anthems, or be conscripted for military service. Their persistent house-to-house evangelism, for which they are renowned, displays an excess of zeal in comparison to the level of commitment that is normally expected in conventional Christianity. Reciprocally, Jehovah's Witnesses view all other religion as contrasting with "the truth," with which they are uniquely entrusted. Christianity is particularly viewed as reprehensible, since the early Church possessed this truth and the exclusive means of salvation but fell into error after the death of the early apostles.

In view of this stark contrast between Jehovah's Witnesses and mainstream religion, it is perhaps unsurprising that much of the plethora of literature on the Watch Tower organization is confrontational and designed to persuade them of the error of their beliefs and practices. However, the organization did not set out to be sectarian; indeed, the Second Adventist movement from which it emerged was a current within 19th-century conventional Christianity in the United States. These Adventist groups draw largely on the teachings of William Miller (1782–1849), a Baptist preacher in Vermont, whose study of the Bible led him to believe that Christ's return was imminent and could be expected in 1843. He based this conclusion on Daniel 18:14: "Unto two thousand and three hundred days; then shall the sanctuary be cleansed." A tradition already existed in biblical exegesis for regarding prophetic days as years (the "year-for-a-day" rule), and Miller concluded that the start-date for the calculations was 452 B.C.E., being with the date of Artaxerxes' decree authorizing the rebuilding of Jerusalem after the Babylonian Exile. When the failure of Miller's prediction became apparent, he revisited his calculations and recognized an error: he had incorrectly assumed the existence of a year 0 between 1 B.C.E. and 1 C.E. This observation enabled him to designate 1844 as the world's last year. Miller had not predicted a specific date in 1843 but specified 18 April and subsequently 22 October as likely dates in 1844. When the predicted event did not materialize, most of Miller's followers became disillusioned and left him, and the failed event became known as the Great Disappointment.

Religion is remarkably resilient to failed prophecy, however, and the remaining Millerites found two ways of dealing with the 1844 prediction. One method began with Hiram Edson, who claimed to have experienced a vision one day in a corn field in which God revealed to him that the 1844 date was correct but that it referred to spiritual rather than physical happenings. At that point in time, Christ had entered a new stage in his ministry. He had taken up his rule in heaven and commenced his "investigative judgment"—the task of determining which of the dead were worthy of entering his kingdom. This explanation was accepted by Ellen G. White (née Harmon, 1827–1915), who became the founder-leader of the Seventh-day Adventists. The second solution was further recalculation, and this path was favored by the Second Adventists, or Second Advent Church, some of whose members were associated with C. T. Russell (1852–1916), who was to become the founder-leader of the Watch Tower organization.

C. T. RUSSELL AND THE *WATCH TOWER*

C. T. Russell was born in Allegheny, now part of Pittsburgh, Pennsylvania. Although raised as a Presbyterian, he turned to Congregationalism and subsequently associated with a number of Second Adventists, some of whom survived the Great Disappointment and came to embrace Adventism through being unable to accept the teachings of mainstream Christianity. These included George Storrs (1796–1879) and George Stetson (1814–1879), both of whom had come under the influence of Henry Grew (1781–1862), a Baptist preacher in Hartford, Connecticut, who was vehemently opposed to the slave trade but was also unable to accept three mainstream Christian doctrines: the Trinity, hell-fire, and the immortality of the soul—heresies for which he was dismissed. Both Storrs and Stetson came to be known to Russell. Also worthy of mention is Dwight Moody (1833–1899), a well-known evangelist who emphasized the role of modern Israel in the divine plan. As far as we know, he never met Russell, but Russell writes favorably about him in *Zion's Watch Tower*.

Russell himself was concerned about the three Christian teachings that troubled Grew and found himself unable to accept eternal damnation and the doctrine of predestination that was associated with it in Calvinist forms of Protestantism. He had come to abandon the Christian faith, and for two years he explored oriental religious teachings but failed to find them satisfying. One day in 1869 he was passing a rather drab-looking building, almost by accident, and felt constrained to go in. It was a gathering at which Jonas Wendell (1815–1873), a Second Adventist preacher and an erstwhile follower of Miller, was giving an address. This struck a chord with Russell and marked the commencement of his return to the Christian faith.

Russell began to organize a small group of sympathizers who met together regularly to study the Bible from 1870 until 1875. The group appears to have come to agreement on a number of key theological points. They could not accept that the soul was inherently immortal but regarded immortality as a gift from God, only available to some. They laid great stress on Christ's atonement for sin, in particular emphasizing its function as a "ransom sacrifice" for sin. They also affirmed that, while Christ had come to earth with a physical body "in the flesh," his return would be as an invisible presence. Further, the object of Christ's return was not to destroy the wicked. The group deplored the belief of some Adventists that Christ's return would be accompanied by a burning of the earth, with only the Second Adventists surviving: Christ would come to bless the earth, not to destroy it. It should be noted that the group based its conclusions on the study of the Bible, not on any special divine revelation. In common with the Adventist tradition, the Bible students and subsequent Watch Tower leaders have never claimed special revelations or visions: the Jehovah's Witnesses claim nothing more than can be deduced from the Bible, if it is read with discernment and prayer.

In 1876 Russell received a copy of *The Herald of the Morning*, a journal edited by Nelson H. Barbour (1824–1905), another Millerite who had experienced the Great Disappointment. Barbour accepted the doctrine of the invisible presence but argued that it had already come. Much of Barbour's work was concerned with end-time calculations, expanding on and correcting those of Miller and concluding that Christ's invisible presence commenced in 1874. It should also be noted that, although some of Barbour's material is predictive, this 1874 date is being given retrospectively here. Barbour once wrote that "Prophecy is prewritten history and requires *time* for its fulfillment." However, it sometimes takes hindsight to identify key events, and the claim that the happenings are invisible rules out the possibility of having to deal yet again with failed prophecy.

Impressed by Barbour's writing, Russell contacted him, and they arranged a meeting in Philadelphia. Russell had been more concerned with the nature of the atonement and Christ's ransom for the sins of humankind than in end-time calculations, but he was persuaded by Barbour's end-time chronology, and they decided to work together. Russell was able to provide financial backing for *The Herald of the Morning*, as well as contribute material to it, and the two men worked jointly on a volume entitled *Three Worlds and the Harvest of This World*, which was published in 1877. The "three worlds" were not earth, heaven, and hell but rather the antediluvian world, the present world, and the world to come. The book sets out a detailed chronology for God's plan of redemption, much of which probably owes more to Barbour than to Russell. The central message is that Christ has already returned, having come as a "thief in the night" (1 Thessalonians 5:2). His coming was not in a spectacular "glorified" form but as an invisible "presence," which the authors argue is the correct translation of the Greek word *parousia*, often wrongly rendered as "coming." This Second Presence, which occurred in 1874, would be followed by a "harvesting period" that will end in 1878, when Christ will enter his kingdom with his faithful ones.

Three Worlds and the Harvest of This World divides post-diluvian history in two distinct periods—Jewish and Gentile—the former period extending from the death of Jacob (to whom God gave the name Israel) to the defeat of King Zedekiah by the Babylonian king, Nebuchadnezzar. The Babylonian captivity marks the beginning of "the times of the Gentiles," when the Jews found themselves under foreign rule. This period was due to end, however, and the authors set the date of 1914 for the expected return of the Jews to God's favor. In the same year, Russell published his own work, *The Object and Manner of the Lord's Return*. This was a much shorter and simpler work than *Three Worlds and the Harvest of This World* as it contains no end-time calculations and focuses on Christ's redemption of humanity and his invisible presence.

Russell's relationship with Barbour continued until August 1878, when Barbour published an article in *The Herald* magazine that appeared to deny the ransom theory of atonement. Russell was outraged. Not only did he pen a response, but he ended the relationship and withdrew financial support for the journal. Firmly believing that the ransom theory had to be defended, he decided to produce his own journal, which he called *Zion's Watch Tower and the Herald of God's Presence*. The first edition appeared in July 1879 and was initially published monthly. It had a circulation of no less than 6,000 copies. Tract distribution was also regarded as important, and the pamphlets *Tabernacle Teachings* and *Food for Thinking Christians* were widely distributed. Some of Russell's larger pamphlets were reissued as special supplements to *Zion's Watch Tower*. Russell's key themes were the message that humanity was living in its last days and that Christ's return was imminent. Christ's return, however, was not to destroy the world but to bless it, and as Russell's controversy with Barbour demonstrated, of key importance was the doctrine of Christ's death as the "ransom sacrifice" for sin. It has been suggested that Russell's innovation was the combination of eschatological and soteriological doctrines. His Adventist precursors had either focused on end-time calculations or doctrines of atonement; Russell's originality lay in his bringing the two themes together.

Russell's differences with mainstream Christianity went beyond the doctrines of predestination and eternal damnation. Mainstream Christianity typically taught the immortality of the soul. Russell argued that this was erroneous, since the earliest Christian tradition, as expressed in the Bible, was that of bodily resurrection. Further, he argued, survival after death was not an automatic expectation but something that God had to bestow. Russell's followers therefore set themselves up as rivaling mainstream Christianity, rather than yet another form of Adventism. Indeed, Russell swiftly came to dissociate himself with the Adventists: an early edition of *Zion's Watch Tower* states that "We are neither 'Millerites' nor 'Adventists'" (*ZWT* 1881/10:3). It had been characteristic of Protestantism to regard the Roman Catholic Church as apostate. Russell went further, and in an 1879 edition of *Zion's Watch Tower*, he declared that all other churches, and not merely Rome, constituted the "harlot" to which the Book of Revelation refers.

The following year, 1880, witnessed an expansion in Russell's activities. Russell made plans to visit congregations throughout Pennsylvania and New York. Hitherto they had simply received copies of *Zion's Watch Tower* and perhaps discussed its themes. Tracts were delivered by colporteurs (now called pioneers), 300 of whom existed in 1885. In 1890 Russell began "newspaper gospeling," telegraphing his sermons to newspapers in the United States, Canada, and Europe, to be syndicated. It was reckoned that some of Russell's sermons appeared in as many as 2,000 newspapers.

Russell wanted to consolidate the movement he had started. The increasing circulation of his literature necessitated his own purpose-built premises; until then Russell had relied on commercial firms to print his literature. In 1880, Bible House, a four-story building in Allegheny, was completed, with printing facilities and meeting accommodation, and it became the organization's headquarters. The next stage of institutionalization was legal incorporation. In 1884, Russell formed the Zion's Watch Tower Tract Society, which was incorporated in Pennsylvania as the Watch Tower Bible and Tract Society of Pennsylvania for "the dissemination of Bible Truths in various languages by means of the publication of tracts, pamphlets, papers, and other religious documents." Russell was concerned that his supporters should feel part of a unified movement. This was particularly important for individuals who had decided to break with their mainstream congregations and who lacked a local ecclesia (congregation) for Watch Tower study. In 1886, Russell issued a special invitation for his entire group of supporters to come to Allegheny to participate in the annual Memorial of the Lord's Evening Meal. This event paved the way for the practice, begun in the 1890s and which Jehovah's Witnesses continue, of having conventions (or assemblies). Russell would address the assembled gathering and expound the Bible. One listener describes him thus:

> When on the platform before an audience, he always wore a long black cloak and a white necktie. His voice was not loud, and he would never use a microphone or a loudspeaker, for they had not been invented; yet, somehow his voice always carried to the most distant part of the auditorium. He could hold the attention of a large audience for not just one hour but sometimes two or three hours. He would always begin his lecture with a gentle bow to the audience. While speaking, he did not stand still like a statue, but he was always on the move, gesticulating with his arms and stepping from side to side or from front to back. I never once saw him carry any notes or a manuscript in his hands—only the Bible, which he used very frequently. He spoke from the heart and in a manner that was very convincing. Usually the only article on the platform in those days was a small table with a Bible on it and a pitcher of water and a glass from which the speaker occasionally took a sip of water. (*Proclaimers*: 55)

Russell's six-volume *Millennial Dawn*, later renamed *Studies in the Scriptures*, was published in 1886. The first volume was entitled *The Divine Plan of the Ages*, and it dealt with the three dispensations from Adam to the present time and its millennial hopes. The series reinforced the ideas of Christ's invisible second presence, the "harvesting period" from 1874 to 1878, and 1914 as the end of the Gentile times, with the expectation that the present religious and political systems would come to an end.

In 1891, Russell traveled abroad, visiting Britain, Continental Europe, and part of Russia. This was the first of a number of such tours and served to establish branches in London, England, in 1900 and Germany in 1903, as well as enabling conventions to be held outside the United States. In 1909, the society moved its offices to New York. Two considerations prompted the move: the premises of the Bible House in Allegheny were proving too small, and it was also felt that a more prestigious city would facilitate the circulation of Russell's sermons to the media and his literature to the public. Accordingly, two properties in Brooklyn, New York, were purchased, one of which continues to serve as the society's in Columbia Heights. It was decided to call the building the "Brooklyn Bethel" rather than "Bible House," and the name "Bethel" has subsequently designated Watch Tower Society's premises, providing residential accommodation for those who produce its publications or administer its regional activities. Russell's followers became known as "Bible students." This was an informal designation until 1914, when the name "International Bible Students Association" was adopted for the legally incorporated British branch and subsequently for other national branches.

One particular achievement in propagating Russell's message was his *Photo-Drama of Creation*. This was a presentation, initially shown in January 1914 to an audience of 5,000 Witnesses at The Temple in New York and later at other venues on both sides of the Atlantic, as well as Australasia. The work combined motion and still pictures, telling the story of God's plan for humanity stretching from the time of Adam to the present and beyond. Russell appeared in motion as narrator—a particularly remarkable innovation since there had previously been few successful attempts to combine motion picture with sound.

Russell's later years were marred by a number of controversies. There was some dissent among some of his followers in 1894 and again in 1908 and 1909. The 1894 dissenters felt that Russell's control of the organization was too authoritarian; the latter expressed doctrinal disagreements. Russell experienced matrimonial problems, and the relationship between him and wife became strained, finally leading to a legal separation in 1908. Maria Russell, his wife, had enjoyed a prominent place in Russell's organization, not only as one of the founding directors, at one point as secretary and treasurer, but also as a *Watch Tower* contributor and traveling speaker. *Watch Tower* sources speculate that she may have been influenced by some of the conspirators or possibly suffragettes, but, whether this was so, Russell came to find her unduly domineering and critical with regard to editing the *Watch Tower*. There were also sexual allegations: the Russells had a foster daughter, Rose Ball, who was allegedly the victim of sexual harassment by Russell. Although Maria made allegations to this effect in court, Ball was never called as a witness, and the accusation remains unsubstantiated. Finally, there was the "miracle wheat" scandal. A Virginian farmer reported finding wheat that bore a phenomenal yield. In 1911, J. A. Bohnet, one of the society's directors, wrote to *Zion's Watch Tower*, stating that he had purchased some wheat, and he would sell it at a dollar a pound, donating the proceeds to the society. The Brooklyn newspaper *The Eagle* got hold of the story and accused the society of profiteering. Russell sued for defamation, but lost the case.

The outbreak of World War I in 1914 was probably the greatest factor in attracting public hostility to the Watch Tower organization. On one level, the war provided some confirmation of the end-times, and some of the Bible students expected to be translated into heaven in October of that year. Russell had been on one of his many traveling tours in the United States and had returned to New York from a convention at Saratoga Springs. On the morning of Friday, 2 October, he entered the Bethel's dining room where the staff was already seated, and, instead of his customary "Good morning!" he clapped his hands and announced, "The Gentile times have ended; the kings have had their day." A. H. Macmillan, who recorded this incident, recounts that Russell announced a change of program in the convention and called upon him to give an unscheduled address on Sunday morning. Macmillan, who no doubt thought he had given his last public address the previous Wednesday, elected to speak on Psalm 74:9 — "We see not our signs; there is no more any prophet: neither is there any among us that knoweth how long" — arguing that the "little flock" should not have expected visible events like translation into heaven.

Regarding participation in the conflict, it was not yet the society's official policy to insist that its members refuse to bear arms. However, the Watch Tower's attitude to the war was becoming increasingly negative. A *Watch Tower* article entitled "Christian Duty and the War" (1 September 1915) urged readers not to work for the munitions industry, "except as the money would be absolutely necessary to provide food and shelter for their families and themselves," advocated neutrality and nonparticipation on both sides, and deplored the churches' support for war, arguing that patriotism was not a virtue to be displayed at any cost (261). Such comment paved the way for the much greater hostility against the Bible students under Rutherford's leadership, for Russell did not live to see the conclusion of World War I. On one of his preaching tours, he became seriously ill and was taken aboard his train and advised to return to Brooklyn. He did not survive the journey, dying in Pampa, Texas, on 31 October 1916.

RUTHERFORD BECOMES THE NEW PRESIDENT

Russell's death raised the inevitable issue of the succession of leadership. Affairs proved acrimonious: Marley Cole, a Jehovah's Witness author, describes it as a "wholesale fight for supremacy within the Board of Directors." This power struggle was not so much about who the new president should be, as about the society's methods of operation, who was entitled to a place on the Board of Directors, and whether authority primarily resided with the board or the president. Immediately following Russell's death, an interim Executive Committee was set up, drawn from the Board of Directors, consisting of A. I. Ritchie, who was then vice president; W. E. Van Amburgh, who was secretary-treasurer; and J. F. Rutherford, who was appointed as legal adviser to the committee. As legal adviser, Rutherford expressed disquiet with the way the society's affairs had been run under Russell's leadership. The society's Charter of 1884 named seven directors who were granted the authority to fill vacancies arising within their ranks. Once elected, a board member held office for life. At the society's annual general meeting, shareholders were entitled to elect the office bearers (president, vice president, and secretary-treasurer) to the board on a yearly basis. A share could be purchased for 10 dollars, and there was no limit to the number of shares any individual could hold.

Rutherford's legal opinion was that, whatever the Charter stated, this method of operation was in conflict with Pennsylvanian state law, which he argued did not permit directors to remain in office in perpetuity. Since state law had precedence over any company's charter, the society was under a legal obligation to elect its board annually and not merely the office bearers. No such elections had taken place for 20 years and were long overdue. Elections were scheduled for January 1918. Two opposing factions emerged within the board, and Rutherford removed four board members from office, including A. I. Ritchie, Robert H. Hirsh, Isaac F. Hoskins, and J. Dennis Wright, arguing that they were never elected, and replaced them with A. H. Macmillan, W. E. Spill, J. A. Bohnet, and G. H. Fisher. Whether Rutherford acted legally remains a matter of controversy; the matter was never brought to court, and Rutherford's opinion prevailed.

One member wrote to the *Watch Tower*, arguing that the policy of buying votes was unfair and that poorer members should not be excluded from helping to determine the society's affairs. Accordingly, a referendum was organized in which individual ecclesias were invited to take a straw poll of individual members and declare the popularity of the various candidates. Shareholders were asked to bear in mind the referendum results when voting. Rutherford was elected president; Macmillan was appointed vice president; Van Amburgh became secretary-treasurer; and Spill, Pierson (Pierson had been co-opted to the Board to replace Russell after the president's death), Bohnet, and Fisher took their positions on the newly elected board. Rutherford's rise to power may seem surprising. In Russell's last will and testament, he was only mentioned as part of a reserve pool from which the Watch Tower Editorial Board might be drawn. Macmillan had been Russell's personal assistant, and he claimed that Russell had invited him to be his successor but that that he did not wish to assume office, naming Rutherford in his place.

It is also possible that Paul S. L. Johnson had aspirations to lead the organization. Russell had sent him to England in 1916 to assess the London branch's progress and assist in its running. Suspecting that a plot was afoot to make the London branch secede from the Watch Tower organization, Johnson dismissed its directors, H. J. Shearn and William Crawford, and attempted to gain control of the branch's finances. When Rutherford, who had by then assumed office, heard of Johnson's activities, he demanded that he be dismissed and return to England. Johnson sent numerous cables to Rutherford, claiming that he was the present-day steward in Jesus' "parable of the penny" (Matthew 20:1–16) and was thus justified in his actions. This was one of several attempts to find antitypical references to himself and his opponents, and some of his colleagues regarded such biblical interpretations as bizarre. After returning to Brooklyn, he continued to oppose Rutherford.

THE FINISHED MYSTERY AND ITS AFTERMATH

Upon his death, Russell left notes for a seventh volume of *Studies in the Scriptures*, a commentary on Ezekiel and Revelation, along with an interpretation of the Song of Solomon. Rutherford sought to have this work completed and assigned Clayton J. Woodworth and George H. Fisher the task. The book, *The Finished Mystery*, was launched on 17 July 1917. A copy was left at everyone's place at the lunch table at the Brooklyn Bethel. The book immediately proved controversial: Johnson initiated a protest, with heated exchanges between his supporters and those of Rutherford lasting for some five hours.

Two issues, it appears, were being debated. First, there was the question of authenticity: to what extent did the completed volume remain true to Russell's intentions? The publication details state that it was written by Russell in 1886, although the Watch Tower Society acknowledges Woodworth's and Fisher's roles in bringing the book to final publication. However, the style is strikingly different from Russell's other writings, being a verse-by-verse commentary on the three biblical books rather than a more discursive piece of prose. Further, unlike the six volumes published during Russell's lifetime, *The Finished Mystery* included a number of cartoons, satirically attacking mainstream Christianity and its clergy. Second, the dissenting members felt that undue consultation had taken place during the book's production, arguing that it was the prerogative of the Watch Tower editorial committee to produce Watch Tower publications, rather than Rutherford acting on his own authority. However, Russell's will specifically referred to the publication of the *Watch Tower* magazine, not to other books and brochures; hence, it is not altogether clear that Rutherford was acting against Russell's wishes.

The Finished Mystery caused even greater controversy outside the Watch Tower Society. On 30 December 1917, *The Bible Students Monthly* magazine ran an article entitled "The Fall of Babylon," which included extracts from *The Finished Mystery*. Ten million copies were printed for wide circulation as a tract. Inside the tract was an advertisement for the book, with a picture depicting a crumbling building with Protestant and Catholic clergy clinging to falling bricks that were variously labeled "Romanism," "Protestantism," "doctrine of the trinity $(3 \times 1 = 1)$," and "eternal torment theory." The clergy were outraged, describing the book as "seditious," and the rumor spread that the book was partially funded by the German government because of its apparent support for conscientious objectors to World War I. Copies of the book were seized by U.S. and Canadian authorities, and on 12 February 1918 it was formally banned in Canada, and in the same month the United States. The Army Intelligence Bureau of New York raided the society's Brooklyn headquarters. The society decided to respond to the seizures by publishing a further article in the second issue of *Kingdom News*. It was entitled "*The Finished Mystery* and Why Suppressed—Clergymen Take a Hand." A petition was also composed, to be sent to President Woodrow Wilson, protesting against interference with their work by the clergy and the state and requesting the lifting of the ban.

On 24 February, Rutherford gave a lecture in Los Angeles, California, which attracted some 3,500 attendees. The event was given considerable coverage in the *Los Angeles Tribune* the following day, prompting the Army Intelligence Bureau to take possession of the Los Angeles headquarters. On 4 March, several Watch Tower leaders were arrested, including Van Amburgh, Macmillan, Woodworth, and Fisher, and, on 14 March, the U.S. Department of Justice ruled that the distribution of *The Finished Mystery* violated the Espionage Act and must therefore cease. Rutherford and the other leaders were tried, and all but one was sentenced to 20 years' imprisonment in Atlanta's penitentiary.

Many in the public were not content to let the law run its course, and the Bible students became subject to many attacks, ranging from lynching to destruction of their premises. So great was public disapprobation of the organization that such incidents continued into the 1920s. Meanwhile, with the ending of World War I, the situation of Rutherford and the other Watch Tower leaders was reviewed, and they were released on bail on 26 March 1919. On 19 May 1919, the Federal Second Circuit Court of Appeals reversed their convictions, and the following year the attorney general ordered that further prosecutions be withdrawn. However, Rutherford and the other leaders had by then spent nine months in prison in a damp cell with few amenities, which had a permanent effect on Rutherford's health, making him prone to a recurring lung disorder.

The opposition of the clergy, combined with the internal schisms within the Watch Tower Society, no doubt contributed to Rutherford's increasing awareness of the need for a corporate identity and the conviction that belonging to the Watch Tower organization was a necessary condition of salvation. This being so, there was a need to promote the society's message—a particularly urgent task in the face of the belief that humanity was living in the last days. Rutherford's strategy was to introduce a uniform system relating to the use and distribution of the society's literature and the method of governance and accountability of individual congregations. Until 1925, the society had in effect been a federation of individual "ecclesias," many of which did not use Watch Tower publications for Bible study, preferring to discuss the Bible directly and make their own arrangements for worship and preaching. Rutherford desired to introduce a system of reporting on the numbers of publications distributed and the number of hours spent on preaching work and wanted to insist on a uniformity of practice relating to regular Bible studies. A number of congregations declined to fall in with these requirements, and some of the less-dedicated members who lacked sufficient motivation to "advertise the kingdom" fell away. William J. Schnell (1956), an active member of the society for 30 years, before leaving in 1952, reported that around three-quarters of the movement's loose adherents left during the 1920s. Although it is difficult to substantiate this figure, the period saw a falloff in numbers and the formation of a number of Russellite splinter groups, some of which continue to this day.

Keen to proclaim the message of the kingdom, Rutherford took a number of initiatives. On release from prison, one of his first activities was the organization of the Cedar Point Convention in Ohio, which took place during 1–8 September 1919. At its peak, some 7,000 attendees were present at the convention, and 200 were baptized. A large banner was displayed on the platform bearing the letters "GA." Having been kept in suspense during the week as to their significance, attendees heard Rutherford reveal on the final day that they stood for *Golden Age*—a new society publication that they would receive regularly.

The 1919 convention fostered a greater awareness of the worldwide nature of the Bible students' task and paved the way for Rutherford's "Millions Campaign," which began in 1920. In that year, Rutherford published his famous *Millions Now Living Will Never Die.* This short work, little more than a hundred pages in length, was important on two fronts. First, it contained the basic material for public talks that Rutherford delivered at various locations countrywide. Second, it introduced a number of new components in the Bible students' understanding of history. In particular, Rutherford focused on the two key years 1918 and 1925. Using calculations based on presumed biblical dates, he concluded that the first year marked the return of the Jews to God's favor. This was signaled by the Balfour Declaration of 1917, which allowed the return of significant numbers of Jews to Palestine. (The apparent discrepancy of a year is explained by the fact that the Jewish year begins in October and thus straddles two years, as defined by Western calendars.) Second, the date of 1925 marked the end of the 70 "jubilees" (Leviticus 25:8), at which time "the earthly phase of the kingdom shall be recognized." It was expected that the year would be marked by the resurrection of the patriarchs Abraham, Isaac, Jacob, and many other "faithful ones of old," who would then assume office as the leaders of the new order of affairs, which would begin on earth (Rutherford, *Millions Now Living Will Never Die*, 88–89).

The early 1920s saw the beginnings of the society's house-to-house work. Until then, the Bible students had promoted Russell's *Studies in the Scriptures*, but after the publication of *Millions Now Living*, Rutherford published his own writings. *The Harp of God* was completed in 1921 and became used in conjunction with house-to-house work. It was subsequently translated into 22 different languages, with a total print run of more than 5.8 million copies. Other innovations included a correspondence course offered to the public, who were asked to complete a weekly questions sheet to check their understanding of the material. In 1922 the society purchased 24 acres of land on Staten Island, New York, where they built a radio station. With the code name WBBR, its first broadcast was put out on 24 February 1922, marking the beginning of 35 years of broadcasting.

The objective of proclaiming the kingdom message gained further impetus at the 1922 assembly, held once again in Cedar Point, Ohio. On this occasion, the banners bore the letters "ADV," and the same letters were displayed on trees and signposts in the convention area. Once again, Rutherford revealed the meaning of the cryptic message in his address on the final day. He reminded the audience that the Gentile times ended in 1914 and went on to speak out against the League of Nations, which had come into existence immediately after World War I. Shortly before its inception, the Federal Council of Churches had declared that the league was the "political expression of the kingdom of God on earth." Rutherford described the statement as blasphemous, since the year 1914 heralded Satan's ejection from heaven down to earth, where he would continue to rule earthly affairs until Armageddon commenced. The league was therefore appealing to Satanic government as a means to solve humankind's problems. By contrast, Rutherford asserted, his followers should fight Babylon the Great, proclaiming Jehovah as God and supporting the Christ's reign as the King of kings. "Therefore," Rutherford continued, revealing the meaning of "ADV," "advertise, advertise, advertise, the King and his kingdom" (*Yearbook*, 1975:131).

The principal method of advertising the kingdom was the house-to-house work, which commenced in 1919. Until 1918, the task of distributing books was only required of designated colporteurs and pioneers, the latter being full-time workers for the society. Rutherford wanted to widen the responsibility of placing Watch Tower publications in the hands of the public. In order to facilitate the work, the society prepared testimonies, which were memorized and recited at the doors, and pressure to publicize the kingdom message was progressively increased. Elders were required to undertake door-to-door work if they wanted to remain in office, and initially the first Tuesday of each month was designated as the "Service Day" for book selling. This was changed to Sunday and became a weekly rather than a monthly responsibility for all members. On Wednesdays, the scheduled day for prayer meetings, congregations were asked to include testimonies from members relating to their field service.

The house-to-house work was backed up by the use of the technology of Rutherford's time. Loud-hailer vans were used to proclaim the message, and the gramophone (record player) was used by missionaries to play recordings of Rutherford's speeches to interested households. These practices were fairly short-lived, however. Although households could be lent gramophones for a period, the main drawback was that they were not interactive, and the Bible students came to prefer to initiate a dialogue with householders, enabling them to ask questions and receive responses.

Some comment is needed about the year 1925, the year in which Rutherford predicted the "return of the princes." The year ended, of course, without any such occurrence, to Rutherford's embarrassment. He emphatically affirmed that this event was certain, describing is as "indisputable" in *Millions Now Living*, and he later admitted at the Brooklyn Bethel that he had "made an ass of himself." At a convention in Basel, Switzerland, the next year, the following exchange occurred:

Question: Have the ancient worthies returned?
Answer: [by Rutherford] Certainly they have not returned. No one has seen them, and it would be foolish to make such an announcement. It was stated in the *Millions* book that we might reasonably expect them to return shortly after 1925, but this was merely an expressed opinion. (*Yearbook*, 1980)

Rutherford later wrote:

There was a measure of disappointment on the part of Jehovah's faithful ones on earth concerning the years 1914, 1918, and 1925, and disappointment lasted for a time. Later the faithful learned that these dates were definitely fixed in the Scriptures; they also learned to quit fixing dates for the future and predicting what would come to pass on a certain date, but to rely (and they do rely) upon the Word of God as to the events that must come to pass. (*Vindication*, vol. 1, 1931:339)

Whether Rutherford's words were totally heeded is discussed later: there were expectations surrounding 1975.

Rutherford did not give up hope for the ancient worthies' miraculous resurrection, and at his behest the society purchased a piece of land in San Diego, California, in 1929, on which a large Spanish mansion was built to accommodate some of the patriarchs upon their return. The house was named "Beth Sarim" ("House of the Princes"), and in the meantime, Rutherford used it as his winter residence on the grounds that his chronic lung disorder—contracted during his prison stay—required him to live in a warm climate. Rutherford did not give up hope that the house might actually offer hospitality to the returning patriarchs. As late as 1939, he wrote in his *Salvation*, "if and when the princes do return and some of them occupy the property, such will be a confirmation of the faith and hope that induced the building of Beth Sarim" (311). The house was finally sold in 1948, six years after Rutherford's death.

The 1925 failed prediction was particularly disastrous, since it was specific and capable of falsification, making backtracking difficult. The disappointment heralded a drop in membership. In 1919, Memorial attendance was reported at 17,961. This number rose dramatically over the next few years, reaching 90,434 in 1925. In 1926 there was a slight drop-off to 89,278, but by 1928, the reported attendance was a mere 17,380 (*Your Will*, 1957; *Yearbook*, 1958). The declining attendance cannot wholly be attributed to Rutherford's error regarding the returning patriarchs. There were other factors: as Rutherford progressively attempted to unify the organization, many congregations refused to be part of Rutherford's theocratically governed institution, preferring to retain their own autonomy. Rutherford succeeded in transforming the movement from a federation of individual ecclesias that elected their own leadership to a centrally controlled body—but at a price.

The 1920s witnessed other significant changes in the society. The progressive distancing between the Bible students and mainstream

Christendom was further underlined by the students' stance on Christian festivals, which took rise during this period. Members had long been aware that there was no historical basis for the date of 25 December as the day of Jesus' birth, although it had been customary to hold a celebratory Christmas dinner at the Brooklyn Bethel. Increasingly, however, they became concerned about the pagan associations of the date, coinciding, as it did, with the Roman Saturnalia. In 1926, members in the United States, Britain, and Switzerland decided to make that year's festival the last. Two years later, Richard H. Barber, one of the Watch Tower headquarters staff, gave a radio broadcast on Christmas celebrations during which he pointed out their pagan roots. The talk was published in *The Golden Age* (*GA* 1928 12/12), after which the practice was discontinued.

Shortly after the reappraisal of Christmas celebrations came a similar reevaluation of the commemoration of birthdays. As with Christmas, it had been common practice for members to celebrate their birthdays, and the book *Daily Heavenly Manna*, which provided members with day-by-day inspirational thoughts bore the subtitle *and Birthday Record*, and it was customary for one's friends to write their names against their birth dates. On 15 February 1909, Russell had been brought onto the platform at a convention in Jackson, Florida, to receive birthday greetings from the audience as well as a number of boxes of fruit as a birthday gift. However, having considered whether Jesus' birthday should be celebrated, the society came to the view that all birthday celebrations should cease. Birthdays, it was reasoned, were not part of the early Church's festivities; they are only twice mentioned in the Bible, in the context of pagan religion, both with unfortunate consequences—the Egyptian pharaoh's birthday (Genesis 40:20) and the birthday of King Herod, the Roman governor of Judaea (Matthew 14:6).

Eager to weed out all traces of paganism from the Watch Tower organization, Rutherford was troubled by Russell's teaching, expressed in his *Studies in the Scriptures* (1890)—in particular the third volume, which includes a special appendix on the topic—that the Great Pyramid of Giza was "God's stone witness" (310). The Great Pyramid, Russell contended, was a fulfillment of Isaiah's prophecy:

> In that day shall there be an altar to the Lord in the midst of the land of
> Egypt and a pillar at the border thereof to the Lord. And it shall be for a

sign and for a witness unto the Lord of hosts in the land of Egypt. (Isaiah 19:19–20)

Its proportions, he claimed, bore cryptic corroboration of God's plan of redemption for humanity, as well as the date of Christ's Second Advent and the sequence of events to be expected in the millennial age. He wrote, "The Pyramid Refutes Atheism, Infidelity, and all Evolution Theories, and Verifies both the Plan of the Bible and Its Appointed Times and Seasons" (Russell: 313; text as original). Rutherford saw no need to appeal to the artifacts of foreign religion for corroboration, believing that all the truth necessary for salvation could be found in the Bible itself. He wrote two *Watch Tower* articles defending his opinion, stating in the first:

> Manifestly God's purpose was that his people should trust in him and in his Word which he gives them. There is no intimation that they were to refer to the great pyramid for corroborative evidence, although at the time of the giving of the law covenant the pyramid was undoubtedly built. (*WT* 28 11/15:340)

One further change merits brief mention. In 1891, *Zion's Watch Tower* introduced the "cross and crown" symbol, depicting a laurel wreath intercepted by a diagonal cross. The symbol became the society's logo and was used as a lapel badge by many members. By 1928, it was felt that the symbol had pagan connotations, the laurel wreath being associated with the ancient Romans; the society's belief was that Jesus was crucified on an upright stake, rather than a cross, as portrayed by mainstream Christianity. On 15 October 1931, the *Watchtower* appeared without this symbol, and the wearing of the badges ceased.

The distinctive character of Rutherford's Bible students combined with a perceived need to distinguish themselves more plainly from the Russellite groups that had splintered off. Accordingly, Rutherford devised a new name for the organization. The name was announced at a convention in Columbus, Ohio, in 1931. On this occasion, cryptic banners and plaques bore the letters "JW." On 26 July, the final day, Rutherford's gave the address "A New Name," and to the delight of his audience, he revealed that from that point forward, the Bible students were to be known as "Jehovah's Witnesses." The new name did not have status in law; the change did not mark any change in the legal status of the names Watch Tower Bible and Tract Society of Pennsylvania or Peoples Pulpit Association. These names, under which the society was incorporated, remained.

The name change reflected an increasing emphasis on the name "Jehovah," a topic to which several *Watch Tower* articles had previously been devoted. Witnesses hold that the name Jehovah is the personal name for God, in contrast with other forms of appellation, which they believe to be generic, such as "God" or "Lord." "Jehovah" is held to be the correct rendering of the Hebrew tetragrammaton ("JHVH" or "YHWH"). Although mainstream scholars have claimed that the name Jehovah derives from incorrect transliteration in the Latin Vulgate, Witnesses will point out that the authentic pronunciation cannot be truly known, since the Jews were forbidden to pronounce the divine name. In any case, the Witnesses have never embarked on a quest for any such authenticity and indeed pronounce the divine name differently in their various languages. The importance they attach to the name "Jehovah" lies in the fact that they regard it as a personal name, facilitating closeness in their relationship with God.

If the 1920s marked a downturn in allegiance, the Jehovah's Witnesses experienced renewed growth in the 1930s. However, there was a problem. Russell originally taught that his Bible students contributed to the 144,000 anointed ones who would experience Christ's heavenly rule. Russell made no claims to exclusivity for his organization, but Rutherford emphasized the apostate nature of Christendom, as well as the Russellite groups that had separated themselves from the Jehovah's Witnesses. The number 144,000 would therefore be drawn from a limited number of sources: those early Christians who were loyal to Christ before the days of Christian apostasy, Russell's Bible students who remained faithful to the Watch Tower organization, and the emergent Jehovah's Witnesses. It might have been plausible enough to maintain that only such a small number of faithful existed if human affairs had come to an end around 1918, but the world's continued existence meant everincreasing numbers joining the organization. While it was impossible to count the total number of people who comprised these categories, it must have been apparent that the number 144,000 would soon be exceeded, if indeed this had not already happened. Although the Watch

Tower literature does not mention this consideration, it would be surprising if this point had not been obvious to Rutherford.

Another issue served to resolve this problem. The Book of Revelation referred to 144,000 people who take their place in heaven, but it goes on to mention an innumerable "great crowd" who surround God's throne and sing praises to "the Lamb" (that is, Jesus Christ). In the early 1930s, there were numerous people who supported the organization's work, but they had not formally committed themselves to membership. In his third volume of *Vindication* (1932), Rutherford referred to them as the "Jonadabs," and this label became widely used among Jehovah's Witnesses. The name alluded to Jonadab (or Jehonadab), whom King Jehu encountered on one of his military expeditions. Jonadab was not Jewish, but he persuaded Jehu of his integrity and support and was invited to come on board Jehu's war chariot (2 Kings 10:15–16). Thus the Jonadabs were those who shared the same cause as God's people but did not formally belong. The identity of this "great crowd" was made explicit by Rutherford at an assembly in Washington in May and June 1935. An eyewitness reports that Rutherford asked, "Will all those who have the hope of living forever on the earth please stand?" whereupon more than half the audience stood up, followed by loud cheering from the others. They were the antitypical Jonadabs.

The "great crowd" expects to experience eternal paradise on earth, rather than heavenly rule with Christ. Although Witnesses show deference to the dwindling number of anointed ones who still remain on earth, those who expect an earthly calling do not see themselves as second-rate citizens, believing that God has his purpose for creating the two different callings and that the joys of a perfect earth are indeed considerable. Although it is not explicitly stated that the composition of the 144,000 was completed in that year, there are instances of Witnesses who have subsequently claimed to belong to the anointed class. The anointed are particularly recognizable at the annual Memorial service, being the only ones who are expected to partake of the "emblems," the symbols of bread and wine; the remainder of the congregation simply handle them and pass them on in silence. After Rutherford's 1935 statement, some Witnesses reconsidered their membership of the heavenly class and ceased to consume the emblems, believing that their aspirations were earthly rather than heavenly.

POPULAR AND LEGAL OPPOSITION

Rutherford's exhortation that Witnesses should "advertise the kingdom" encouraged evangelical zeal, as members distributed literature and went about their house-to-house witnessing. However, this aroused opposition, resulting in many arrests throughout the United States, Canada, and Europe, usually on charges of breach of the peace or selling literature without a license. Litigation reached a scale that prompted the society, both in the United States and Germany, to set up its own legal departments to defend their members and appeal where courts gave unfavorable decisions. Witnesses were prepared for legal opposition, however. In some cities, members deliberately engaged in civil disobedience so that the police would be unable to cope with the sheer number of arrests. In 1933, they set up a system whereby carloads of Witnesses from outside a trouble spot could be summoned at short notice. Up to 200 carloads of Witnesses could be available for this purpose, and law enforcement often had insufficient cells for their imprisonment.

The wave of nationalism that spread throughout the United States raised another issue—the flag salute. Even before Adolf Hitler became chancellor of Germany in 1933, the Watch Tower Society expressed its opposition to physical declarations of allegiance to civil governments. A booklet published in 1931 entitled *The Kingdom, the Hope of the World* drew attention to the biblical story of Daniel's three friends who refused to comply with King Nebuchadnezzar of Babylon's command to bow down to a gold image (Daniel 3:1–26) and whom God rescued from immolation. On 3 June 1935, Rutherford spoke against saluting the American flag, and a few months later eight-year-old Carleton B. Nichols Jr. of Lynn, Massachusetts, declined to salute the flag and join in the singing of a patriotic song at school. In a radio broadcast on 6 October 1935, Rutherford explained that saluting the flag was an expression of support for earthly Satanic ruling powers and hence was idolatrous. The Nichols case was the first to be brought to court. Contrary to their expectation, the case was not upheld on the grounds of religious liberty. In summing up, the judge said, "The flag salute and pledge of allegiance here in question do not in any just sense relate to religion. . . . They do not concern the views of any one as to his Creator. They do not touch upon his relations with his Maker."

The most notable flag salute case was *Minersville School District v. Gobitis* (the court papers consistently listed the family's name incorrectly as Gobitis). It first came to court in 1937, and the Witnesses were initially more successful. Impressed by Rutherford's stance on flag saluting and encouraged by local pioneers Lillian Gobitas and her brother William—then only 11 and 10 years old, respectively—declined to salute the flag at school. They were expelled, and the American Civil Liberties Union assisted their father, Walter Gobitas, in filing a suit in the Federal District Court of Philadelphia in 1937. The trial commenced the following year, and the Gobitas family was successful. However, the School Board refused to accept the children back and appealed the verdict. The United States Court of Appeals once again found in favor of Gobitas in November 1939. A further appeal brought the case to the U.S. Supreme Court, and Rutherford himself testified on the family's behalf. This time the verdict went against the Witnesses, and at the most inopportune time, since World War II had already began, and patriotism was at its height. The verdict was followed by physical attacks on Witnesses. In Kennebunk, Maine, their Kingdom Hall was burnt down, and Witnesses' businesses were often boycotted.

Between 1940 and 1943, the Supreme Court delivered 19 verdicts against the Jehovah's Witnesses. Most damaging to their morale was the unfavorable verdict delivered in 1942 against Rosco Jones, who had distributed Watch Tower literature in Opelika, Alabama, without a license tax. The decision not only meant that Witnesses were obliged to pay for a license but that authorities could withdraw the license at any time.

The year 1943 marked a turning point in the Witnesses' legal affairs, however. On 3 May 1943, the Supreme Court found in favor of the Witnesses in *Murdock v. Commonwealth of Pennsylvania*, declaring that it was unconstitutional to demand payment of a license tax before obtaining permission to distribute religious literature. This decision reversed the 1942 *Jones v. City of Opelika* case and heralded a number of more favorable decisions. In particular, a further flag salute case, *West Virginia State Board of Education v. Barnette*, on 14 June 1943, resulted in the ruling that "no official, high or petty, can prescribe what shall be orthodox in politics, nationalism, religion, or other matters of opinion or force citizens to confess by word or act their faith therein."

WORLD WAR II

The issue of allegiance to the state had far more serious consequences for the Jehovah's Witnesses in Germany. The Witnesses' attitude toward the Third Reich at its inception is not altogether clear. Much controversy continues to surround the "Declaration of Facts" that was adopted at the 1933 Berlin-Wilmersdorf Convention. The Witnesses' detractors claim that the Bibelforscher (as they continued to be called in Germany) attempted to curry favor with Hitler and even went as far as displaying the swastika flag and singing the German national anthem as a prelude to the event. Such allegations are surprising, particularly in view of the society's firm stance against expressions of allegiance to civil governments, and it is not supported by photographic evidence. Much more likely is the explanation that the Wilmersdorf Tennishallen had been used on the preceding day by the Sturmabteilung (SA), the Schutzstaffel (SS), and Nationalist Socialist Groups, who might well have displayed flags on the building's exterior. If this were the case, Witnesses probably would have left them in position, since their mere presence would not require any display of allegiance. The accusation about the national anthem is probably a misunderstanding. Watch Tower sources state that the opening hymn was "Zion's Glorious Hope," which was invariably sung to Haydn's "Austria"—coincidentally the tune of the national anthem. At that time, the Witnesses were happy to draw on mainstream Christian hymns—a practice that they have now reappraised as they have progressively distanced themselves from Christendom.

Of much greater significance is the Declaration of Facts, which was agreed upon by the convention, in which the Bibelforscher appeared to declare support for the "high ideals" of the Nazi regime. The purpose of the declaration was to persuade Hitler not to ban the Bibelforscher's activities, and the convention desired to demonstrate that its ideals were not hostile to those of the Third Reich. Part of the text reads as follows:

> A careful examination of our books and literature will disclose the fact that the very high ideals held and promulgated by the present national government are set forth in and endorsed and strongly emphasized in our publications and show that Jehovah God will see to it that these high ideals in due time will be attained by all persons who love righteousness and who obey the Most High. Instead, therefore, of our literature and our

work's being a menace to the principles of the present government we are the strongest supporters of such high ideals. For this reason Satan, the enemy of all men who desire righteousness, has sought to misrepresent our work and prevent us from carrying it on in this land.

For many years our organization has put forth an unselfish and persistent effort to do good to the people. Our American brethren have greatly assisted in the work in Germany, and with money freely contributed, and that at a time when all Germany was in dire distress. Now because it appears that Germany may soon be free from oppression and that the people may be lifted up, Satan, the great enemy, puts forth his endeavors to destroy that benevolent work in this land. (*Yearbook*, 1934:131–34)

Two and a half million copies of the declaration were distributed and sent to every government official.

Many, including some Jehovah's Witnesses at that time, believed that the declaration should have been more condemnatory of the Nazi regime and that it was particularly inappropriate that Rutherford should refer to it as promoting "high ideals." Although the State persecution of the Jews was only at its beginning at the time of the convention (Dachau was the first camp and was completed in 1933), Hitler's *Mein Kampf* was published in 1927, and restrictions and boycotts were already being applied to Jews. However, the nature of the Jehovah's Witnesses' theology probably caused them to infer that the persecution of Jews was part of the "fiery trials" that they could be expected to undergo in the end-times. Such a belief is, of course, less plausible in hindsight, but it is certainly the case that the Witnesses would have wished to theologize the Jews' plight, rather than to campaign on their behalf. The declaration was designed not as political action but rather as an attempt to ensure their own rights to spread their organization's message.

The Jews were persecuted for supposedly genetic characteristics. The Witnesses, by contrast, were deemed to be "ideologically unfit" (Liebster and Chu, 1998, 5). This "ideological unfitness" was due to a number of factors. Their apolitical stance meant that they would not demonstrably support the Third Reich; they declined to participate in national festivals, and, in common with their American peers, they would not salute the country's flag or follow the expected practice of using the greeting "Heil Hitler!," claiming that doing so would give to a human being the honor that was due to God. The Witnesses' radical critique of Christendom did not endear them either to the Church or the state, and their insistence on house-to-house calling and distributing their literature provoked much opposition from the clergy. It must be said, however, that the Witnesses' opposition was not blatant or campaigning. They did not organize protest marches or publicly burn copies of *Mein Kampf* or their draft papers, nor did they particularly make an issue of failing to offer the Nazi salute. Sheer avoidance of these practices was sufficient: one woman, for example, is reported to have walked through the streets carrying heavy shopping bags in both hands so that she would be unable to salute her friends in the expected way. Watch Tower publications, however, did take the German government to task for its treatment of Jews, in contrast with the mainstream churches. For example, Pius XII was afraid of offending the Roman Catholics living in Germany, many of whom were serving in the German armies. An edition of *The Golden Age* in 1933 stated:

> Probably there is nothing so indicative of primitive consciousness in the entire Nazi program as the anti-Jewish sentiment it so passionately advocates. (*GA*, 1933:209)

Of course, the Jehovah's Witnesses' stance as conscientious objectors in the war and their refusal to undertake military service was a position that inflamed their many opponents.

Because of their unpopularity in Nazi Germany, the punishments that ensued for being a Witness varied. School teachers were prohibited from teaching in school, and Witnesses' children were forbidden to be taught with their Christian peers. Other Witnesses found themselves dismissed from jobs, their businesses boycotted and even put into liquidation, and deprived of unemployment benefits and pensions. Being married to a Witness was in itself grounds for divorce. Watch Tower literature, when found, was confiscated and destroyed.

Most serious of all, of course, were arrest and imprisonment. The Jehovah's Witnesses were among the first groups to be taken to the prewar German camps as political prisoners. They constituted somewhere between 5 and 10 percent of the camp population. Instead of the Jews' Star of David, they were obliged to wear a purple triangle. They were the only Christian group to have a symbol of their own: other Christian political prisoners had a red triangle on their camp uniforms. There was another respect in which Witnesses were unique: all of them had the opportunity to be discharged from the concentration camps, but on the condition that they underwent the process of "swearing off." This involved signing a document declaring that they regarded the society's teachings as false and that they would no longer participate in any of its activities or undertake house-to-house work, but instead become loyal to the state.

The proportion of Bible students who "swore off" remains contested. Watch Tower sources support those historians who claim that only a small number participated (Buber-Neumann, 1950; Hackett, 1995; Kogon, 1950), while Gestapo files suggest that more than half defected (Penton, 2004). The declaration for signing was not standardized until 1938, hence much depends on whether one is referring to this document or to earlier declarations and what the import of the latter was. It seems likely that more Witnesses would sign at an early stage (some apparently took the initiative in doing so) to avoid being consigned to the concentration camps, or as a piece of "theocratic strategy" to enable them to continue with their evangelizing. Those in the camps, in contrast, were likely to be more resolute, having already refused to defect, and also being subject to peer pressure from their fellow prisoners.

Once in the camps, Witnesses endeavored to maintain exemplary standards of behavior. They did not attempt to escape and accepted assigned tasks, so long as they did not require overt declarations of allegiance to the Third Reich. Even SS officers acknowledged that they were "quiet, industrious, and sociable men and women, who were always ready to help their fellow creatures" (Hoess, 1959:97). Because commodities were so scarce in the camps, it was not uncommon for other prisoners to fight over the ownership of half a shoelace when one of the inmates died. There is no record of Witnesses ever having committed such an act, and all the testimonies about their demeanor point to the contrary. Because of their integrity, they were entrusted with tasks that kept them close to the SS officers—for example, doing their laundry at their homes—but they never abused any such positions. The one thing they consistently refused to do was obey orders to harm or kill. Witnesses never mistreated other prisoners. The one instance where they would not cooperate was when their faith appeared to be compromised.

At the outbreak of the war, there were around 25,000 Jehovah's Witnesses in Germany, all of whom were affected by the Third Reich. On the instruction of German courts, approximately 500 children were taken from their parents. Some 13,400 Jehovah's Witnesses spent time—often years—in camps or prisons. Around 2,000 Witnesses died in concentration camps, and some 270 were executed. When one recalls that some six million Jews died in the Nazi Holocaust and that one-third of the world's Jewry were obliterated, it may seem that, relatively speaking, the Witnesses' ordeal was somewhat less. No doubt this is to be explained in terms of the type of opposition to Nazism that the Witnesses posed. Because their opposition was ideological rather than supposedly genetic, the Nazis felt no need to exterminate Jehovah's Witnesses. The Nazis' purposes would have been better served if they could have broken the Witnesses' faith and elicited conformity; they believed that the Witnesses, potentially, were therefore better alive than dead. The 250 Witnesses who were deliberately killed were, in the main, shot or beheaded rather than taken to the gas chambers; they were made an example so that other Witnesses would be encouraged to renounce their faith and sign the declaration that would ensure their freedom.

WAR AND BLOOD TRANSFUSION

One further consequence of war requires mention: blood transfusion. Although their negative stance on transfusion has come to be commonly associated with Jehovah's Witnesses, this procedure was not widely used as a standard medical practice before World War II. The prohibition therefore did not exist at the Bible students' inception, and neither Russell nor Rutherford makes reference to it. Members had, of course, been familiar with the commandment given to Noah proscribing the consumption of blood, reaffirmed by the early disciples at the First Jerusalem Council (Genesis 9:3–4; Acts 15:28–29), but this was a dietary law, which entailed the avoidance of meat that substantially contained the animal's blood. In 1927, a lengthy article in the *Watch Tower* explained the society's position. The availability of blood transfusion raised the question of whether the biblical injunction to "refrain from blood" applied to any method of ingesting blood, including transfusion. A *Watchtower* article on 1 December 1944 first mentioned the issue, and the following year a full-length feature set out the society's position on the matter.

KNORR SUCCEEDS AS PRESIDENT

The war years were marked by a further important change in the society. Rutherford's health was failing, and he died on 8 January 1942. The appointment of his successor was swift and unanimous. On 13 January, Nathan H. Knorr (1905–1977) was elected as president of the Watch Tower Bible and Tract Society of Pennsylvania and the Watchtower Bible and Tract Society of New York. Knorr had been vice president of the society, and had co-led a procession in London in 1938 with Rutherford, where Witnesses displayed placards bearing the words "Religion is a Snare and a Racket"—a favorite slogan for their "information marches" in major cities during the 1920s and 1930s.

Rutherford's administrative contribution to the society had been organizing it into a coherent and unified structure and theologically distancing the Witnesses from mainstream Christendom. Knorr recognized the need for a firmer international structure to facilitate overseas mission, and perhaps even more importantly, the need for extensive and systematic training of every missionary, both at home and abroad. One of Knorr's first achievements was establishing the Gilead School of Ministry; the plan was approved in September 1942, and on 1 February 1943, the school was opened at Kingdom Farm in South Lansing, New York, with 100 students in attendance. The syllabus, which was described as the Advanced Course in Theocratic Ministry, encompassed study of the Bible as well as proficiency in public speaking. Arrangements were made for similar training to be available at the congregational level, and at the "Call to Action," assemblies held throughout the United States on 17 and 18 April 1943, the scheme was announced and a booklet entitled *Course in Theocratic Ministry* was launched. To familiarize members more thoroughly with the Bible, a small book, *Equipped for Every Good Work*, was published. It provided an introduction to each book of the Bible along with background information about its presumed author, date, and purpose. It was introduced at the Glad Nations Theocratic Assembly, which took place in Cleveland, Ohio, on 4 through 11 August 1946. At the same convention, the key text *Let God Be True* was introduced. For several decades, this remained the key work for use in home Bible studies, and by 1971 more than 15 million copies had been circulated in 54 languages. Additionally, the new periodical *Awake!* was issued, replacing *Consolation* (formerly *The Golden Age*).

Knorr believed that global expansion could not effectively be accomplished without familiarity with the various lands in which mission was taking place. The ending of World War II in 1945 facilitated increased travel, and Knorr was able to visit, together with the society's secretary, Milton G. Henschel, the Branch Offices in Britain, France, Sweden, Belgium, The Netherlands, and Scandanavia. A further world tour in 1947 took Knorr to the Pacific, Australasia, Southeast Asia, India, the Middle East, the Mediterranean, Central and Western Europe, Scandinavia, England, and Newfoundland. Between 1947 and 1952, the society increased the number of branch offices from 25 in 1942 to 57 in 1946. In 1955, the society divided the world into 10 zones, each presided over by a "zone servant," later called a "zone overseer," and the number of Kingdom preachers reaching 456,265 in 1952.

Another important project during Knorr's time of office was work on the *New World Translation* of the Bible. In common with mainstream Christianity, Jehovah's Witnesses used the King James Version in Britain and the American Standard Version in the United States, both of which were well known and readily available. These translations had their drawbacks, however, although the latter had the perceived merit of using the divine name "Jehovah." In both texts, the language was archaic, and they did not rely on the best-available ancient manuscripts. Some texts were inimical to the Watch Tower Society's theology. For example, the First Epistle of John states, "For there are three that bear record in heaven, the Father, the Word, and the Holy Ghost: and these three are one" (1 John 5:7). The verse would be an embarrassment to an organization that denied the doctrine of the Trinity, if it were not for the fact—also acknowledged by mainstream biblical scholars—that these words are not in the original Greek. Translation commenced on 29 September 1949, and, remarkably, the *New World Translation of the Christian Greek Scriptures* was released on 2 August 1950. Work on the "Hebrew Aramaic Scriptures" (the society's preferred term for "Old Testament") was completed in 1960, although further revisions were made during the following decade.

The membership of the committee of translators remains undisclosed. Knorr introduced the policy of ensuring that all Watch Tower publications remained anonymous, believing that only God and not human individuals should receive the honor for such work. It seems likely, however, that Frederick Franz and George Gangas, both of whom were proficient in Greek, were part of the translation team. Inevitably, the translation has been attacked by critics, who allege that it is tendentious, being slanted in favor of the Watch Tower's theology. Although this is certainly the case, it is important to remember that the Witnesses are not unique in bringing their own doctrines into the text. Being believers in scriptural inerrancy, they have sought to bring out in translation what they regard as the true meaning of scripture. It is certainly the case that they have corrected some errors found in the King James Version, but most important to the Witnesses is the fact that their translation makes use of (they would say "reinstates") the name "Jehovah" 237 times in Greek and 6,827 times in Hebrew.

THE END OF THE MILLENNIUM?

Mention was made earlier of the Witnesses' reluctance to set dates for end-time events following the disappointment of 1925. However, it did not escape their attention that the year 1975 was potentially significant. Since their presumed date of Adam's creation was 4026 B.C.E., the year 1975 fell exactly 6,000 years later, and thus, arguably, marked the end of the sixth millennium, heralding a new 1,000-year period. Might this date mark the commencement of the final 1,000 years of the seventh sabbatical "day," in which Jehovah's kingdom on earth would commence, heralded by the Battle of Armageddon? Such expectations were raised by a Watch Tower book published in 1966, *Life Everlasting in Freedom of the Sons of God*. The contents included a chronological table, beginning in 4026 B.C.E. as the date of Adam's creation, and ending with 1975 as the "end of the 6th 1,000-year day of man's existence (in early autumn)" (31–35). The reference to early autumn related to the Jewish year, which begins in autumn. The body of the text explains:

> According to this trustworthy Bible chronology six thousand years from man's creation will end in 1975, and the seventh period of a thousand years of human history will begin in the fall of 1975 C.E.
>
> So six thousand years of man's existence on earth will soon be up, yes, within this generation. (29)

This was later backed up by statements in the *Watchtower*. These were relatively few and fell short of making firm predictions. One article reads as follows:

> Are we to assume from this study that the battle of Armageddon will be all over by the autumn of 1975, and the long-looked-for thousand-year reign of Christ will begin by then? Possibly, but we wait to see how closely the seventh thousand-year period of man's existence coincides with the sabbathlike thousand-year reign of Christ. If these two periods run parallel with each other as to the calendar year, it will not be by mere chance or accident but will be according to Jehovah's loving and timely purposes. Our chronology, however, which is reasonably accurate (but admittedly not infallible), at the best only points to the autumn of 1975 as the end of 6,000 years of man's existence on earth. It does not necessarily mean that 1975 marks the end of the first 6,000 years of Jehovah's seventh creative "day." (*WT* 68 8/15:494)

Franz, then the society's vice president, introduced *Life Everlasting in Freedom of the Sons of God* at the assembly in Baltimore in the same year, and said:

> "What about the year 1975? What is it going to mean, dear friends? Does it mean that Armageddon is going to be finished, with Satan bound, by 1975? It could! It could! All things are possible with God. Does it mean that Babylon the Great is going to go down by 1975? It could. Does it mean that the attack of Gog of Magog is going to be made on Jehovah's Witnesses to wipe them out, then Gog himself will be put out of action? It could. But we are not saying. All things are possible with God. But we are not saying. And don't any of you be specific in saying anything that is going to happen between now and 1975. But the big point of it all is this, dear friends: Time is short. Time is running out, no question about that." (*WT* 66 10/15:631)

Although official written statements stopped short of making definite predictions, leaders were at times quite explicit about the 1975 expectation. Franz apparently went so far as to name a precise date — 5 September 1975 — as the end of the present "wicked system," in a public address in Australia earlier that year. Many Witnesses were persuaded that 1975 would mark the end of the present system on earth and possibly the beginning of Armageddon. Some made a point of undertaking additional service to the Watch Tower organization; others planned financially. For example, in *Jehovah's Witnesses: The Global Kingdom* (1985), Marley Cole reports buying a large house in Georgia, intending to sell it to provide financial security during Armageddon (332). When no significant end-time event happened in 1975, many members were disillusioned, and a number left the organization.

Of course, the society could not ignore the unfulfilled expectations and made two comments. First, the expectation was not strictly a failed prophecy, since Jehovah's Witnesses do not claim to prophesy independently from scripture. The incorrect date was, rather, a human error based on faulty inferences from scriptures, which themselves remained infallible. As the *Watchtower* explains:

> If anyone has been disappointed through not following this line of thought, he should now concentrate on adjusting his viewpoint, seeing that it was not the word of God that failed or deceived him and brought disappointment, but that his own understanding was based on wrong premises. (*WT* 76 7/15; quoted again in *WT* 80 3/15)

Second, the society looked again at the Bible and located the source of the error. As they explained, the year 1975 was exactly 6,000 years after the creation of Adam, but Adam's creation did not coincide with the end of the sixth creative day. Although Witnesses believe that the date of Adam's creation can be calculated, the Bible does not state the length of the time period that elapsed between this event and God's resting on the seventh day. The Book of Genesis merely says, "After that God saw everything he had made and, look! [it was] very good" (Genesis 1:31, NWT). Once again, Witnesses learned to be cautious of setting precise end-time dates. Despite the embarrassment of the false expectations, the loss of members was more than compensated for by the evangelical zeal of this period. The number of peak publishers and Memorial attendees climbed continuously and almost doubled between 1968 and 1976. Publishers increased from 1,221,504 to 2,248,390, and Memorial attendance soared from 2,493,519 to 4,972,571 (Penton, 1985, 96).

RESTRUCTURING THE SOCIETY

The 1970s heralded some important changes in the Jehovah's Witnesses that were not so visible to the outside world. In the organization's earlier years, the society was defined as the anointed Christians together with the Governing Body. The use of elections as a means of appointing office bearers presented few problems since the anointed could be guaranteed to run the organization. The Book of Acts recorded that elders and deacons were appointed by "the stretching forth of the hand" (Acts 14:23), and it was assumed that this referred to the practice of voting. Under Rutherford's leadership, voting was abolished, and a 1938 *Watch Tower* article explains that the phrase refers to the practice of the laying on of hands as an act of ordination (*WT* 38 6/1; *WT* 38 6/15).

Voting was still dependent on subscription within the incorporated Watch Tower Bible and Tract Society of Pennsylvania when Knorr assumed office. Knorr objected to this practice, arguing that it made the election of the Governing Body dependent on the financial means of individual members. In any case, the society was coming to the view that government should be theocratic, not democratic. Accordingly, the company's charter was revised, and a new system came into force on 1 October 1945. Membership in the incorporated society, which had previously been unlimited, would now be reduced to between 300 and 500 people, all of whom would be chosen by the Board of Directors.

As time went on and early affairs continued, the "remnant" was declining and the "great crowd" increasing. The restructuring was designed to serve a number of functions: to give greater involvement to the "great crowd" and provide less reliance on the dwindling numbers of anointed, and also to attempt to understand and apply biblical principles of organization, as experienced in the early Church. As a result, the society decided congregations should no longer be governed by a single "congregation overseer" but by a number of elders with a rotating chairman. As before, these office bearers would not be elected but appointed by the Governing Body, and only men would be eligible. A further category of office bearer was also introduced: the ministerial servant. Ministerial servants could deal with such physical aspects of a Kingdom Hall as coordinating the house-to-house work, keeping records, and dealing with financial accounting.

The Governing Body also underwent some reorganization. In 1971, it consisted of the seven anointed members who served on the Board of Directors of the Watch Tower Bible and Tract Society of Pennsylvania. The number was increased to 11, although there was to be no fixed number of members, and the chairman would rotate annually by alphabetic order of surname. In addition, on 4 December 1975, it was decided that the society's work would be carried out by six committees: a Personnel Committee, Publishing Committee, Service Committee, Teaching Committee, Writing Committee, and Chairman's Committee. At branch level, instead of a single branch overseer, each branch would be governed by a committee of at least three members, depending on its size. The Writing Committee would deal with "spiritual food"—publications and translation work; the Teaching Committee would oversee the schools, assemblies, Bethel instruction, and outlines of material for teaching; the Service Committee would supervise the evangelization work and activities of congregations; the Publishing Committee would manage the physical production and distribution of the society's publications, as well as the financial, legal, and business matters relating to them; the Personnel Committee would provide for the personal and spiritual needs of Bethel families; the Chairman's Committee would deal with such urgent matters as disasters, campaigns, reports of persecution, and other emergencies, which it would refer to the Governing Body. Additionally, branch committees would be set up, with between three and seven members, according to need, and have a rotating chair.

As time progressed, it became necessary once again to reappraise the role of the heavenly class in the running of the society's affairs, since the heavenly class continued to decrease in numbers, and many of them came to lack the required physical and mental abilities. In 1992, it was decided that membership of all of these, with the exception of the Governing Body's six committees, would be open to the earthly class. The Chairman's Committee would include the current chairman of the Governing Body, its immediate past and future chairmen. Some thought also had to be given to the meaning of the interpretations of prophecy with which Jehovah's Witnesses have so typically been associated. What did it mean to say that "this generation will by no means pass away until all these things occur" (Matthew 24:34)? Few remained who were alive in 1914, and this small number would soon expire completely. An article in the *Watchtower* (*WT* 95-11-1) explained that the word "generation" did not necessarily mean a group of people who were born within the same time period but could simply mean a "race" or a group, and Matthew's statement could not be used to determine the times of the end. The article cited Jesus' description of the Pharisees as a "generation of vipers" (Matthew 23:30–36) in evidence of this interpretation.

A further organizational change was implemented in 2000. When Henschel assumed the presidency of the society in 1992, he was 72 years old. This made him the second-youngest member of the Governing Body at the time, the average age of which was 82. Being drawn exclusively from the heavenly class, the aging Governing Body seemed to suggest that the society would soon be left without any leadership. In 2000, the seven directors of the Watch Tower Bible and Tract Society of Pennsylvania—all members of the Governing Body—resigned en masse, including Henschel, who also resigned from the presidency of the Watchtower Bible and Tract Society of New York. The seven directors of the Watch Tower Bible and Tract Society of Pennsylvania were replaced by seven new leaders, none of whom were Governing Body members. Three additional corporations were created: the Christian Congregation of Jehovah's Witnesses was set up to deal with religious and educational issues; the Religious Order of Jehovah's Witnesses would oversee the full-time workers; and the Kingdom Support Services would be responsible for the society's buildings and vehicles.

The declared reason for these major changes was that it freed the Governing Body to focus on the "ministry of Word," without having to entangle itself in the physical running or the society's affairs. Some critics speculated that the restructuring was a cynical attempt to avoid impending litigation. (Some former members threatened legal action relating to blood transfusion.) However, the main consequence of the change was that it separated the Governing Body from the structure of the Watch Tower organization. The former could continue, at least in the meantime, to be made up exclusively of anointed ones, while the organization has no further necessity for the heavenly class to have a role in its day-to-day affairs. For the first time in its history, the Watch Tower Bible and Tract Society of Pennsylvania and the Watchtower Bible and Tract Society of New York have two different presidents: Don A. Adams (b. 1926) in Pennsylvania and Max H. Larson (b. 1915) in New York. Neither belongs to the anointed class—another break from tradition. Unlike past leaders Russell, Rutherford, Knorr, and Franz, whom most members knew of and could name, relatively few Witnesses recognize their names, and their assumption of the office was not formally announced in the *Watchtower* or any recent *Yearbook*. This serves to indicate that the presidency is now more of an administrative than a spiritual role and hence is of little interest at rank-and-file level.

JEHOVAH'S WITNESSES IN THE 21ST CENTURY

The zeal and determination of Jehovah's Witnesses in proclaiming their message has resulted in remarkable and consistent growth, apart from a few years following the society's difficulties in 1925 and 1975. Jehovah's Witnesses keep meticulous statistics, and the latest statistical information shows a Memorial attendance in 2006 of 16,675,113 in a total of 236 countries and 99,770 congregations. Not all attendees are Witnesses, since the Memorial service is open to the public, and Witnesses are encouraged to bring friends. A more conservative but nonetheless impressive statistic relates to the number of publishers in that year. The "peak" number, that is the total number who undertook house-to-house ministry, was 6,741,444, and the average number was 6,491,775. These statistics include unbaptized supporters, since children are encouraged to become involved in house-to-house work, as are candidates preparing for baptism. Although it is sometimes said that the Jehovah's Witnesses are one of the world's fastest growing religious organizations, their current worldwide growth is only slightly above the world's population increase. In 2006 the latter was estimated to be 1.167 percent, while Jehovah's Witnesses' reported growth was 1.6 percent. It is not possible to establish to what extent this growth is due to evangelism or to reproduction.

The society's rate of growth is spread fairly evenly worldwide. However, its most concentrated presence, as a proportion of total population, is in the Caribbean and Latin America. It is weakest in Islamic countries, in India, and further East. The Witnesses appear to have greater success evangelizing within predominantly Christian countries. This may be due to the fact that the Bible is better known in such countries, but lack of religious tolerance elsewhere has impeded the work of Witness pioneers and their converts. The smaller Islamic countries that belonged to the former Soviet Union—notably Azerbaijan, Kazakhstan, Turkmenistan, and Uzbekistan—have been relentless in their persecution of Witnesses, breaking up meetings, imposing fines and prison sentences, and burning literature. Elsewhere in the former Soviet bloc, Witnesses face opposition from Eastern Orthodoxy: hostility is most severe in Georgia, although it remains one of the countries with the highest concentration of Witnesses. Communism has been a serious opponent, and in China, Jehovah's Witnesses continue to experience problems of recognition as a legal religion. Despite opposition, Witnesses continue to preach, even if doing so involves infringing on the law of the land. They do not actively campaign for change but work determinedly and unobtrusively, believing that Jehovah's law takes precedence over human law and that they have an obligation to ensure that every nation participates in Jehovah's kingdom.

The Bible affirms that members of "all nations and tribes and peoples and tongues" will stand before God's throne (Revelation 7:9), and hence Jehovah's Witnesses are of necessity a global community. The Watchtower publication *Revelation—Its Grand Climax at Hand!* (1988) describes Jehovah's Witnesses as "the only truly united multinational organization on earth today" (122–23), and Jehovah's Witnesses possess many features of a multinational company. The society operates as a single integrated unit worldwide. The *Watchtower* is available in 154 languages, and the Watch Tower Society takes considerable pains to ensure that copies of the *Watchtower*, *Awake!*, and other literature are not only translated accurately but have the same illustrations and layout, with only minor adaptations to accommodate cultural expectations in a few countries. Although the articles tend to be "digest' in character, they are carefully researched, and authors are instructed to produce four independent sources to corroborate their material. The *Watchtower* is used as the basis for Bible study and is the focus of the second Sunday meeting at the Kingdom Hall. Witnesses study the Bible through Watch Tower literature rather than read it in a direct sequential way. Discussion is designed not to elicit different points of view, since sharing the one single "truth" is held to be much more important than eliciting opinions. Care is taken to ensure that worship is uniform: passages for study, songs, and themes for talks are determined by the society's headquarters, with the result that any Witnesses who travel abroad can be ensured that, apart from language differences and some variation in a leader's talk, the meeting will be the same as that of one's home country.

Because of the size to which the Jehovah's Witnesses have grown, it is not possible to maintain an international identity by organizing international conferences. The lifestyle and financial means of the majority of Witnesses prevents much international travel, and there is no auditorium or stadium that can accommodate the sheer number of Witnesses who would attend if circumstances enabled it. The practice of pioneering in foreign countries no longer has the necessity that existed in the society's early days, since Witnesses now have a presence in every land. Although there is still some international travel, evangelism is largely carried out by natives of each country. On occasion, multinational assemblies are held. This is done by grouping together clusters of countries in sectors. For example, a recent assembly in Poland was attended by delegates from the former Soviet Union and other Eastern European countries. In common with district assemblies and conventions, these larger events are open to the public, and Witnesses from other countries are welcome to attend, if circumstances permit. In some countries the sheer size of local circuits precludes plenary meetings, and circuits are therefore divided to sectors, which take turns using the local Assembly Hall for their gatherings.

Technological innovation remains important to the society. Printing facilities are as up-to-date as possible. The society's printery was relocated to Wallkill, New York, in 2004, with two new MAN Roland Lithoman rotary presses and a new bindery capable of producing both paperback and hardback copies. CDs and DVDs help with the dissemination of Watch Tower literature, and in developed countries the CD has replaced the piano or harmonium to provide the music for worship, thus ensuring global consistency, a high standard of musical accompaniment, and performers' anonymity, in line with the society's policy of giving God the glory rather than humanity. The Internet has been used with greater caution. While the society has recognized the necessity of presenting its message in the most modern media and has placed much of its literature on the World Wide Web, rank-and-file members—particularly children—are warned of the dangers of surfing and of harmful associations that might result. Since the early Church's practice was to propagate the gospel from house to house, the Internet cannot serve as a substitute for house-to-house ministry.

Despite technological change, the values and commitments of individual Jehovah's Witnesses remains the same. Practicing Witnesses attend five meetings in the course of a week: the public Sunday meeting, the *Watchtower* study, congregation book study, Theocratic Ministry School, and Kingdom Service Meeting. They are expected to undertake at least ten hours a month of house-to-house ministry, on which they report to the congregation's elders. Witnesses tend to enter trades rather than professions, although some have found their way into higher education. Attendance at three assemblies in the course of the year is recommended, and attendance at the annual Memorial service should be a firm commitment. Witnesses hold family life in high esteem, and marriages should be within the organization to ensure a common purpose within one's marriage, as well as the rearing of children in the faith. The woman's role is supportive to the man's, and there are no concessions toward feminism, which is regarded as unduly political and campaigning. However, some of the Watch Tower researchers and writers are women.

Despite the restructuring of the Watch Tower Society in 2000, the Governing Body still remains the principal earthly source of authority. It continues to be drawn from the anointed class, despite the fact that few remain who belonged to the society in 1935, when Rutherford defined the "great crowd." The 21st century has seen fluctuations in the number of anointed ones who partake at the Memorial, and the year 2006 saw a slight increase from 8,524 to 8,758. Jehovah's Witnesses believe that the anointed class may not yet be complete, as new countries open up and some anointed ones forfeit their heavenly calling and need to be replaced, just as Matthias took up Judas Iscariot's office (Acts 1:26). The average age of the Governing Body has in fact decreased rather than increased, being a mere 68 years at the time of writing. This has been achieved by the appointment of younger members who are deemed to have a place among the anointed. In fact, only two out of the current nine Governing Body members were born before 1935. The society has therefore recognized and addressed the issue of a potentially aging Governing Body and, in addition to the appointment of younger office bearers, has provided them with ample assistance from the society's earthly class of members, who advise, research, and assist in various ways. The introduction of younger members is not simply due to the practicality of perpetuating the Governing Body's existence. Witnesses note that the Book of Revelation affirms that the 144,000 will be drawn from the four corners of the earth (Revelation 7:1), hence there is an expectation that citizens of countries that have only recently been introduced to the society's teachings will be represented among the anointed class who will reign with Christ in heaven.

If the Governing Body were eventually allowed to die out, it is unlikely to be an insuperable problem for Watch Tower leaders, since the final destiny of the anointed ones is heaven, with the earthly class remaining on earth. Without its Governing Body, the Watch Tower Society would therefore be a true replication of its ultimate goal of Christ's completed heavenly rule, with the earthly class striving toward paradise earth. Since its inception, the society has undergone change, and Jehovah's Witnesses do not expect that their organizational structures or understandings of scripture will remain static in the course the 21st century. Witnesses claim that a "greater light of understanding" has been experienced in the past, and they expect it to continue as time advances. They continue to preach an imminent end to the world's present system but no longer name any firm dates, having learned the imprudence of being over-specific, particularly with respect to the years 1925 and 1975, which proved particularly embarrassing for the society. The society acknowledges that even though it regards itself as God's sole vehicle for salvation, this does not preclude human error, and Witnesses look to the future to bring greater understanding of the Bible and its message for humankind.

THE DICTIONARY

– DATES AND NUMBERS –

666. *See* MARK OF THE BEAST.

1874. The date given by **Nelson H. Barbour** and accepted by **C. T. Russell** for Christ's invisible presence or Second Advent. It marked the beginning of the "time of harvest," during which the faithful would take their place in heaven and which Barbour believed would end in 1878.

1878. According to **C. T. Russell**, this year paralleled **Christ**'s **resurrection** and marked the establishment of God's **kingdom**, with the faithful dead being admitted to heaven. Russell regarded the date as signifying the beginning of God's favor returning to the **Jews**. It was, he believed, confirmed by the Berlin Congress that year, at which Lord Beaconsfield gave Turkey voting rights on the condition that it grant civil and religious rights to the Jews. According to **J. F. Rutherford**, the 1878 date begins a 40-year period, culminating in the Balfour Declaration of November 1917, which is taken to legitimate the **Bible** students' belief in the significance of **1918** as a key date in their **end-time calculations**. *See also* DEATH; FAITHFUL MEN OF OLD.

1914. The year of **Christ**'s presence (*parousia*). This is not the date of a second coming: Witnesses hold that 1914 marks the year when **Jesus Christ** began his rule in the heavenly sanctuary, having cast **Satan** out of heaven down to earth. The date thus applies to an invisible, not a visible event, and, contrary to popular belief, has never been revised by **Jehovah's Witnesses**. It is unnecessary for Witnesses to do so, since the claim regarding this event cannot be decisively verified or falsified by any earthly happenings. However, Witnesses perceive such subsequent events on earth as **war**, earthquake, and famine as evidence of the end-times and as suggesting that other more observable events, like the commencement of **Armageddon**, are imminent. *See also* CLEANSING OF THE SANCTUARY; END-TIME CALCULATIONS; PROPHECY.

1918. The significance of this date is multifaceted. According to **C. T. Russell**, its importance lay in its falling 40 years after **1878**, which was the date of the **resurrection** of the sleeping saints. After 1918, no more people would be translated directly into heaven. Later **Bible** students construed the date as marking the end of the "harvesting period" begun in **1914**, having come to believe that 1914 was the year in which **Christ** began his heavenly rule. This would herald the direct translation of the **anointed class** into heaven upon **death**, without any period of soul sleep between their earthly and heavenly existence.

According to **J. F. Rutherford**, the year also signified the return of the **Jews** to God's favor, evidenced by the Balfour Declaration of November 1917, which approved the establishment of a Jewish state in Palestine. The apparent discrepancy of one year is explained by the fact that the Jewish year, on which these **end-time calculations** are based, begins in the autumn. Rutherford noted that the date fell 40 years after 1878, being the beginning of this return. The return of the Jews would herald the messianic **kingdom** on earth. *See also* IMMORTALITY; PARADISE EARTH; SOUL.

1925. This date was first perceived as significant by **J. F. Rutherford**, who regarded it as the year in which the 70 "jubilees" of 50 years each, begun in 1575 B.C.E., would end (Leviticus 25:1–12). The year 1925 would be marked by the return of the **faithful men of old**. Having lived before the time of **Christ**, these "ancient worthies" are believed to be eligible for everlasting life on earth, not heaven, and they would be resurrected at this time to begin this existence. Rutherford had to admit the failure of this prediction but nevertheless commissioned the construction of **Beth Sarim**, a mansion designed to accommodate some of the worthies upon their return, which he continued to expect.

1975. This year was anticipated by **Jehovah's Witnesses** as a potentially significant date, being the 6,000th anniversary of God's **creation** of **Adam**, presumed to have taken place in the autumn of 4026 B.C.E. The date was mentioned briefly in a small number of *Watchtower* and *Awake!* articles and more explicitly in talks given by **Watch Tower Society** leaders. Many Witnesses were promised that "thrilling events" would follow, and they believed that the date closely anticipated the end of the 6,000-year period, marking the transition to the seventh **millennium**. They expected some significant event to occur, possibly the commencement of the Battle of **Armageddon** or the beginning of the **millennial rule of Christ.**

When nothing significant appeared to happen in that year, it was explained that an unspecified period of time had elapsed between the creation of Adam and the end of the first creative day, hence any anniversary of Adam's creation need not be significant for millennial expectations. A significant number of members were disappointed that their expectations were unfulfilled, and some left the society as a result. *See also* END-TIME CALCULATIONS; MILLENNIALISM; PROPHECY.

144,000. Aka **anointed class**, little flock, spiritual Israel of God. This is the number of the faithful who will experience eternal life in heaven as spirit creatures, in contrast with the **great crowd**, who will live eternally in **paradise earth** as humans. The number 144,000 is specified in the Book of **Revelation** (7:4) and is held to be a fixed, not a symbolic number. The number of this anointed class started to be made up after **Pentecost** (33 C.E.) and consists of those followers of **Christ** who remained faithful. Effectively, **Bible** students and **Jehovah's Witnesses** who joined between the formation of **C. T. Russell**'s **International Bible Students Association** and 1935 are expected to belong to this class. The exact membership of the class is known only to God, and some additions continue to be made. Those who belong to this number partake of the emblems at the annual **Memorial** service.

– A –

ABORTION. Defined as the expulsion of an embryo or fetus from a womb, deliberate abortion is regarded as killing, since life is held to begin at the moment of conception. Abortion is therefore totally unacceptable to God. **Jehovah's Witnesses** firmly hold that it may not be used as a method of population or of **birth control** or for preventing the birth of a deformed child. When a woman desires abortion because of a sexual relationship outside marriage, the unwanted pregnancy arises from a previous sinful action; in such a situation offering the child for adoption is considered preferable to avoiding any social stigma. Couples who experience an unplanned pregnancy are reminded of the **Bible**'s teaching that children are a gift from God. Witnesses who are advised that continuing a pregnancy may jeopardize the life of the mother are asked to bear in mind that medical opinion about such matters can be wrong. Choosing between the life of the baby and the life of the mother should only be made at the moment of birth. Witnesses deplore the liberal laws on abortion that exist in many countries and the widespread availability of the procedure. A Witness is not permitted to work in an abortion clinic. *See also* SEX.

ADAM. The first human to be created, on the sixth creative day, as recounted in the Book of Genesis. Watch Tower teachings define the precise year of his **creation** as 4026 B.C.E. Being the creation of God, neither Adam nor his wife Eve—the first woman—had any human parents. Although created as a perfect son of God, Adam succumbed to temptation by eating of the tree of knowledge of good and bad in the Garden of Eden. Having previously been warned by God that the penalty for disobedience was **death**, Adam was cast out of the paradisiacal Garden of Eden and is not expected to be one of partakers in the **resurrection** in **paradise earth**.

Jesus Christ is described as the "last Adam," being Adam's antitype. He is said to resemble Adam in having no human father, and his role is to restore paradise earth. He accomplishes this by being the **ransom sacrifice** for sin.

Witnesses believed that the year **1975** was to be a significant one, believing it to be exactly 6,000 years after Adam's creation. However, there exists an unspecified period of time between Adam's creation and the end of the sixth creative day. It is the end of this **millennium**, not the anniversary of Adam's creation, that is held to have eschatological significance.

ADAMS, DON ALDEN (1925–). President of the **Watch Tower Bible and Tract Society of Pennsylvania** since 2000, in succession to **Milton G. Henschel**. Born in Illinois, Adams' mother, Mary Adams, became a **Jehovah's Witness** in 1938; his father, William Karl Adams, was baptized in 1952. Don Adams began pioneering in 1943, and in 1945 he took up full-time ministry at the Brooklyn **Bethel**, gaining exemption from military service. His two brothers also served at the Bethel. Adams worked with the **Gilead School of Ministry** and also traveled extensively as a **zone overseer**.

Adams came to office as a result of significant structural reorganization of the society in 2000, which involved formal separation of the **Governing Body** and the society's **Board of Directors**. Adams is not reckoned to be a member of the **anointed class**, hence he is the first president not to belong to the **Governing Body**. *See also* PIONEER.

ADVENTISM. A movement in the Protestant tradition that traces its roots to the teachings of **William Miller**, a Baptist preacher who began proclaiming the imminent return ("second advent") of **Jesus Christ** in 1831. Miller's expectations were based on a series of **end-time calculations** from dates and time periods mentioned in the **Bible**. Christ's return was expected in 1843 and subsequently in 1844. When these dates failed to materialize, many of Miller's followers were disillusioned, and the prophetic failure became known as the Great Disappointment. Subsequent Adventists either recalculated dates or concluded that an invisible spiritual event had occurred in 1844—Christ's **cleansing of the sanctuary**—which would be followed by an investigative judgment in which God and Jesus Christ would determine whose names would appear in the Book of Life and hence be eligible for glorification in heaven.

Following the Mutual Conference of Adventists in 1845, Adventism developed into a number of denominations, the best-known of which are the Evangelical Adventists (founded in 1845 but now defunct), the Advent Christian Church, and the Seventh-day Adventists. The Advent Christian Church emerged from the Life and Advent Union, created by John T. Walsh and **George Storrs** in 1863, and is the tradition with which **C. T. Russell**'s Bible students were most closely associated. The Seventh-day Adventists were founded by Ellen G. White in the same year and emphasize the observance of Saturday as the day of worship, together with dietary laws. Adventists typically taught the doctrine of "**soul** sleep," the belief that the dead remain unconscious until the day of **judgment**; "**conditional immortality**," the idea that experiencing a **resurrection** is conditional on one's deeds; and the extinction rather than eternal punishment of the wicked.

ALCOHOL. Alcohol is permitted, but in moderation, since Paul recommends the consumption of "a little wine" (1 Timothy 5:23). It is noted that **Jesus** turned water into wine at the wedding in Cana, hence wine and alcoholic beverages are permitted at **marriages** and other occasions, in moderation. Alcoholic wine is used at the **Memorial** service. **Jehovah's Witnesses** note that drunkenness is condemned in the **Bible** (Proverbs 20:1; Luke 21:34–35) and regard alcoholism as a serious problem. Persistent drinking to excess could result in **disfellowshipping**. Misuse of alcohol, they teach, can cause **health** problems, including harmful effects on unborn children, and can lead to dependence. Additionally, alcohol can cause harmful effects on one's spiritual life: drunkenness can lead to other misdeeds, and one has to be careful not to cause others to "stumble." Being in the company of heavy drinkers can constitute "bad **associations**" (Proverbs 23:20).

ANCIENT WORTHIES. *See* FAITHFUL MEN OF OLD.

ANGELS. These are spirit creatures, also referred to as "holy ones" or "Elohim" and metaphorically as "morning stars" and "sons of God." They serve as messengers on God's behalf and using speech to communicate. Angels take an interest in earthly affairs, although direct intervention is rare, and their support is spiritual rather than physical. They are ungendered (Matthew 22:30) but have individual personalities and names. Two angels are explicitly named in scripture:

Michael (the archangel) and Gabriel, and they are organized into ranks, which include the archangel, princes, cherubs, seraphs, angels, and armies. They are capable of choosing between right and wrong, hence the existence of **Satan**, who is a fallen angel.

Witnesses do not believe the **Bible** to endorse the notion of personal "guardian angels," and they dissociate themselves emphatically from the upsurge in interest in angels in "new spirituality" or New Age.

ANIMALS. Brought into existence by God as part of the six-day **creation**, animals are a separate creation from humanity and not related to humans by **evolution**. God gave **Adam** dominion over the animal kingdom, which entails permission to use animals for bearing burdens and agriculture and to kill animals for food and clothing. Animals should nonetheless be treated with kindness. Distinctions between clean and unclean animals are regarded as pertaining to the Mosaic Law and not the new covenant, hence **Jehovah's Witnesses** are not subject to dietary restrictions, apart from the prohibition on **blood**.

Harmony among the animal realm and between humans and animals is portrayed as a feature of the expected **paradise earth**. Although animals are viewed as living souls, they have no hope of **resurrection** and thus will be subject to birth and **death** in the coming **kingdom**. *See also* IMMORTALITY; SOUL.

ANOINTED CLASS. Aka little flock. These are the **144,000** members mentioned in the Book of **Revelation** (Revelation 14:1), who entertain the "heavenly hope" and will rule with **Christ** in heaven. The number is made up from Christ's followers from the Day of **Pentecost** (presumed date 33 C.E.) and those whom God has called, up to the present day. Those who belonged to the **International Bible Students' Association** up to 1931 are generally reckoned to be anointed ones, but in 1931 it was decided that the organization's scope should be broadened to encompass Christ's "other sheep" (John 10:16), initially known as **Jonadabs** and later as the **great crowd**. Although 1935 is regarded as the date after which the anointed class became virtually complete, the exact identity of all 144,000 members is not known for certain, and the **Watch Tower Society** acknowledges the possibility that their number has been added to after that date.

Only a few of the anointed class now remain on earth. They are known as the **remnant** and are distinguishable by their consumption of the **Memorial emblems** at this annual event. The **Governing Body** consists entirely of anointed ones. To qualify as a member of the anointed class, one must be dedicated to God and loyal to his organization, to have his spirit, and to be used in his service. Their expectation is to be citizens of heaven under Christ's "heavenly rule," while the great crowd will experience **paradise earth.** They will be like the **angels** and will see God face to face.

God's faithful who died before the time of Christ's death and **resurrection** do not belong to the anointed class; the **Bible** teaches that they "did not get the [fulfillment of the] promise" (Hebrews 11:39) and that there exist those who can expect something better. Hence the patriarchs and the prophets belong to the earthly class.

ANTICHRIST. The term is mentioned five times in John's two epistles and not in the Book of **Revelation**, as is popularly supposed. One occurrence (1 John 2:18) employs the word in plural, thus indicating that "antichrist" does not refer to one single person, like Nero, Hitler, or the wild **beast** mentioned in Revelation 13. The concept designates all who deny biblical teaching concerning **Jesus Christ**, all those who oppose Christ's **kingdom**, and all who persecute his followers. The term denotes individuals, organizations, and nations.

The wild beast of Revelation 13 is held to represent human governments and thus forms part of the antichrist. The concept also embraces those who claim that Christ works through human governments, since Christians are "no part of the world" (John 17:14), or political organizations that make quasi-messianic claims. *Watchtower* articles explicitly mention **communism** in this regard and also the **United Nations.** Roman Catholicism has also been labeled antichrist because of its support for political systems, especially Hitler's regime. All human political systems will be destroyed at **Armageddon** and hence cannot offer **salvation.**

Religious antichrists include all those who espouse any form of **false religion.** Particular mention is made of those who propagate false teachings regarding Christ's person and work, for example, that he was not fully human (docetism), that he was not the unique son of

God, that he is part of a **Trinity**, or that he did not offer a **ransom sacrifice** for sin. Apostates also form part of the antichrist.

APOSTASY. The term refers (a) to defection of the organization's members and (b) to the ways in which **Christendom** has departed from the presumed authentic practices of the early Church. **Jehovah's Witnesses** hold that apostasy is predicted in the **Bible** as one of the signs of the last days. Apostasy is more than lapsed practice. The term connotes a willful defection and rebellion against God. In the case of individual members, it refers to those who have undergone **disfellowshipping** and actively oppose the faith and those who have deliberately decided to leave the organization and promote opposing views.

Christendom's apostasy is held to have begun under the early Roman Empire, when **pagan** practices were imported, for example, the celebration of pagan festivals, which resulted in the celebrations of **Christmas** and **Easter**. Christendom also allowed the introduction of Greek philosophical ideas, like mind-body dualism, with the resultant doctrine of the **immortality** of the **soul** in place of the **resurrection** of the body. The **Watch Tower Society** also deplores the way in which clergy persecute Witnesses, their over-liberal attitudes to sexual morality, their support of world governments and **war**, and in general the false teachings they propagate. *See also* SEX.

APPOINTED TIMES OF THE NATIONS. *See* GENTILE TIMES.

ARMAGEDDON. Aka Har-magedon. The final battle between God's invisible army of **angels** and **Satan**'s forces, described in the Book of **Revelation** (Revelation 16:13–16). It occurs on a cosmic scale and hence is not to be confused with any major earthly conflict. Although the name appears to denote the Plain of Megiddo, no single physical location is large enough for this conflict.

Jehovah's Witnesses teach that, following a heavenly battle that commenced in **1914**, Satan was cast down from heaven when **Jesus Christ** established his messianic **kingdom** there. Satan's rule over the earth intensified after he amassed support from its kings, political rulers, and people. The "spiritual prosperity" of Jehovah's Witnesses infuriates Satan, who plans his attack. **Jehovah** wants to cleanse the world of all evil, hence at Armageddon these competing cosmic forces aim for power over the earth. Satan's earthly armies will be attacked by Christ, also described as **Michael**, with his heavenly forces. Jehovah's supporters will not participate in this conflict but will receive his protection.

Most of the earth's inhabitants will fail to recognize the signs of the imminent conflict or to heed the divine warning, hence most will die. Satan and his demon angels will be imprisoned in an abyss for 1,000 years. The "**great crowd**" who acknowledge Christ's kingship will be spared; Christ will rule the earth; and during the ensuing **millennium**, the earth will be restored. Evil, conflict, and pollution will be eliminated, and **paradise earth** will be created. *See also* MILLENNIAL RULE OF CHRIST.

ASSEMBLIES. In addition to meeting congregationally, **Jehovah's Witnesses** regularly assemble in their **circuits** and **districts**. The term normally designates such meetings, although it has been used synonymously with "**convention**." Circuit meetings are normally held in **Assembly Halls**, where these meetings are available, but district meetings are normally too large and require obtaining large public buildings or stadiums.

The practice of holding assemblies receives biblical justification: Moses is instructed to hold "solemn assemblies" of the Israelites. The frequency of such meetings is not prescribed in the **Bible**, but typically three are held each year. Although attendance is not an absolute obligation, most Witnesses make every effort to be present. Both children and adults are expected.

Assemblies are essentially for teaching purposes, and they include congregational singing, **prayer,** talks on biblical themes, and sometimes dramatizations. They are not business meetings and do not include reports, financial statements, discussions of policy matters, or announcements not relevant to the functioning of the assembly. *See also* SONGS.

ASSEMBLY HALL. A building used for **circuit assemblies** and other large gatherings of **Jehovah's Witnesses**. Witnesses initially rented accommodations but found it preferable to acquire their own premises, usually by converting such unused buildings as cinemas, theaters, or factories. Circuit assemblies are normally held twice annually for spiritual edification and **baptism.** As far as possible, construction work is carried out by members of local **congregation**s, who also finance the projects. The **Watch Tower Society**, however, must approve the construction after analyzing the costs and benefits. An assembly hall frequently incorporates a **kingdom hall**. The first assembly hall was built in Long Island City, New York, in 1965.

ASSOCIATIONS. Jehovah's Witnesses attach great importance to the company one keeps as a means of faith maintenance, and *Watchtower* publications frequently quote the text, "Bad associations spoil useful habits" (1 Corinthians 15:33). Bad associations (also described as wrong or harmful associations) result from excess mixing with people who do not belong to the organization or being exposed to ideas that counter Watch Tower teachings. Examples of bad associations include literature that promotes immoral ideas, radio, television, cinema, the **Internet**, and gatherings of people at social events or in interest groups. Regularly exposing oneself to religious ideas that originate from the mainstream churches, particularly writings that support higher criticism of the **Bible**, can prove dangerous and are strongly discouraged. Bad associations expose the believer to the standards of the world, which is ruled by **Satan**, and to its thinking, and can thus prove harmful to one's spiritual and moral welfare.

While the **Watch Tower Society** does not prohibit such activities as radio and television, **Jehovah's Witnesses** are advised to discriminate carefully, using a "good **conscience**" in relationship with God and his word, as found in the Bible. Witnesses tend to associate mainly with each other, attending any social events and entertainments collectively. Ideally, **marriage** partners and friends should be fellow-believers, although there can be areas of life, like **education** and employment, that raise difficulties in this regard. One of the reasons for not pursuing higher education relates to the likely associations that a student will encounter. Parents are advised to supervise their children carefully to ensure that they are not adversely affected by bad associations. Witnesses who have nonbelieving marriage partners are advised to avoid separating, although such situations can create problems of conscience at times. Members who have undergone

disfellowshipping may not have social relationships with members in good standing because the latter must avoid harmful associations.

Right associations are said to be harder to find than wrong ones, and the society believes that they are not to be found in **Christendom**.

AWAKE! One of the **Watch Tower Society**'s principal publications. Originally published in 1919 as the *Golden Age*, its name was changed to *Consolation* in 1937. The latter was reckoned to be an apt title in the face of the impending **World War II**. In 1946, the name was again changed, becoming *Awake!*, an allusion to Romans 13:11: "it is already the hour for you to awake from sleep, for now our salvation is nearer than at the time when we became believers." The sister magazine to **Watchtower**, it was published semimonthly until 2007, when it became a monthly periodical, and it covers a wide range of topics. Its themes are not exclusively biblical, although it presents **Jehovah's Witnesses**' teachings on the topics presented where appropriate. Subjects include events and issues in the news, societal issues, and practical advice on themes relating to **health** and safety, as well as discussion of religious matters. At the time of writing, *Awake!* is available in 81 languages, and it is circulated to more than 34 million people worldwide. *See also* BIBLE.

– B –

BABEL. *See* BABYLON.

BABYLON. Aka Babel; Babylon the Great. An ancient city held to have been established by **Nimrod** (Genesis 10:10). Since it is described as Nimrod's **kingdom**, it is inferred that Babylon's government was civil rather than theocratic, hence the city was ruled contrary to God's will. The name has negative connotations for Judaism and Christianity, being the place into which the **Jews** were taken captive. The evil nature of Babylon is demonstrated by its triad of gods (held to be a precursor of the Christian **Trinity**), its use of images in **religion**, its priesthood, its belief that life after **death** was inevitable, and its **occult** practices.

Babylon is identified in the Book of Daniel as one of four great empires destined for destruction. The book recounts a dream of King Nebuchadnezzar of Babylon, in which he sees a statue with a gold head, silver chest and arms, a bronze belly and thighs, and feet of iron mixed with clay (Daniel 2:37–43). This last component is held to signify the empires' crumbling foundations, which herald its inevitable destruction, as well as the unacceptable mingling of religion and civil government—a significant aspect of **Christendom**'s **apostasy**.

Christendom is thus the most reprehensible part of antitypical Babylon. Although mainstream Protestantism has characteristically identified Babylon with Roman Catholicism, from the **Watch Tower Society**'s inception, **Bible** students and **Jehovah's Witnesses** have applied the term to Christendom more widely. **C. T. Russell** defined it as "the nominal Church." More widely, Witnesses have come to identify three principal aspects of Babylon: **false religion**, earthly government, and commerce.

In the Book of **Revelation**, the term *Babylon the Great* is used, signifying a "mystic Babylon," which is not to be identified with the ancient city since the city of Babylon was destroyed centuries before John was writing. Babylon the Great is described as a harlot, who rides a ten-horned scarlet **beast** and who becomes drunk with the blood of the faithful (Revelation 17:1–17). Witnesses hold that such references allude to the "world empire of false religion," with the harlotry consisting of the union of religious and political powers, who have persecuted the followers of true religion. This empire is the enemy of God's people and will be destroyed in the Battle of **Armageddon**.

BAPTISM. Aka water baptism. **Jehovah's Witnesses** practice adult baptism, acknowledging that this has been an authentic Christian rite dating back to **Jesus** himself, who instructed his disciples to administer it (Matthew 28:19). John the Baptist (aka John the Baptizer) is regarded as the first person authorized by God to administer the rite for repentant **Jews** professing their guilt at infringing the Law. When Jesus presented himself to John for baptism, he did so with a different purpose, being sinless: his was a self-presentation to accomplish **Jehovah**'s will, and his act was vindicated by the divine voice from above declaring that he was God's beloved son.

Baptism by Jesus' disciples again assumed a different meaning, being a symbol of complete dedication of one's life to God and an opportunity to enter the **kingdom** of heaven. Baptism was initially administered to Jews but later to **Gentiles**. It is initiatory, unlike that of John, the initiatory rite for Jews being circumcision. Witnesses teach that baptism is necessary for **salvation** but do not regard it as a "sacrament." Baptism is for adults, not babies or young children, since it requires personal decision and understanding of the faith, rather than the desire of one's parents. Witnesses point out that there are no references to infant baptism in the **Bible**. Baptism is carried out by total immersion in water, as described in the **Christian Greek Scriptures**.

A number of conditions must be satisfied for a candidate to qualify for baptism. He or she must have repented; must have undergone conversion; must have received instruction; must be completely dedicated to Jehovah and to doing his will; must already be expressing the faith by living an appropriate lifestyle, including regular attendance at **Kingdom Hall** meetings, proclaiming God's word; and must be living a morally upright life, consistent with the organization's expectations. Candidates are subjected to more than 100 questions by appointed **elders** to determine their readiness, and not all are accepted. Baptisms are usually conducted at **circuit assemblies** or **conventions**. *See also* SIN.

BARBER, CAREY W. (1905–2007). Born in Wiltshire, England, Barber moved to Winnipeg, Canada, and was baptized as a **Bible** student in 1921. Together with his twin brother, he served at the **Bethel** from 1923 until 1948, when he was appointed as a traveling **overseer**. He was appointed to the **Governing Body** in 1977 and served until his **death** in 2007.

BARBOUR, NELSON H. (1824–1905). An early associate of **C. T. Russell**, Barbour was raised as a Presbyterian but joined the Methodist Episcopal Church, where he began to study for the ministry. After questioning mainstream teachings on election and universal **salvation**, he became an independent preacher in the **Adventist** tradition. A Millerite Adventist, Barbour experienced the **Great Disappointment** of 1944 and was led to revise his **end-time calcula-**

tions, concluding that **Christ** would return in 1873 but that his presence would be invisible. His reasoning is expressed in his *Evidences for the Coming of the Lord in 1873, or the Midnight Cry* (1869).

Barbour edited the magazine *Herald of the Morning*, a copy of which Russell received in January 1876. They met the following year and collaborated on *Three Worlds and the Harvest of This World* (1877). In light of his discussion with Barbour, Russell was prompted to explore end-time **prophecy**, having previously been more interested in soteriology, and he came to write *The Object and Manner of Our Lord's Return* (1877). Russell and Barbour jointly revived *Herald of the Morning*, which had ceased publication, but in 1878, Barbour composed an article denying the substitutionary theory of atonement. This offended Russell, who wrote a reply, and the journal continued to publish doctrinal discussion between Barbour, **John H. Paton**, and Russell. Believing that this only served to confuse readers, Russell decided to withdraw his support, and the two separated.

In 1879, Barbour traveled as a preacher, visiting England, Canada, and Australia. His views proved unacceptable to other Adventists. The periodical *Advent Christian Times* warned readers against Barbour, Russell, and Paton, and Barbour was expelled from the New York Conference of the Advent Christian Church. *See also* ADVENTISM; *PAROUSIA*; PREDESTINATION.

BEASTS. The imagery in Daniel and the Book of **Revelation** makes considerable reference to beasts. The serpent and the dragon are taken to refer to **Satan**, while other beasts typically refer to the earth's political powers that have ruled at various points throughout history. Daniel has a dream in which he sees four beasts resembling a lion with eagle's wings; a bear; a four-winged, four-headed leopard; and a ten-horned ferocious beast (Daniel 7:1–8). **Jehovah's Witnesses** equate these with **Babylon**, Medo-Persia, Greece, and Rome, referring to their successive waves of military conquest. In Revelation, mention is made of a beast with "ten horns and seven heads, and upon its horns ten diadems, but upon its heads blasphemous names" (Revelation 13:1). This vision is taken to refer to seven kings or empires. Six are mentioned in the **Bible**, namely Egypt, Assyria, **Babylon**, Medo-Persia, Greece, and Rome. In a similar vision in Revelation 17.10 of the scarlet-colored beast on which Babylon rides, it is stated that the last king is yet to come. This last king is a two-horned beast (Revelation 13:11–13) and is identified with Britain and America (Anglo-America). Witnesses perceive this as a reference to the persecution of the Witnesses from December **1914**—as public dislike for their opposition to **World War I** increased—until 18 June **1918**, when **J. F. Rutherford** and other leaders were sent to prison for proclaiming their faith. All these world powers are destined for calamity, as is evidenced by **World War I** and **World War II**, but they will be finally defeated at **Armageddon**. *See also* MARK OF THE BEAST.

BEELZEBUB. *See* SATAN.

BEREAN BIBLE INSTITUTE. Founded in Melbourne, Australia, in 1917 by R. E. B. Nickolson, the organization is based on the teachings of **C. T. Russell** rather than **J. F. Rutherford**, and it rejects the so-called "seventh volume," *The Finished Mystery* (1917). The institute aims to promote the study of the **Bible** and proclaim God's coming **kingdom**. Its principal periodical is the *People's Paper and Herald of Christ's Kingdom*, and several of its publications are available online. It maintains links with other groups that broke away from the **Watch Tower Society** after Rutherford took office. This Australian organization should not be confused with a U.S. entity bearing the same name and which is not derived from the Watch Tower organization. *See also* DAWN BIBLE STUDENTS ASSOCIATION.

BEREAN BIBLE STUDIES. Home-based **Bible** study groups, previously called Dawn Circles for Bible study, they assumed this name around the turn of the 20th century. The name derived from the inhabitants of Berea (Beroea), whom Paul and Silas found studying the scriptures carefully (Acts 17:11). This method of Bible study directs Bible students to read and interpret scripture through Watch Tower material. On 1 March 1905, the *Watchtower* printed a list of 30 questions, directing readers to Watch Tower literature and biblical references to locate the answers. In house groups, "Berean questions" were used by the book study **overseer**, who checked for comprehension of the passage being studied. Beginning in 1922, Berean questions became a regular feature in the *Watch Tower*. **C. T. Russell**

strongly encouraged his supporters to use Berean methods of study, using the **Watch Tower Society**'s literature to interpret scripture, rather than direct systematic study of the Bible. Under **J. F. Rutherford**'s leadership, the use of Berean Bible Study rather than Free Bible Study became mandatory. Such meetings are now called **Congregational Book Studies**, and they presuppose that "understanding the Bible today [is] dependent upon association with [**Jehovah**'s] organization" (*WT* 61 11/1).

BETH SARIM. Literally "House of the Princes." **J. F. Rutherford** predicted that the ancient patriarchs mentioned in Hebrews 11 (the "princes" Abraham, Joseph, David, and others) would rise from the dead to herald the coming **kingdom**, in fulfillment of Psalm 45:16, and assume control of earthly affairs. The year set for this event was **1925**, and Rutherford conceded his error when this event did not occur. He did not abandon this hope, however, and had a house built in San Diego, California—Beth Sarim—to accommodate some of the expected princes and give tangible expression to the **prophecy**. Rutherford, in need of a warm climate because of his **health**, meanwhile occupied the house, which is depicted in his *Salvation* (1939), with an accompanying explanation. Beth Sarim was sold shortly after Rutherford's death. **Jehovah's Witnesses** now teach that the earthly **resurrection** of the "ransomed dead," including these patriarchs, is to be expected after **Armageddon** and not before. *See also* DEATH; PARADISE EARTH; SALVATION.

BETHEL. A branch office consists of a Bethel home, which specializes in the production and distribution of Watch Tower publications and oversees the organizational needs of the country it supervises. It provides a home for its workers, in which they live as a community. Until 1908, the **Watch Tower Society**'s headquarters was known as **Bible** House and was located in Allegheny, Pennsylvania, but owing to the organization's expansion, new offices were purchased in Brooklyn, New York, in 1908, and the name "Bethel" was given. The name means "house of God" and is the name of an important biblical city. The Brooklyn Bethel opened in 1909, and in 2007 the society reported 114 Bethels worldwide, with a total of 19,328 volunteer staff of ordained **ministers**.

The Bethel accommodates all aspects of literature production, including research, translation, printing and binding, and physical distribution. Literature encompasses Bibles, books, magazines, brochures, CDs, and DVDs. The society normally seeks men between the ages of 19 and 35 for Bethel work; they must have been baptized members for more than a year; be spiritually, physically, and emotionally fit for the work; and be willing to stay for at least a year. Preference is given to regular **pioneers**. Assignments are also given to **Jehovah's Witnesses** who have specialist nonpublishing skills, for example, in accountancy, information technology, and construction. In such cases, the age restriction does not apply, and married couples are eligible. Housekeepers also work for the Bethel homes.

The Bethel operates as a religious community and an administrative unit. The day begins with worship, and there are devotional meetings at other times. Members may use the library facilities for personal study and research. Work is carried out from Monday through Friday and on Saturday mornings. Members are assigned to a local **congregation**, where they worship on Sundays and attend weekly meetings. *See also* BAPTISM.

BIBELFORSCHER. Literally "**Bible** students" in German, the name continued to be used in Germany for some time after the **Watch Tower Society**'s adoption of the name "**Jehovah's Witnesses**" in 1931. The Bibelforscher were banned by Adolf Hitler in 1935 and persecuted by the Third Reich. Approximately 13,400 Bibelforscher spent time in prison or concentration camps during **World War II**. Some 2,000 perished, and 270 were executed before the survivors were finally liberated in 1945.

BIBLE. The principal source of authority for **Jehovah's Witnesses** that has been studied since the inception of **C. T. Russell**'s **Zion's Watch Tower Tract Society**. During the society's early years, **colporteurs** distributed Russell's *Studies in the Scriptures*. In 1921, **J. F. Rutherford** published *The Harp of God*, which introduced the key ideas of the Bible and was accompanied by a correspondence course.

Witnesses hold that the writing of the Bible commenced some 3,500 years ago, preceding the composition of any other religion's scripture. Subsequent writing continued over the ensuing 16 centuries and was the work of around 40 authors. The **Watch Tower Society** accepts the Protestant canon, not the Apocrypha; while Russell and Rutherford referred to its two components as the Old and New Testaments, in line with mainstream Christianity, the preferred names are now the **Hebrew-Aramaic Scriptures** and the **Christian Greek Scriptures**.

Witnesses consider the Bible to be the infallible word of God, thoroughly compatible with science, history, and archaeology and affording sound guidance on morals and **health**. It is regarded as a book of **prophecy**, reliably predicting ancient events, the coming of **Jesus Christ**, and signs of the end of the modern era. The society acknowledges that there have been mistakes in the copying of the text but believes that these errors have largely been corrected. There have been attempts to tamper with the text to vindicate false doctrine, for example, the introduction of the **Trinity** in the King James translation of 1 John 5:7. The society's own **New World Translation** is therefore preferred. Witnesses reject the view that the Bible is to be understood "literally" throughout, acknowledging that in places it includes metaphor, symbolic language, and figurative speech.

Witnesses largely study the Bible through the society's own publications, rather than select their own passages for private devotional study. Use of the Bible tends to be organized around themes, to which a variety of biblical sources contribute. At times, books on specific biblical texts are issued, for example, *Daniel's Prophecy* (1999) and *Isaiah's Prophecy* (2000–2001). All the Witnesses' teachings are referenced closely to the Bible. *See also* EMPHATIC DIAGLOTT.

BIBLE STUDENTS. *See* INTERNATIONAL BIBLE STUDENTS ASSOCIATION (IBSA).

BIBLE STUDY. The term can be used generically to refer to any situation in which the **Bible** is read, both in personal devotion and public worship, not necessarily by **Jehovah's Witnesses**. Specifically, the phrase denotes a session led by a **publisher** with an unbaptized inquirer, normally in the inquirer's home, as a follow-up to initial **house-to-house ministry**. Bible study is normally prefaced by a short extempore **prayer**, followed by sequential reading of sections from one of the **Watch Tower Society**'s recommended brochures for this purpose.

The publication *What Does God Require of Us?* (1996) is typically used in this context. The brochure outlines key Christian doctrines, as interpreted by the Watch Tower organization, and these are discussed using accompanying questions, together with biblical cross-references. It is not the Witnesses' practice in such a context to examine a book of the Bible directly and sequentially. Between six and ten sessions are normally required to examine the brochure fully, and inquirers who complete the series of studies may then express an interest in undergoing further preparation toward **baptism.**

Publishers keep records of the Bible studies they conduct, and national and international statistics relating to these sessions are disclosed in the society's annual Yearbooks.

BIRTH CONTROL. Although God instructed the first man and woman to "Be fruitful and become many and fill the earth and subdue it" (Genesis 1:28), **Jehovah's Witnesses** regard this commandment as belonging to the old **covenant** and point out that no such injunction was given to Christians. The purpose of sexual intercourse is therefore not exclusively for reproduction but for the pleasurable expression of love between husband and wife. Contraception is permissible, so long as it is preventative and not abortive, since life is held to begin at the moment of conception. The decision as to whether to practice contraception and, if so, which method is favored is a matter for each couple to determine. The use of the intrauterine device (IUD) is a matter of conscience, since there is disagreement among medical experts about whether it is preventative or abortive. Sterilization is not favored, since it involves mutilation of the human body. It is not explicitly forbidden but is a matter for individual **conscience.** Where the life and health of a mother depends on sterilization, there should be no objection; if conscience allows, the husband may undergo vasectomy to preserve his wife's **health.**

The **Watch Tower Society** points out that the Roman Catholic Church's prohibition on contraception did not occur until the 13th century and that it has no warrant in scripture. *See also* ABORTION; BIBLE.

BIRTHDAYS. Jehovah's Witnesses point out that birthday celebrations were not part of Jewish or first-century Christian practice. Only two birthdays are mentioned in the **Bible**: an Egyptian pharaoh (Genesis 40:20–22) and the Roman governor Herod Antipas (Matthew 14:6–11), neither of whom subscribed to "true **religion**." It is noted that both celebrations were associated with executions. In early years, Bible students observed birthdays, but the practice was abandoned shortly after **Christmas** celebrations were discontinued in 1928.

Birthday celebrations are held to derive from and are associated with **pagan** practices. It has been believed, for example, that one has a mystical relationship with a protective spirit whose birthday one shares. Birthdays are also linked to astrology, being needed for horoscopes. The use of birthday candles is said to derive from Greek fertility rites, and the practice of making wishes is magical and superstitious. Additionally, birthdays involve self-glorification and often materialism.

While Witnesses believe that the birth of a child is a cause for rejoicing, birth is not marked by formal celebrations or any religious rite, like **baptism**. *See also* BABYLON; CHRISTENDOM; EASTER; OCCULTISM.

BLOOD. Blood was first stored during **World War I**, and the use of blood banks only became widespread in the 1940s, largely as a consequence of **World War II**. Statements regarding blood transfusion are therefore not found in the organization's earliest writings. The first *Watchtower* articles on the topic appeared on 1 December 1944 and 1 July 1945. **Jehovah's Witnesses** regard blood as sacrosanct, being the life force of any living being, and the ingesting of blood is seen as contrary to the **Bible**. Proof-texts that are typically cited in support of this are Jehovah's commandment to Noah (Genesis 9:3–4), the prohibition in Leviticus 17:4, and the early Church's pronouncement on blood (Acts 15:28–29). Although Witnesses acknowledge that blood transfusion can have harmful effects, like the transmission of AIDS, they see such facts as vindication of their belief rather than justification of it.

The prohibition includes the storing of blood, including one's own; blood donations and transfusions; and the consumption of meat that still substantially contains an animal's blood, for example, black pudding. Medication that is derived from blood fractions is a matter of individual **conscience**. Witnesses, however, do not object to **organ**

transplantation or donation or to the use of dialysis equipment. Acceptable alternatives to blood are saline solution and blood volume expanders, like Hetastarch. Witnesses typically carry a "No Blood" card on their person at all times to ensure that this belief is respected.

BOARD OF DIRECTORS. Two incorporated Watch Tower organizations exist: the **Watch Tower Bible and Tract Society of Pennsylvania** and the **Watchtower Bible and Tract Society of New York**. Each is overseen by a board of seven men; they are earthly organizations, subject to **Caesar's rule**. Board members were formerly elected by shareholders, who became eligible to vote by purchasing shares at US$10 a share. **C. T. Russell** initially held the majority of shares and thus had control over both societies. Membership to the board was initially by co-option, with the shareholders merely voting the **president**, vice president, and secretary-treasurer into office from the wider board. **J. F. Rutherford** questioned the legality of this system, requiring all board members to be elected.

Until 1971, the Board of Directors of the Watch Tower Bible and Tract Society of Pennsylvania constituted the society's **Governing Body**, and all belonged to the **anointed class**. Since the number of anointed ones on earth was dwindling and since it seemed inappropriate that the Governing Body be bound by earthly civil laws, both organizations were restructured, and thereafter 500 corporation members, most of whom were not anointed, elected the directors, who were now distinct from the Governing Body. **Nathan H. Knorr**, then president of both incorporated organizations, continued to preside over them, as well as occupy a place on the Governing Body. The organizational structure was again changed in 2000, when the entire Boards of Directors of both organizations, including President **Milton G. Henschel**, resigned their positions and were replaced by others, none of whom were anointed, effectively separating the directors from the Governing Body, at least organizationally. *See also* ADAMS, DON ALDEN; LARSON, MAX H.

BOOK OF REVELATION. *See* REVELATION, BOOK OF.

BOOK STUDY. *See* CONGREGATION BOOK STUDY.

BRANCH. A region of the world, usually an entire country and sometimes a cluster of several small countries, in which the **Watch Tower Society** has a headquarters office, presided over by a branch **overseer** who acts as chairman of the branch committee. The branch has jurisdiction over the various **districts**, **circuits**, and local **congregations**, overseeing their preaching work.

BROTHER. A baptized male member of a **congregation**. The term may be employed either as a noun or as a title prefixing one's surname. It is considered acceptable for speakers to use the term to address male and female members of a congregation collectively. The word is used in the **Bible** not merely to signify the kinship of male siblings but also a cousin or close friend. **Christian Greek Scriptures** use the term to signify an entire Christian congregation. **Watch Tower** literature notes the words of **Jesus**, that "whoever does the will of my Father who is in heaven, the same is my brother, and **sister**, and mother" (Matthew 12:50). *See also* BAPTISM.

– C –

CAESAR'S LAW. *See* CAESAR'S RULE.

CAESAR'S RULE. Aka Caesar's Law. The term alludes to the question posed to **Jesus** about tribute money and whether it should be paid to the Roman authorities. Jesus' rejoinder was, "Pay back, therefore, Caesar's things to Caesar, but God's things to God" (Matthew 22:21). Until **theocracy** is established, **Jehovah's Witnesses** live under the jurisdiction of civil governments. Following Jesus' instruction, they consider themselves obliged to fulfill their civil obligations, unless they conflict with divine law, as expressed in the **Bible**. Witnesses are therefore enjoined to be honest and scrupulous in their compliance with the law and to pay their taxes honestly. However, at times they have felt constrained to oppose the law, for example, when conscripted to fight in **wars** or obliged to make open expressions of patriotism, like **flag salutes**.

The society's **elders** implement divine law, not Caesar's law, which will be removed after **Armageddon**. *See also* HIGHER POWERS; THEOCRACY.

CHARITABLE WORK. Jehovah's Witnesses express concern about the world's social problems, and articles in the *Watchtower* and, more particularly, in *Awake!*, address such matters as poverty, famine, crime, drug abuse, and **environmental issues**. Witnesses may work for organizations that seek to remedy such problems, provided they are not run by mainstream churches or other organizations representing **false religion**. The **Watch Tower Society** deplores the high proportion of monies that go into salaries and administrative costs in charitable organizations and counsels its members to evaluate these establishments carefully before making donations. Witnesses prefer to give directly to the needy or donate monies to another **congregation** elsewhere in the world if a disaster occurs, and such activity is coordinated by the **Governing Body**.

Social improvement and reform are not part of the society's main agenda, since the Watch Tower organization's principal task is the proclamation of **Jehovah**'s coming **kingdom**. In this **new world order**, all societal ills will disappear. Witnesses, however, will often teach adults and **children** to read and write in countries where there is a poor literacy rate; this enables them to study the **Bible** and the society's literature. Witnesses will also help to better society by paying taxes to the state, which they seek to do honestly. Within congregations, they recognize the importance of caring for the physical and emotional well-being of their members and seek to ensure that the sick and infirm are visited and cared for.

CHILDREN. Children are regarded as a gift from God, and it is natural for married couples to want to become parents. They should be properly cared for, with adequate provision for their material, emotional, and spiritual needs. Parents have a duty to ensure that they receive a good **education**, which goes beyond acquiring the abilities of reading, writing, counting, and practical training for the home or workplace. It should include spiritual and moral values, most notably the fear of **Jehovah**, honoring one's parents, knowing God's law, and obedience. As part of their spiritual education, children are expected to attend **congregation** meetings with their parents. There are no special classes for children, such as Sunday School: children are expected to participate fully in meetings and from a very early age contribute comments and ask questions. Parents are urged to spend time with their children for both recreation and **Bible** study. High moral standards are sought, and **Jehovah's Witnesses** disapprove of the trend toward permissiveness, which they perceive outside the organization. Disobedient children within society are regarded as one of the marks of the last days (Matthew 10:21).

Witnesses expect their children to work hard at school but not necessarily to accept the pressures in the West to aspire to higher education, which can encourage undue competition, materialism, and harmful **associations**. Aiming for part-time employment, coupled with work for Jehovah's organization, may be thought preferable.

Witnesses acknowledge that children need to be disciplined from time to time. The Bible offers guidance for this: a reprimand is preferable to corporal punishment (Proverbs 17:10), but the latter may be necessary if a verbal rebuke proves ineffective. As an extreme measure, a child can be expelled from a congregation, and baptized minors can undergo **disfellowshipping**, although such cases are rare. *See also* BIRTH CONTROL.

CHILIASM. *See* MILLENNIALISM.

CHRIST. The title applied to **Jesus**, being the Greek equivalent of the Hebrew-derived "messiah," meaning "anointed." **Jehovah's Witnesses** teach that Jesus was not born as the Christ but was anointed by **Jehovah** at his **baptism**, after which he preached the message of the coming **kingdom**. The title is applied to Jesus' preexistent form as **Michael**: he is regarded as the only begotten son of God but not as God himself. He was not the cocreator with God, since **creation** was accomplished by God's power working through the **holy spirit**. The title also refers to Christ in his heavenly glory, since he rules in heaven with the **144,000** members of the **anointed class**, having authority over the earth. *See also* 1914; MILLENNIAL RULE OF CHRIST; RANSOM SACRIFICE.

CHRISTENDOM. Not to be identified with Christianity, the term denotes those parts of the world where the Christian religion, as practiced by the churches, prevails. True Christians, **Jehovah's Witnesses** claim, do not want to be part of this system, since it is apostate and corrupt. It has failed God, having made the same mistakes as the **Jews** in ancient times. It has failed to heed God's prophetic warnings, declines to use the personal name of God—**Jehovah**—and it has not kept itself pure from the practices of foreign, pagan religions. Christianity's **apostasy** has been evident from the time of the Emperor Constantine, where it absorbed the ideas of the Romans and Greeks, as it demonstrated by the doctrines of the **creeds**, as well as the celebration of such festivals with **pagan** origins as **Christmas** and **Easter**.

Further, Christendom is divided, both politically and spiritually, unlike Jehovah's own organization. It is tied to political organizations and supports **war**: Witnesses note that both **World War I** and **World War II** began within Christendom. Christendom is therefore a substantial part of the politico-religious systems that are ruled by **Satan** and hence does not preach the doctrine of Satan's being cast out of heaven to rule the world.

Christendom is therefore construed as having failed God and hence is bound for destruction during the Battle of **Armageddon**. However, there still exists a **remnant** who has steadfastly maintained the **truth** and who will be able to participate in the coming **kingdom**. *See also* PROPHECY.

CHRISTIAN CONGREGATION OF JEHOVAH'S WITNESSES. Formed as a consequence of the institutional reorganization during the year 2000, this arm of the **Watch Tower Society** attends to its special full-time service: those who work in **Bethels**, special **pioneers**, and traveling **overseers**. It oversees congregations and corresponds with them regarding the appointment of elders, ministerial servants, and those in special full-time service. *See also* ADAMS, DON ALDEN; KINGDOM SUPPORT SERVICES, INC.; RELIGIOUS ORDER OF JEHOVAH'S WITNESSES.

CHRISTIAN GREEK SCRIPTURES. The second major section of the Christian **Bible** consisting of 27 books, from Matthew to **Revela-**

tion. This section is called the "New Testament" by **Christendom**, but this term is judged inappropriate by **Jehovah's Witnesses**. Witnesses prefer to distinguish the two major sections of scripture on the grounds of language, prefacing the word "Greek" with "Christian" to distinguish this section of the Bible from the Septuagint (the early Greek version of **Hebrew-Aramaic Scriptures**). These scriptures are regarded as canonical and divinely inspired. They are attributed to eight authors: Matthew, Mark, Luke, John, Paul, James, Peter, and Jude. The Gospel of Matthew, it is believed, was originally written in Hebrew, but only the Greek text remains available. *See also* NEW WORLD TRANSLATION (NWT).

CHRISTMAS. This festival was originally celebrated by the **Watch Tower Society** but was discontinued after 1928 as part of **J. F. Rutherford**'s attempts to free the society from **pagan** elements. **Jehovah's Witnesses** decline to celebrate Christmas, principally on account of its presumed pagan origins. Christmas was not celebrated by the early Christian Church, and they do not believe that **Jesus** was born on 25 December—a date fixed by Christendom in the 4th century. The festival originated when Christianity became the official religion of the Roman Empire and replaced the festival of Saturnalia, coinciding with the winter solstice. Christmas symbols bear pagan connotations: for example, Christmas lights represent the return of the sun, and Father Christmas is a composite figure derived from miscellaneous religious traditions, not all of which are Christian. Additionally, 25 December is held to be the birthday of **Nimrod**, who is held to be the originator of the **Babylonian apostasy**.

Witnesses believe that it was unlikely that shepherds, who feature in the **Bible**'s account of Jesus' birth, would be out in the fields during winter. The more likely date for Jesus' birth is reckoned to have possibly been near the beginning of October, 2 B.C.E. (*WT* 79 12/15).

Witnesses disapprove of the commercialism of Christmas, which they believe encourages greed and materialism. They have no objection, however, to family gatherings, good meals with friends, or giving presents, which they will do at any time of the year. Some Witnesses introduce "present days" for their families, when gifts may be exchanged. *See also* BIRTHDAYS; EASTER.

CIRCUIT. The term's original use is biblical, designating the itinerary of the judges in the **Hebrew-Aramaic Scriptures** (1 Samuel 7:15), and also of **Jesus** and his disciples undertaking their mission (Matthew 10:16), as well as early church missionaries like Paul. **Jehovah's Witnesses** apply the term to a cluster of **congregations**, which are grouped by locality, and about 20 of these form a circuit. Each circuit has a circuit **overseer**—an **elder** who travels on a week-to-week basis, visiting each congregation twice a year. Many circuits have their own premises called **Assembly Halls**, where circuit **assemblies** are held for the purposes of devotion, teaching, and **baptism**. *See also* BIBLE.

CIVIL AUTHORITY. *See* CAESAR'S RULE.

CLEANSING OF THE SANCTUARY. This expression alludes to the holiest area in the Israelites' tabernacle (Leviticus 16:32) and subsequently the Jerusalem Temple, where the high priest entered the Holy of Holies (the sanctuary) only once a year on the Day of Atonement. This ancient Hebrew practice was mirrored in **Jesus'** cleansing of the Temple (John 2:13–17) and the miraculous rending of the Temple veil, which hid the sacred sanctuary area, at the time of Jesus' **death** (Matthew 27:51). After the destruction of the Temple by King Nebuchadnezzar's army—presumed to have occurred in 607 B.C.E.— Daniel prophesied an end to the days in which God's sanctuary would remain defiled (Daniel 8:14). This **prophecy** is believed to have two fulfillments: one in the restoration of the Temple after the **Jews'** return from exile and subsequently in present-day end-time events. Daniel's prophecy refers to "a time, times, and half a time," which the **Adventist** tradition equated with the period of 2,300 "days" mentioned in Daniel 8:14.

Adventists typically identified the cleansing of the sanctuary with the purification of the earth by fire following **Christ**'s second coming, thus conceiving of it as a physical occurrence. However, following the **Great Disappointment** brought about by **William Miller**, James White (the husband of Ellen G. White) claimed that 1844, the apparently failed date for Christ's return, marked the spiritual event of Christ's entering the most holy place of the heavenly sanctuary, an antitypical Day of Atonement. Applying the "**day-for-a-year rule**,"

C. T. Russell concluded that the 2,300-day period ended in the spring of 1846. In common with other Adventists, he associated the defilement of the "sanctuary" with Roman Catholicism, which had become corrupt in its teachings and practices and by its associations with earthly governments. Russell identified the formation of the Evangelical Alliance that year as a key event in purging Christianity of several important deficiencies.

J. F. Rutherford provided a different interpretation, preferring to link the cleansing of the sanctuary to current events in Palestine, as well as to the internal disputes within the **Watch Tower** organization. He viewed it as a progressive process rather than an episodic event. The Holy Land, he argued, was the "soul" of God's sanctuary and was in the process of restoration by the return of the Jews from **1918**. The year 1918 also marked the beginning of Christ's rule in heaven, which was followed by a cleansing that "began in earnest" in 1922. Rutherford perceived the year 1926 as significant, since the international convention in London on 25 through 31 May passed a resolution condemning the **League of Nations**. Rutherford also regarded his own purging of the Watch Tower Society of dissenters as part of the cleansing, in particular those who advocated the system of elective **elders**, which was abolished in 1932. After the 1930s, the term *cleansing of the sanctuary* is only rarely used in the society's literature. **Jehovah's Witnesses** now believe that the 2,300 days started in June 1938, lasting until October 1944 and that the expression relates to the Witnesses' persecution during the **war** years and Rutherford's further reforms to the society. *See also* ADVENTISM; END-TIME CALCULATIONS.

CLERGY. The **Bible** students and subsequent **Jehovah's Witnesses** have always remained a lay movement, without any professional clergy, and they insist that all Witnesses are "**ministers**." Witnesses hold that the early Church did not have any division between clergy and laity and had no religious specialists who received payment for their services, used titles like "Reverend" or "Father," wore ecclesiastical robes, or assumed special powers, like the forgiveness of **sins** or the authority to celebrate sacraments.

Distinctions between priesthood and laity are believed to be characteristic of **Babylonian** religion, which has entered **Christendom**.

Watch Tower literature condemns such **apostasy** and accuses clergy of frequently keeping their laity in ignorance or poverty, spreading **false religion**, and persecuting true Christians. Christian clergy, for example, expressed opposition to **C. T. Russell**'s posthumous *The Finished Mystery* (1917) and were believed to have instigated the arrests of **J. F. Rutherford** and his associates. Witnesses point out the various respects in which clergy are deemed to have compromised the Christian faith. Examples include acceptance of Charles Darwin's theory of **evolution**, rejection of the inerrancy of the Bible, support for **war**, the ordination of **women**, and tolerance of homosexuality.

Witnesses are committed to training their members for their work, and **elders** are selected from within their **congregations** to preside over affairs.

COLE, MARLEY (1916–). A news reporter and an active **Jehovah's Witness.** He is principally known for his book *Jehovah's Witnesses: The New World Society* (1955), which was promoted and distributed by the **Watch Tower Society** and recounts the history, teachings, and practices of the organization. The work was reissued in 1985, with an appendix that includes frank discussion of members' expectations for **1975** and the aftermath. This was followed by *Triumphant Kingdom* (1957). His writings also include *Living Destiny: The Man from MatthewMarkLukeJohn* (1984), a harmonization of the gospels, and *David* (1996). His autobiography, *Harvest of Our Lives*, was published in 1996.

COLPORTEUR. One who sells or distributes literature, particularly religious publications. The term is no longer used by **Jehovah's Witnesses**. Those who promote the **Watch Tower** organization's message outside their own congregation are now known as "**pioneers.**" **C. T. Russell** strongly encouraged his **Bible** students to act as colporteurs, commencing in 1881, when a *Watch Tower* article advertised, "Wanted—1,000 preachers." The goal of 1,000 preachers was not attained, although some 300 supporters volunteered by 1885 and 625 by 1909. The favored tract for distribution was initially Russell's "Food for Thinking Christians" (1881), although volumes of his *Millennial Dawn* (1886) were also placed in the public's hands. Colporteurs often traveled on foot or by bicycle, and within a short time they succeeded in reaching Britain, the rest of Europe, Scandinavia, Burma, and Australia, among other countries.

Russell endeavored to ensure that publications were not merely accepted by the public. A 1917 *Watchtower* article explained that pastoral workers would call on inquirers who had accepted the society's literature, inviting them to attend special talks or **Berean Bible Studies**. When pastoral workers were unavailable, colporteurs typically undertook follow-up activity themselves.

COMMUNISM. Jehovah's Witnesses do not hold that the government of the early Church was communist. Although it practiced the common sharing of possessions, it did not strive to be the godless earthly social system that gained prominence in the mid-20th century in the Soviet Union and Eastern Europe and which extolled a classless society with equal distribution of wealth and common ownership of the means of production and subsistence. **Watch Tower** publications express disapproval of communism on the grounds that it is godless and continues to perpetuate class and inequality. In any case, no human government can bring about **paradise earth**.

Witnesses viewed the former Soviet Union's policies of glasnost and perestroika in the late 1980s and the collapse of communism in Eastern Europe in the early 1990s as improvements in human civil affairs, affording better opportunities to evangelize in Russia and Eastern European countries and enabling them to claim substantial expansion there. The organization does not view the demise of communism as a fulfillment of biblical **prophecy**, although the conflicts in which it has been involved are included among the **wars** and threats mentioned in the **Bible**, and which are signs of the end of the present system of earthly affairs. *See also* PARADISE EARTH.

CONDITIONAL IMMORTALITY. Aka conditionalism. The doctrine that immortality is not an inherently human condition but one that has to be earned or obtained as a gift from God. Its corollary is the doctrine of "soul sleep": the dead are oblivious until those who are worthy of **resurrection** are awakened. Since the wicked have not earned immortality, they will not experience eternal punishment, but merely oblivion. The term is not used by the **Watch Tower Society**, since it implies that the **soul** is an immaterial entity, distinct from body, which it denies. However, **Jehovah's Witnesses** subscribe to the view that eternal life will not be enjoyed by all, but only the **great crowd**, the **anointed class**, and the resurrected dead who proved faithful, and that there will be no eternal **hell** for the unrighteous.

Conditional immortality was preached by some of the early **Adventists**, including **George Storrs**, and it is linked to the notion that the purpose of Christ's return would be to bless and not to destroy. *See also* ADVENTISM; DEATH.

CONDITIONALISM. *See* CONDITIONAL IMMORTALITY.

CONGREGATION. The term admits of a variety of meanings. The **Bible** initially uses the word to designate the "congregation of Israel," being God's chosen people, who were commanded to obey his laws. Subsequently, **Jehovah's Witnesses** have used the term as synonymous with "spiritual Israelites," by which they mean the **144,000** members of the **anointed class**. It is also used to mean the totality of true worshippers, that is, the anointed class, together with the "other sheep" and unbaptized associates.

At a local level, the **congregation** is the local community of Witnesses who meet regularly for worship and study, normally in a **Kingdom Hall**. As with the congregation of Israel, association depends on obedience to God's law and true worship of **Jehovah**. The **Watch Tower Society** notes that not everyone was included in the congregation of Israel and that one could be cut off for serious misconduct; in a similar manner, apostate members are subject to **disfellowshipping** from a congregation. It is highly important that a congregation be a group of Christians who are united together with no rival bodies.

Until 1972, each congregation had a **presiding overseer** who exercised control over its affairs. This changed in 1972, when congregations became governed by a body of **elders** with a rotating chairman and the assistance of **ministerial servants**. In 1983, further change was made, and the presiding overseer became a permanent chairman overseeing the body of elders. Only men, not **women**, are eligible for these offices. Members meet three times a week for worship. There is a public lecture followed by study of a biblical theme using the *Watchtower* magazine. Bible study is held weekly at a member's home, and the **Theocratic Ministry School** meets for training for preaching and **house-to-house ministry**. *See also* APOSTASY; BAPTISM.

CONGREGATION BOOK STUDY. One of five weekly **meetings** that members of a **congregation** are encouraged to attend. Formerly known as **Dawn Circles for Bible Study** and also Berean Circles for Bible Study, the Congregation Book Study is carried out in small groups of about 15 people or fewer in someone's private home, and the session focuses on a predetermined part of a recent book or booklet published by the **Watch Tower Society**. A book study **overseer,** formerly called a "conductor," presides over the meeting: this is usually an **elder**, and he is supported by other strong active **publishers**. Members are generally assigned to a study group.

Attendees are urged to prepare for these studies by reading the prescribed portion in advance, making notes, and, if possible, looking up accompanying biblical references. Questions are provided in each study publication, and the overseer may use these to check for comprehension and encourage comment. The purpose of these meetings is to foster the spiritual well-being of a congregation and reinforce members' confidence in their faith. A well-conducted book study also sets an example to other publishers who can learn how a **Bible** study should be conducted in inquirers' homes. All who attend are encouraged to participate actively. Punctuality is expected, and members should dress smartly, not casually. *See also* BEREAN BIBLE STUDIES; DAWN BIBLE STUDENTS ASSOCIATION.

CONGREGATION SERVANT. *See* PRESIDING OVERSEER (P.O.).

CONLEY, WILLIAM H. (1840–1897). First president of **Zion's Watch Tower Tract Society** in 1881. Little is known about Conley, apart from his being part of **C. T. Russell**'s nucleus of five founder-members, consisting of Russell, his father, his sister Margaret, and Conley and his wife. He was not an office bearer in the **Watch Tower Bible and Tract Society of Pennsylvania** when it became incorporated in 1884. Russell's group celebrated the Passover in Conway's home in Allegheny, Pennsylvania, in April 1880 and 1881. His home is described as "commodious," and he was a director of Riter and Conley, a metal fabrication firm. There appears to be no reference to him in Watch Tower sources after 1881, apart from the publication of a letter in *Zion's Watch Tower* on 11 June 1894, in which he responds to a pamphlet written by Russell entitled *A Conspiracy Exposed and Harvest Siftings*. Russell composed the pamphlet to rebut false accusations against dissenting members, and Conley stated that he never denied the doctrine of the **ransom sacrifice**. It is unknown whether Conley dissociated himself from the organization and if so why. *See also* MEMORIAL.

CONSCIENCE. Neither the **Bible** nor the **Watch Tower Society** provides definitive guidance for all moral situations, and there are gray areas that are left for individual decision. The Bible teaches that, in addition to God's law, there is a law written on one's heart (Romans 2:14–15), which serves as an inner faculty for ethical judgment. Examples of borderline ethical decisions cited in the *Watchtower* include working as a hospital technician, where tests may be used for **blood** transfusion purposes, or deciding whether to stand when a national anthem is played. Choosing one's friends, deciding what music to listen to, or pursuing higher **education** may also be matters of conscience.

Conscience is not infallible and hence requires training; it can be corrupted by **false religion**. It is reckoned to be superior to a detailed set of codified rules but does not provide a carte blanche for one's actions. **Jehovah's Witnesses** are urged to invoke biblical principles in using one's conscience, especially respect for headship, honesty, hatred of what is bad, pursuit of peace, obedience to authority, devotion to **Jehovah**, not being part of this world, avoiding bad **associations**, modesty in dress and demeanor, and not causing others to stumble. *See also* FLAG SALUTE.

CONVENTIONS. In the early years of the **International Bible Students Association**, gatherings to which all members were invited were held near Pittsburgh, Pennsylvania, and were followed by a "love feast." These meetings were not open to the public, but in 1892, some outsiders who expressed an interest in **Christ**'s **ransom sacri-**

fice were permitted to attend. In 1893, the first convention outside Pittsburgh convened, and from 1900 onward, general conventions grew in popularity, reaching a record attendance for any single event in 1958 when 253,922 people assembled at Yankee Stadium and the nearby Polo Grounds in New York. Large gatherings of **Jehovah's Witnesses** have been called **assemblies**, but the term *convention* was substituted when assemblies were declared illegal in the United States during the war years.

Conventions are national or international gatherings essentially for the purposes of teaching and devotion. However, until 1945, they included business matters, and resolutions were discussed and adopted. In the postwar period, the **Watch Tower Society** has become organized along more theocratic lines, and business matters are conducted at an Annual Business Meeting of the **Watch Tower Bible and Tract Society of Pennsylvania**, which is attended by and composed of a corporate membership of between 300 and 500 men chosen by its **Board of Directors**.

In the past, conventions have provided the platform for key strategies within the organization. Important landmarks include the 1922 Convention in Cedar Point, Ohio, where **J. F. Rutherford** delivered his address *Millions Now Living Will Never Die!* and exhorted **Bible** students to "advertise, advertise, advertise the **kingdom**." The 1931 Convention in Columbus, Ohio, was used to announce the organization's new name, "Jehovah's Witnesses." Also noteworthy is the 1933 Berlin-Wilmersdorf Convention, where the controversial "**Declaration of Facts**" was approved, which has sometimes been construed as supportive of Adolf Hitler's government. The 1935 Convention in Washington, D.C., formulated the definitive meaning of the "**great crowd**."

Attendees may be referred to as "delegates," but there are no longer business matters to vote on, and **congregations** do not appoint designated people to represent them. All Witnesses are encouraged to attend, and the gatherings are open to the public. *See also* MEMORIAL; MILLIONS CAMPAIGN; THEOCRACY.

COTTAGE MEETINGS. *See* DAWN CIRCLES FOR BIBLE STUDY.

COVENANT. An agreement or legal contract, generally entered into by two parties. In the **Bible**, the term denotes an agreement between **Jehovah** and various pre-Christian patriarchs, notably Noah, Abraham, Moses, and King David. A covenant entails a dependable promise, generally involving the protection and preservation of God's people. Thus, the Abrahamic covenant afforded the prospect of a land, populated by innumerable descendants of Abraham. The Davidic covenant promised an everlasting **kingdom** for David's progeny. The prophet Jeremiah spoke of a "new covenant" (Jeremiah 31:31–34), which rendered the old one obsolete. The new covenant comes through **Jesus Christ** and offers a heavenly calling to the **anointed class**, who aspire to Jehovah's kingdom in heaven. The **great crowd** is assured of everlasting well-being in **paradise earth** and partakes of God's covenant similar to the way foreigners could enjoy the benefits of the Jews' covenant with God. **Jehovah's Witnesses** believe that the term *covenant* is preferable to the term *testament* when applied to the two sets of scriptures, since "covenant" is a more accurate translation of the Greek *diathēkē*, which is rendered as "testament" in mainstream Christianity.

COVINGTON, HAYDEN COOPER (1911–1979). Legal counsel for the **Jehovah's Witnesses** from 1939 to 1963, Covington studied at the San Antonio Bar Association School of Law and was admitted to the bar in Texas in 1933. He was baptized in 1934 and acted as attorney on 111 legal cases against Witnesses, 44 of which went as far as the U.S. Supreme Court, pertaining to human rights and freedom of **religion**, particularly the rights of Witnesses to undertake **house-to-house ministry** and distribute literature. He worked closely with **J. F. Rutherford** and, upon **Nathan H. Knorr**'s assumption of office in 1942, he became vice president of the **Watch Tower Bible and Tract Society of Pennsylvania**. He resigned in 1945, having come to the belief that he belonged to the earthly class rather than the **anointed class**. He was **disfellowshipped** in 1963 (the precise reason is contested) but was later reinstated. He acted as defense lawyer on behalf of boxer Muhammad Ali (Cassius Clay), who refused to be drafted into the U.S. Army in 1967, enabling him to be cleared by the Supreme Court in 1971.

CREATION. Jehovah's Witnesses accept the **Bible**'s account of a six-day creation. However, a "creative day" is not equivalent to 24 hours. Its precise length is unspecified but may be thousands of years in duration. God's first creation was his "only begotten son," who assisted him with the creation of the **angels**. As the Bible teaches, the six "days" respectively saw the creation of light, sky, dry land and vegetation, the visibility of heavenly bodies, fish and birds, and finally **animals** and humanity. Witnesses reject the view of Western mainstream scholarship, which alleges that the Bible draws on **Babylonian** creation myths. The theory of **evolution** is likewise denied. Although the various stages of creation cannot be dated, a date can be given for the creation of **Adam** by means of examining the Bible's genealogical information. *The Truth Shall Make You Free* set this date at 4028 B.C.E., although later **Watch Tower** teaching revised this to 4026 B.C.E., which is now the generally accepted date. *See also* CHRIST; JESUS; MICHAEL.

CREATIONISM. The belief, championed by the Moral Majority in the United States, that the earth was created less than 10,000 years ago in six 24-hour days, normally coupled with the belief that all geological strata were formed as a result of the great flood of Noah's time. **Jehovah's Witnesses** do not accept these tenets and do not view creationism as the only alternative to **evolution**. **Jehovah's Witnesses** view creationism as incompatible with scientific theory. Geologists have discovered fossils that are millions of years old, astronomers have located stars whose light has taken billions of years to reach the earth, and nuclear physicists believe that the radioactive elements have also had lives of billions of years. The **Watch Tower Society** therefore endorses the view of scientists who hold that the age of the earth is between 10 and 20 billion years and concludes that creationism is unscientific.

Watch Tower sources contend that the "creative days" referred to in the **Bible**'s account of creation should not be understood as literal periods of 24 hours. They point out that the word "day" in scripture admits of a variety of senses, including an unspecified period of time. The length of a creative day is not defined, hence Witnesses find themselves able to believe that the earth is billions of years old without compromising scientific integrity. Their rejection of creationism, however, does not entail that species evolved from common ancestries over this lengthy time period. *See also* CREATION.

CREEDS. The **Watch Tower Society** has never formulated any independent creed or statement of doctrine on the ground that the **Bible** is the sole source of authority. Although **Jehovah's Witnesses** study the Bible through Watch Tower literature, all the society's teachings purport to be Bible-based, and any changes or developments in doctrine are justified by its interpretation of scripture.

Not only does the society consider it unnecessary to formulate a creed that is separate from the Bible, Witnesses contend that creeds do not go back either to **Jesus** or the early Church. The Apostles' Creed was not written by the twelve apostles but dates from around 340 C.E. The Nicene Creed was originally formulated by the Council of Nicaea in 325 and underwent further amendment at the Council of Chalcedon in 451 C.E. The creeds are rooted in theological controversy, which served to divide rather than unite Christians, and they draw on concepts from Greek philosophy, thus demonstrating the apostate nature of mainstream Christianity. They have given rise to doctrines that Witnesses deny, like Christ being God incarnate and the doctrine of the **Trinity**. The recitation of the words of the creed during a service is "vain repetition," and Witnesses deplore the fact that many clergy no longer believe the statements of the creeds and contend that this is further evidence of hypocrisy and falling away from the truth. *See also* BABYLON; PAGANISM.

CROSS. While acknowledging the importance of **Jesus Christ**'s death as a **ransom sacrifice** for **sin**, **Jehovah's Witnesses** do not use the symbol of the cross and insist that Jesus' death was not on a cross but on a "torture stake"—an upright piece of wood—which they believe correctly translates the Greek word *stauros* in the **Bible**, as **J. F. Rutherford** pointed out in *Riches* (1936). At one time, a "cross and crown" symbol was used by Bible students. It featured a laurel wreath with a cross going through at an angle, and it was worn as a lapel badge and displayed as a logo on copies of the *Watch Tower* from 1891 to 1931. Witnesses dislike the cross symbol, partly because of its associations with apostate Christianity but also because they regard it as a **pagan** symbol, being used, for example, as a symbol of Tammuz in ancient Chaldean religion. *See also* APOSTASY; BABYLON.

– D –

DAWN BIBLE STUDENTS ASSOCIATION. A breakaway group of **Bible** students who draw on the teachings of **C. T. Russell** rather than **J. F. Rutherford** and subsequent **Jehovah's Witnesses**. The association was founded by Norman Woodworth and John E. Dawson, who worked initially in **WBBR** but who came under criticism for presenting the views of Russell rather than Rutherford. They left the organization in 1929, joining an independent Brooklyn **ecclesia**. In 1931, a **convention** was held, at which a central committee was set up, and the following year Dawn Incorporated of New York was founded. The Dawn Bible Students specialize in media ministries. Initially a radio program entitled *Frank and Ernest* was aired featuring characters portrayed by Woodworth and Dawson, respectively. The show was renamed *The Voice of Tomorrow* in October 1940. The radio dialogues were reprinted in *Radio Echo*, renamed *The Dawn* in 1932. The latter continues to circulate, with copies in French, German, Greek, Italian, Spanish, and Polish. The organization also exploited the early use of tape recordings and has made low-budget films. Members meet in ecclesias and organize conventions worldwide. *See also* JOHNSON, PAUL S. L.

DAWN CIRCLES FOR BIBLE STUDY. Aka Praise, Prayer, and Testimony Meetings. Initially called "cottage meetings," they were renamed Dawn Circles for **Bible** Study in 1895. Encouraged by **C. T. Russell**, Bible students met in private homes to study the Bible via Russell's writings, principally his volumes of *Millennial Dawn*, which were read paragraph by paragraph. These studies were subsequently based on **J. F. Rutherford**'s writings and on *Watch Tower* articles. Presided over by a book study **overseer**, the meetings also included **prayer**, hymn singing, and personal testimony. Around the turn of the century they assumed the name **Berean Bible Studies**.

DAY-FOR-A-YEAR RULE. This principle for interpreting biblical **prophecy** originated with the Protestant Reformers, including John Wycliffe, Martin Luther, and John Calvin, among others. It was used particularly for **end-time calculations** within **Adventism**, notably by **William Miller** and Ellen G. White. The rule involves regarding the word "day" in prophetic writings as meaning a year, and it is justified principally by Ezekiel's statement, "A day for a year, a day for a year, is what I have given you" (Ezekiel 4:6). In accordance with the biblical calendar, the length of a year is regarded as 360 days and can be regarded as being synonymous with "time."

Thus, Daniel's prophecy, "seven times themselves will pass over you, until you know that the Most High is Ruler in the kingdom of mankind" (Daniel 4:32), is taken to specify the length of the **Gentile times**, being 2,520 (7 times 360) "days"—in other words years—running from 607 B.C.E. (the presumed date of King Nebuchadnezzar's destruction of Jerusalem) to **1914** C.E.

DEATH. The condition in which life, thinking, and consciousness ceases, human death is taught to be a consequence of **sin**, a state inherited from **Adam**'s disobedience to God. Since the death of **animals** and plants has no such origin, it is regarded as a natural process, which is expected to continue even into **paradise earth** after **Armageddon**. Being "enslavement to corruption" (Romans 8:21), death is to be regarded as an enemy, whose destruction is made possible by **Christ**'s **ransom sacrifice**.

With the exception of the **144,000** members of the **anointed class** who died after **1918**, when their **resurrection** began, those who die are in an unconscious state, which the **Bible** compares to sleep. Those in this condition are said to inhabit **Hades** (Sheol in Hebrew), to which **Jesus** descended between the time of his death and resurrection. Members of the **great crowd** can expect resurrection during the **millennial rule of Christ** after Armageddon. During this period, death will give up many of its victims. God will determine which of the dead merit resurrection, and they will have a further opportunity to accept his teachings. Nonacceptance will result in the "second death," which is mentioned in the Book of **Revelation** (8:11). This second death differs from humanity's inherited death, being a state of total oblivion from which no release is possible.

Since the dead are unconscious, they cannot be contacted by the living, and any attempts to do so, for example by spiritualist mediums, are strongly condemned. *See also* CONDITIONAL IMMORTALITY; FUNERALS; HELL; OCCULTISM.

DECECCA, GIOVANNI (1879–1965). Born in Calitri, Italy, his early life was that of a shepherd boy. DeCecca's family immigrated to the United States in 1900, and in 1904 he was visited by a **Watch Tower Society colporteur**, who interested him in **C. T. Russell**'s *Studies in the Scriptures*. In 1906, he attended a convention in Asbury Park, New Jersey, where he met Russell and was baptized. After undertaking colporteur work, he joined the Brooklyn **Bethel** staff in 1909. He supported **J. F. Rutherford** during the leadership controversies in 1917 and 1918 and served a prison sentence with Rutherford and other leaders in 1918 and 1919 as a result of charges arising from the publication of *The Finished Mystery* (1917). He received a shorter sentence from that of the other leaders—10 years instead of 20—for no obvious reason.

DECLARATION OF FACTS. Aka Wilmersdorf Declaration. At the Berlin-Wilmersdorf Convention on 25 June 1933, delegates approved a document drawn up by **J. F. Rutherford** as an attempt to persuade Adolf Hitler to allow the **Bibelforscher (Jehovah's Witnesses)** the freedom to practice their religion under the Third Reich. This declaration briefly set out the history, aims, and practices of the Witnesses, asking that arrests, imprisonment, and other forms of state persecution cease. Two and a half million copies were circulated in Germany and sent to all high officials of the government. The document has been criticized for expressing support for the "high ideals" of the Third Reich and for failing to condemn its anti-Semitism. The full text of the declaration was included in the 1934 *Yearbook of Jehovah's Witnesses*. *See also* WORLD WAR II.

DEMONSTRATION. The most frequent use of the term among **Jehovah's Witnesses** is to refer to a presentation in the form of a dialogue, skit, sketch, or short dramatization, typically given at **assemblies** or **conventions**. Any form of presentation to a gathering of Witnesses, other than a traditional talk or lecture, can be referred to as a "demonstration." The script is generally on an outline supplied by the **Watch Tower Society** and is completed by local members within the **congregation**, who can practice their performance at Service Meetings. The use of demonstrations is not simply to transmit the organization's message in a more palatable way: **women** are permitted to take part, since the provision of demonstrations is not a direct form of address to a congregation.

The term has additional meanings. In the **Bible** it can mean "evidence" or "conviction," as in the description of **faith** as an "evident demonstration of realities though not beheld" (Hebrews 11:1). It can also be used in the popular sense of "protest," although Witnesses are not permitted to take part in political or campaigning activities of this kind.

DEVIL. *See* SATAN.

DISASSOCIATION. The process of voluntarily renouncing membership of the **Jehovah's Witnesses**, dissociation differs from **disfellowshipping** in that the former is effected by the member and does not involve a judicial committee. One may renounce one's membership either by words or by actions. A disassociating Witness may write a formal letter of resignation—the preferred course of action—or one's actions may indicate withdrawal if the member joins a secular organization, for example, taking up employment in the armaments industry.

Disassociation is not the same as spiritual weakness or lack of effort in accomplishing the **Watch Tower Society**'s work. The society accepts that members can err or fail to fulfill their publishing or study obligations and recognizes that the **Bible** teaches that they should be supported and encouraged (Romans 14:1).

Disassociation results in a formal announcement being made to the **congregation**, who will give the excluded member the same treatment as a disfellowshipped one. He or she may not communicate with a Witnesses or be allowed in his or her company, although it is permissible for disassociated members to continue to live at home with their immediate family. The society not only wishes to maintain loyalty, but seeks to prevent bad **associations** by imposing exclusion. Disassociated members can apply for reinstatement by demonstrating repentance and approaching their congregation's **elders**, who will provide appropriate admonition and advice before reviewing the former member's position. *See also* SHUNNING; WAR.

DISFELLOWSHIPPING. Expulsion of a member for misconduct. **Jehovah's Witnesses** claim biblical support for this, noting that **Jews** could be expelled from synagogues (John 9:22) and that early Christians could be cast out of the community following two admonitions (Titus 3:10–11). Disfellowshipping can be employed for sexual misconduct, theft, alcoholism, worshipping at a mainstream church, or teaching or practice that might cause schism within the organization.

There is a set procedure for disfellowshipping. A charge must come from within the **congregation**, and at least two eyewitnesses must be forthcoming before a formal investigation can be carried out by a small panel. Two admonitions are normally given to enable the offending member to mend his or her ways. Once disfellowshipped, the disciplined member may not associate with other Witnesses and may not enter their homes. He or she may attend a **Kingdom Hall** but must act in an "orderly" way; he or she may not speak or be greeted by members. The misdemeanor and its sanction are reported to the society to prevent the offender from rejoining another congregation, since the sanction of disfellowshipping is to prevent harmful **associations**.

Elders visit a disfellowshipped member annually to determine whether a return might be possible. A disfellowshipped member can be reinstated after an extended period of time, but only following open confession and sincere repentance, which are formally accepted by the original disfellowshipping committee. The reinstatement is then announced to the congregation. *See also* ALCOHOL; BABYLON; BIBLE; DISASSOCIATION; SEX; SHUNNING.

DISTRICT. The term derives from the **Bible**, particularly the books of Ezra and Nehemiah, where a "jurisdictional district" is a region of local government defined within Israel, **Babylon**, and Medo-Persia, normally centered on a city. The early Church entrusted specific apostles with the responsibility of evangelizing and overseeing designated geographical regions.

The **Jehovah's Witnesses** base their organizational system on biblical principles, with a district as a group of **circuits** in geographical proximity, each with its own district **overseer**. As well as serving obvious administrative purposes, the system of circuits facilitates the **assembly** of Witnesses in substantial numbers at district **conventions**.

DIVORCE. *See* MARRIAGE.

DOOR-TO-DOOR MINISTRY. *See* HOUSE-TO-HOUSE MINISTRY.

DRUGS. There is total opposition to recreational drugs within the **Watch Tower** organization, and total abstention is required. The commandment "You must love **Jehovah** your God with your whole heart and with your whole **soul** and with your whole mind" (Matthew 22:23) cannot be carried out if one's state of consciousness is altered by drugs. They are reckoned to be harmful to **health**, stunt growth, cause hallucinations, and lead to addiction. They are linked to crime, and, when drug-users share syringes, they risk the spread of such medical conditions as HIV and AIDS. Watch Tower sources are unimpressed by the claim that marijuana is less harmful than drugs like heroin and LSD and that it can be used for therapeutic purposes. It is argued that marijuana use can lead to the use of more dangerous drugs, and it could only have therapeutic value if it were properly manufactured and prescribed as a medicine.

Jehovah's Witnesses also contend that drugs are associated with spiritism. The Greek word that is rendered as "those who practice spiritism" (Revelation 22:15) is *pharmakoi*, which can alternatively be rendered as "druggers," according to the **New World Translation**. Parents are advised to counsel their **children** against the use of recreational drugs. If someone has to work beside a drug user, for example, in group work at college, he or she should avoid socializing with that person to minimize harmful **associations**.

Witnesses have no objection to drugs that are prescribed by qualified medical practitioners for therapeutic purposes, apart from products that involve **blood** fractions, like gamma globulin. Whether one accepts such types of medical treatment is a matter of individual **conscience**. *See also* OCCULTISM.

DUNN, HENRY (1801–1878). One-time secretary of the British and Foreign School Society, Dunn worked for Protestant missions in Italy after his retirement. His various books and tracts include *The Destiny of the Human Race* (1863) and *The Study of the Bible* (1871). **C. T. Russell** and **George Storrs** were influenced by his writings and published four extracts from the latter volume as articles in *Zion's Watch Tower*. His *Tracts for Thoughtful Christians* (1866) addresses the themes of **hell**, eternal punishment, and **predestination**. His ideas on two types of **salvation** and the times of restitution were of particular interest to Russell.

– E –

EASTER. The festival of Easter is not celebrated by **Jehovah's Witnesses**, who contend that it was not instituted by **Jesus Christ**, who merely instructed that the **memorial** should be celebrated to commemorate his impending **death**. There is no mention of Easter celebration in the **Bible**, and it was not practiced by 1st-century Christians. Witnesses note that the computation of the date of Easter was set nearly three centuries after the **resurrection**, at the Council of Nicaea in 325 C.E. By that time, **Christendom** had become apostate, being the religion of the Roman Empire.

The **Watch Tower Society** teaches that the origins of Easter and its associated customs have **pagan** roots and thus belong to **false religion**. The word *Easter* is Anglo-Saxon and refers to the Saxon goddess Estera, to whom spring offerings were sacrificed. The festival is thus associated with the returning of spring, hence fertility. Easter eggs connote new life that blossoms in spring as well as pagan theories of cosmogony. The hare or rabbit ("Easter bunny") was a pagan fertility symbol, supposedly responsible for the laying of the eggs. Hot cross buns derive from the ancient Roman practice of marking bread with a cross for use at their public pagan sacrifices, and the lighting of bonfires is thought to be Celtic or possibly pagan in origin.

Witnesses nonetheless maintain the importance of Christ's resurrection. However, they do not set aside any special day to celebrate it but simply accept it as a matter of faith. They acknowledge that it provides hope for the dead, who can look forward to everlasting life, as well as inspiration to the living to serve **Jehovah**. *See also* APOSTASY; DEATH.

ECCLESIA. The etymological meaning of the term is "called out," and the word is applied in the **Christian Greek Scriptures** to the early Christian **congregations** who are called out from the world. It is held that Noah and his family constituted the first ecclesia, being separated by **God** from the sinful antediluvians. Israel subsequently became God's ecclesia until the inception of the Christian Church in 33 C.E.

The name was applied to **C. T. Russell**'s original congregation in Pittsburgh, Pennsylvania, where he and his followers met for study and **prayer**, and the term was subsequently used by other groups of **Bible** students. The term designates a community, not a building, unlike "church," which Bible students and subsequent **Jehovah's Witnesses** have avoided. Russell's organization operated as a federation of ecclesias, which voted congregationally, electing their own **elders**, and were only loosely associated with each other. Under **J. F. Rutherford**'s leadership, the term was changed to "company" in 1931, until the congregational structure was abolished in 1938 in favor of theocratic government.

At various points in **Watch Tower** history, the term *congregation of God* denoted the **144,000 anointed** ones. After 1938, the term *ecclesia* was no longer applied to congregations. *See also* THEOCRACY.

EDUCATION. **Jehovah's Witnesses** view secular education as important, since it enables the acquisition of knowledge and skills that are necessary for being an effective **minister**. Witnesses do not have their own religious schools but are willing for **children** to be educated within the state system. Children are encouraged to work conscientiously and to manage their time well. Where religious education is taught, Witness children may participate, provided that the teaching is objective and factual. They do not participate in acts of worship, like school **assemblies** that assume a religious nature or in the celebration of such festivals as **Christmas**, **Easter**, Mother's Day, Halloween, or **birthdays**. In poorer countries where state education is not provided, the **Governing Body** has instructed Witnesses to provide literacy classes for their children. There have been occasions where Witness children have been excluded from secular schools, for example, when they refused to salute the U.S. flag or use the greeting "Heil Hitler" in Nazi Germany. In the United States, the

Witnesses set up their own "**Kingdom** Schools," using Witness and non-Witness teachers to educate children who had been expelled for refusing to salute the flag.

Most Witnesses do not pursue higher education. It is not forbidden but is a matter of **conscience**. Higher education creates the risk of detracting from one's spiritual work and can result in harmful **associations** with fellow students who may lack integrity. It is therefore recommended that, if possible, Witnesses who undergo higher education should continue to live at home. Those who seek education beyond school level are urged to consider their motives for doing so: education should not be for personal status or for a high salary.

The best education should be in accordance with biblical standards. Witnesses believe that this entails parental responsibility for their children's education, providing verbal instruction and discipline. **Jesus** is regarded as the supreme teacher, and thus the finest education is education in God's law, which comes from the study of the **Bible**. *See also* BIRTHDAYS; FLAG SALUTE.

ELDER. Each **congregation** is governed by a number of older men who preside over the congregation's affairs. They are primarily responsible for teaching and "shepherding" (counseling). In 1972, the **Watch Tower Society** introduced a system of rotation, whereby five or more elders are appointed to five corresponding offices: **congregation servant**, assistant congregation servant, **Bible** study servant, *Watchtower* study servant, and **Theocratic Ministry School** servant. The congregation servant acts as the chairman, and each year every elder assumes the preceding office. Thus, the assistant congregation servant becomes the congregation servant, and the latter falls back to being Theocratic Ministry servant. Some variations in this pattern are possible where the number of elders is more or less than five, and ministerial servants can be assigned the role of Theocratic Ministry School servant, but no other elder's office, if a fully qualified elder is unavailable. Elders work collectively and have equal authority.

The word *elder* is explained as meaning "older man," and elders should be older, both in years and in membership within the organization. They must be able to teach, since duties include giving talks at congregational meetings, and be able to advise and encourage members. The required qualifications for eldership are set out in scripture, particularly in Paul's letters to Timothy and Titus (1 Timothy 3; Titus 1). Organizationally, they are appointed by a committee established for this purpose by the **Governing Body**. Once an elder, the office is lifelong, unless one is subject to disciplining, even though the elder may no longer be able to perform his duties. *See also* WOMEN.

ELIJAH VOICE SOCIETY. A breakaway group from the **Stand Fast Bible Students**, it was founded in 1923 by John A. Hardersen and C. D. McCray. It was vehemently opposed to **flag saluting**, purchasing Liberty Bonds, and any associations with the Red Cross, considerably before other **Bible** students expressed such opposition. The group has been described as a "Seventh Volume Group," since it accepts the authenticity of *The Finished Mystery* (1917). Its main periodical is the *Elijah Voice Monthly*, and it has produced tracts entitled *The Bible Reflector*.

EMBLEMS. Commonly referred to as "elements" in mainstream Christianity, the term denotes the symbols of bread and wine that are used at the annual **Memorial** service, representing the body and **blood** of **Christ**. The practice is held to originate in **Jesus'** last evening meal with his disciples in an upper room in Jerusalem, where he took bread and wine and gave them to his disciples with the instruction, "Keep doing this in remembrance of me" (Luke 22:18), thus indicating that this practice should be perpetuated.

The bread is unleavened, since Jesus' evening meal is believed to have been a Passover celebration. Leaven also connoted impurity, and Christ, whose sacrifice for the world's **sin** was anticipated, is regarded as sinless. The wine was a substitute for the **blood** used at communion offerings prescribed in the Book of Leviticus (Leviticus 1), indicating the propitiatory nature of Christ's **ransom sacrifice**. The emblems are tokens of the new **covenant** Christ offers his followers, who become his "spiritual brothers," unitedly sharing in the benefits afforded by this sacrifice. **Jehovah's Witnesses** point out that Judas Iscariot, who betrayed Jesus, was dismissed before the emblems were distributed and hence was not party to this covenant. They also note that there is no record of Jesus himself partaking; being sinless, he had no need to do so.

The emblems are only consumed by members of the **144,000 anointed class**, since it is noted that Jesus was addressing the "little flock" (Luke 12:32) and that Jesus would not eat and drink with them again until his heavenly rule (Luke 22:14–17). The **great crowd**, who are now the majority—usually the totality—of a **congregation**, merely handle the emblems and pass them on. The participation of the anointed ones in the Memorial is held to be highly important, and if they are unable to attend the service through indisposition, **elders** will bring the emblems to their homes.

No miracles are associated with the emblems, like transubstantiation or consubstantiation. If the emblems were to transform themselves in some literal sense into the body and blood of Christ, Witnesses would regard this as cannibalism, and it would violate their prohibition on the consumption of blood. The emphasis in the Memorial is remembrance and thanksgiving.

EMPHATIC DIAGLOTT. An interlinear word-for-word translation of the New Testament (**Christian Greek Scriptures**), comprising the Greek and English text, compiled by Benjamin Wilson in 1864, based on J. J. Griesbach's Greek text (1806). In 1902, the copyright was purchased from Fowler and Wells in New York and donated to the **Watch Tower Bible and Tract Society**, which reprinted it in 1927. It is frequently referred to by the society, which claims that it supports their translation of certain problematic texts, for instance, the rendering of *parousia* as "presence" (e.g., Matthew 24:3), and "the Word was a god" at John 1:1. Although the society argues that Wilson, being outside the organization, was impartial, critics of the society's **Bible** translation have pointed out that Griesbach's text is dated and that Wilson was a Christadelphian and therefore prone to bias against mainstream renderings of the text. *See also* NEW WORLD TRANSLATION (NWT).

END-TIME CALCULATIONS. The method of constructing a chronology of occurrences pertaining to the eschaton was first devised by Joachim of Floris (c. 1130–1202) and taken up within Second **Adventism** in the 19th century. Calculations do not relate to one single eschatological event but to several decisive occurrences leading up to **Armageddon**. Methods of calculation are complex, and different Adventists drew different conclusions. The principal events that were timetabled by Adventists and subsequent **Bible** students included **Christ**'s second presence, the beginning of the new **millennium**, the **cleansing of the sanctuary**, Christ's assumption to the throne in heaven, the translation of the **anointed class** into Christ's **kingdom**, the end of the **Gentile times** and the return of the **Jews** to God's favor, the return of the "ancient worthies," and the commencement of the Battle of Armageddon.

Adventists employed three key considerations in devising the calendar of events: the date of **Adam**'s creation, Daniel's **prophecy** concerning "a time, times and half a time" (Daniel 7:25), and Daniel's prophecy relating to "seven times" (Daniel 4:25, 4:32), which was connected with the seven 50-year Jubilee periods mentioned in Leviticus and assumed to commence from the **death** of the patriarch Jacob. Adventists held that the creation of Adam was thought to define the beginning of the first millennium and that King Nebuchadnezzar's invasion of Jerusalem marked the end of the Jewish times, after which they were governed by Gentile authorities. The deciphering of the end-time calendar assumed that there were different "dispensations" of equal length—a type and an antitype.

Key end-time dates rely on the dating of historical events, like the fall of Jerusalem and the fall of **Babylon**, whether one should build a year zero into one's calculations, and whether the events that the various Adventists highlighted are physical or spiritual happenings. Bible students and **Jehovah's Witnesses** have reckoned that the creation of Adam occurred in 4026 B.C.E., rather than 4004 B.C.E., the latter being the date defined by Bishop Ussher of Armagh and subsequently widely accepted within Adventism. **C. T. Russell** regarded 606 B.C.E. and subsequently 607 B.C.E. as the date of the commencement of the Babylonian captivity, in contrast with the majority of historians, who would set 586 B.C.E. as the correct date. Despite occasional questioning of the date, Witnesses have been reluctant to revise it because of its impact on their **1914** date, which is still regarded as crucial.

Adventism has explained some delayed expectations by the notion of a "harvesting period," arguing that three and a half years elapsed between the beginning and end of Christ's ministry. This explains why a **1918**/1919 as well as a 1914 date has been postulated. The

Watch Tower organization acknowledges that its end-time calculations have undergone revision over time and describes these as "adjustments in view." However, they have not straightforwardly replaced one date with another. Physical expectations can be
"spiritualized, and Bible students, in common with the Adventist
movement, have frequently averred that they have alighted on a correct date, but for the wrong event.

ENVIRONMENTAL ISSUES. Beginning in the early 1970s, *Watchtower* and *Awake!* have included many articles on ecological issues,
spanning atmospheric pollution, deforestation, toxic waste, water
pollution and scarcity, among others. The material covers scientific
and political attempts to address environmental problems, for example, the 1997 Kyoto Protocol. **Jehovah's Witnesses** identify materialism as the root of the earth's environmental problems. Such issues,
they believe, are predicted in **prophecy**, and are signs that humanity
is living in the end-times. There is no human solution to these problems, which will only be remedied after **Armageddon**, during the
millennial rule of Christ, when the earth will be progressively re-
plenished. In the meantime, Witnesses recommend a modest lifestyle,
and the organization endeavors to ensure that its resources are not
wasted but reused wherever possible.

In 1913, **C. T. Russell** referred to global warming in *Zion's Watch
Tower*, claiming that the earth's temperature was originally uniform
and only changed after Noah's flood. Russell noted that heat from the
torrid **zones** was now affecting the planet's colder areas, causing the
melting of the polar ice caps. Such phenomena aroused little subsequent interest until the rise of the "green" movement in the early 1970s.

EVOLUTION. From the inception of the **Watch Tower** organization,
Bible students and **Jehovah's Witnesses** have rejected Charles Darwin's theory of evolution, describing it as "pseudoscience." They argue
that scientists disagree about the details of the theory, that evidence of
intermediate species is lacking, that it is not backed up by fossil
records, and that it cannot account for the origins of life itself. More
importantly, Witnesses present theological objections to evolution,
claiming that it is contrary to the Bible, which teaches the separate origin of individual species and the creation of **Adam** as a body that was

vitalized by God's **holy spirit**. Evolutionary theory suggests progression in the development of species, in contrast with the doctrine of the fall, which entails a perfect **creation** that became tainted by **sin**. Many Watch Tower publications have offered criticisms of evolution, including *Evolution versus the New World* (1950), *Life—How Did It Get Here? By Evolution or by Creation?* (1985), and *Is There a Creator Who Cares about You?* (1999). *See also* CREATIONISM; IMMORTALITY; SOUL.

– F –

FAITH. The **Bible** teaches that "faith is the assured expectation of things hoped for, the evident demonstration of realities though not beheld" (Hebrews 11:1). Hence faith is not to be understood as "blind faith" or credulity but is based on evidence, reason, and logic. It is a relationship involving confidence and trust that men and **women** have with **Jehovah** and his organization. God's faithful include the ancient patriarchs who were loyal to Jehovah, those who belonged to the early Church, and those who have found the truth taught by the **Watch Tower Society**. Faith cannot acceptably be placed in political systems, **false religion**, or materialism, which are all characteristic of **Babylon** the Great. Faith is evidenced in works, which include ministerial service and participation in congregational activities. Faith should be accompanied by other qualities, notably virtue, knowledge, endurance, self-control, devotion to God, and love for other human beings. *See also* FAITHFUL MEN OF OLD; MINISTER; POLITICS.

FAITHFUL AND DISCREET SLAVE. Aka faithful and wise servant; faithful steward. This expression derives from a saying of **Jesus** that compares a faithful servant with a wicked one, both of whom are left to look after their master's affairs during his absence, and assures the former of being rewarded on his master's return. **Jehovah's Witnesses** do not equate the faithful and discreet slave with any one individual, but with the body of "spirit-anointed Christians," that is, the **anointed class**, made up of early Christians who preceded the Church's **apostasy**, and, in the 20th and 21st centuries, those who belong to the anointed class of the **Watch Tower** organization. The "evil slave" represents those who have been given responsibility within the organization but have fallen away. The faithful and discreet slave is entrusted with the responsibility of running his master's domestic affairs, and this is paralleled by the Watch Tower Society's responsibility to provide "spiritual food" for its members and those outside the organization.

The "faithful and discreet slave" is sometimes incorrectly identified with the **Governing Body**, which only forms part of the anointed class, even though its members have special responsibility for the organization more widely. It is sometimes claimed that **C. T. Russell** applied the term to himself and that Watch Tower teaching on the topic has now changed. This is not wholly accurate: Russell did not explicitly claim to be the faithful and wise servant; however, a large number of his **Bible** students believed that he was and expressed gratitude for his "spiritual food," as provided in his writings and sermons.

FAITHFUL AND WISE SERVANT. *See* FAITHFUL AND DISCREET SLAVE.

FAITHFUL MEN OF OLD. Aka ancient worthies; great cloud of witnesses. These people are mentioned in Hebrews 11, where the writer itemizes the faithful who lived before the time of **Christ** and who serve as an example and inspiration for God's people in the present time. These individuals include some antediluvians, like Abel, Enoch, and Noah, who remained faithful to God; patriarchs, like Abraham, Isaac, and Jacob; judges of Israel, for example, Gideon and Samson; King David; and also the prophets. Notwithstanding the expression, not all the faithful are men, and at least one is not Jewish: the author includes Sarah as well as Rahab.

It was formerly expected that these faithful people would return before **Armageddon**, and **J. F. Rutherford** initially expected them to arrive in **1925**. Current teaching within the **Watch Tower Society** is that they will participate in the "second **resurrection**," immediately before deceased members of the **great crowd** are restored to life. Like the great crowd, the faithful men of old are not eligible for eternal life in heaven, since their lives on earth predate Christ's **ransom sacrifice**. The author of Hebrews states that "God foresaw something better for us" (Hebrews 11:39), that is, the **anointed class**.

See also BETH SARIM; DEATH; FAITH; PARADISE EARTH; WOMEN.

FAITHFUL STEWARD. *See* FAITHFUL AND DISCREET SLAVE.

FALSE RELIGION. The term encompasses any form of **religion** that deviates from the true religion that pleases **Jehovah**. It is associated with **Babylon** the Great and inspired by **Satan**. False religion contrasts with true religion, implying that the latter can exist and will do so in the imminent paradisiacal world. The **Watch Tower Society** teaches that, although false religion has always existed, there have been brief periods in which true religion has been maintained, in particular during **Jesus**' ministry and the 1st-century Church. At various periods in Jewish history, the **Jews** sought to restore true worship by eliminating foreign idolatrous practices. Although Noah is believed to have maintained a true form of religion, his great-grandson **Nimrod** established an empire in Babylon, causing false religion to spread throughout the world.

False religion takes two major forms: religions that do not acknowledge Jesus' messiahship and his **ransom sacrifice** for sin, and people who profess Christianity but who do not belong to the Watch Tower organization. **Christendom** manifests false religion by introducing such **pagan** teachings and practices as the notion of the **Trinity** or the celebration of the pagan festivals **Christmas** and **Easter** or supporting national governments.

The Watch Tower organization expects that false religion will soon be brought to an end by being defeated at the Battle of **Armageddon**. *See also* PARADISE EARTH.

FIELD MINISTRY. *See* FIELD SERVICE.

FIELD SERVICE. Aka field ministry. The "field" is the totality of non-Christians and is thus defined in **Jesus**' parable of the wheat and weeds (Matthew 13:38). The seeds in the parable represent the truth, which the **publisher** scatters throughout his or her part of the world in the expectation of reaping a harvest. It is regarded as an obligation for active **Jehovah's Witnesses** and encompasses **house-to-house ministry** and **Bible** studies with interested householders. Publishers receive training from the **Theocratic Ministry School** and use the **Watch Tower Society**'s publication *Reasoning from the Scriptures* by way of guidance for this work. Study with householders is normally based on one of the society's publications specially recommended for the purpose. Between 1946 and 1968, the book *Let God Be True* (1942) was used; various others have been used from 1968 onward, and currently the favored publication is the booklet *What Does God Require of Us?* (1996). In the 1950s, much of the field service activity focused on doctrinal issues, like doctrines of the **Trinity** or **hell**, matters on which Witnesses disagreed with mainstream Christianity. Topics for discussion in house-to-house work now tend to focus on social, family, and emotional issues since Witnesses believe that their witnessing should be adaptable. However, dialogue is still anchored to the Bible, without compromising the message.

Publishers are expected to keep records of their field service work and submit a monthly field service report at their local **Kingdom Hall**.

THE FINISHED MYSTERY. The seventh volume in **C. T. Russell**'s *Studies in the Scriptures*, the work was incomplete upon Russell's death in 1916 and was published posthumously the following year under **J. F. Rutherford**'s supervision. Although attributed to Russell, it has been suggested that it was completed by **Clayton J. Woodworth** and George H. Fisher. The book is principally a commentary on the books of Ezekiel and **Revelation**, with explanation of the Song of Solomon. The original edition contained criticism of the U.S. position on **World War I**. The book opposed **war** and quickly became highly controversial for its claim that the New Testament nowhere advocated patriotism. It was also distinctive for its inclusion of numerous cartoons, many of which subjected mainstream clergy to ridicule. By the end of 1917, it had been translated into French and Swedish.

In 1918, the Canadian government banned *The Finished Mystery*, and U.S. authorities demanded the removal of pages 247 through 253, claiming the text was antiwar propaganda. Rutherford and his supporters were arrested and imprisoned on charges of conspiracy to violate the Espionage Act and attempting to cause refusal of duties in the armed forces. A paperback edition of the book, known as "ZG"

("Z" standing for *Zion's Watch Tower* and "G" being the seventh letter of the alphabet, denoting the seventh volume of Russell's series), was produced as a special edition of *Zion's Watch Tower* and published on 1 March 1918. It was withheld because of various legal controversies but finally appeared in 1920.

FISHER, GEORGE H. (?–1926). Fisher, from Scranton, Pennsylvania, was an early **Watch Tower** leader. He was named in **C. T. Russell**'s will as one to be considered for the Watch Tower editorial board if a vacancy arose. Initially a supporter of **J. F. Rutherford**, he was commissioned, together with **Clayton J. Woodworth**, to complete Russell's *The Finished Mystery* (1917). Together with Rutherford and other leaders, he served a prison sentence from 1918 to 1919 following controversies surrounding the book's publication. He was elected to the Society's **Board of Directors** in January 1918 and served on the Watch Tower editorial committee until 1924. In 1926, Fisher accused Rutherford of attending a burlesque show and took steps to have him disciplined by the Watch Tower Society. Rutherford denied knowledge of any such event and, when Fisher died that year, the matter was not pursued.

FLAG SALUTE. Jehovah's Witnesses have declined to salute national flags or make other declarations of patriotism on the grounds that it pays to civil authorities the kind of homage that is only justly due to God. **J. F. Rutherford** first gave instructions to Witnesses to refuse to make flag salutes at a **convention** in 1935, and their refusal aroused public distaste, resulting in Witnesses' **children** being excluded from schools in the United States and Germany. In the United States, several cases were the subject of litigation, the first being *Minersville School District v. Gobitis*, which was first brought to court in 1937. Witness children finally gained exemption in the United States in 1943. In Germany, noncompliance resulted in children being removed from schools to correction centers and adults being subjected to a range of penalties, including consignment to concentration camps. *See also* CAESAR'S RULE; HOLOCAUST.

FRANZ, FREDERICK W. (1893–1992). Raised in a Roman Catholic family in Cincinnati, Ohio, Franz converted to Presbyterianism and commenced training for the Presbyterian ministry at the University of Cincinnati. In 1913, he discovered a booklet entitled *Where Are the Dead?*, by John Edgar, a member of the International **Bible** Students in Glasgow, Scotland. This persuaded him to read **C. T. Russell**'s *Studies in the Scriptures* and become baptized into the Cincinnati Congregation of Bible students later that year.

Immediately following the outbreak of **World War I** in 1914, Franz became a **pioneer-colporteur**. In 1920, at **J. F. Rutherford**'s invitation, he joined the Brooklyn **Bethel** family, where he assumed charge of the colporteur desk. In 1926, he joined the Editorial Department. Franz was also a musician: he was a member of the male quartet on **WBBR** radio and on occasion conducted the **Watch Tower Bible and Tract Society**'s orchestra.

Franz became vice president of the **Watch Tower Society** and its associated bodies in 1945. His travels took him to Spain in 1955, where the **Jehovah's Witnesses**' work was banned; he was arrested and interrogated for taking part in a secret **assembly** in the woods outside Barcelona. He was appointed **president** of the society in 1977, in succession to **Nathan H. Knorr**. While in office, Franz traveled widely on behalf of the society and spoke at many international **conventions**.

FRANZ, RAYMOND (1922–). Born a third-generation member of a family of **Bible** students and nephew of **Frederick W. Franz**, Raymond Franz was baptized as a **Jehovah's Witness** in 1938. He graduated from the **Gilead School of Ministry** in 1944 and engaged in missionary work in the Caribbean before being appointed in 1965 to work at the Brooklyn **Bethel** in New York, where he was commissioned to oversee the publication of *Aid to Bible Understanding* (1969), a five-volume reference work reissued as *Insight on the Scriptures* (2 volumes, 1988). Franz became a member of the **Governing Body** in 1971.

In 1979 concerns arose regarding the consistency between the **Watch Tower Society**'s official teachings and those of Raymond Franz and some other members of the Governing Body. **End-time calculations** and dates and the doctrine of the **144,000** members of the **anointed class** were principal issues. Formal proceedings were initiated the following year, resulting in Franz's **disfellowshipping** in

1981. Franz recounts his experiences and discusses the salient issues in *Crisis of Conscience* (1983) and *In Search of Christian Freedom* (1991).

FUNDAMENTALISM. In its wide sense, the term connotes extremism and fanaticism and has been applied, principally by the media, to a number of the world's religions. In its more precise sense, the term was devised within Protestantism as a response to ideas in Christian scholarship that stemmed from the European Enlightenment. These include theological liberalism, including the application of source criticism and historiographical methodology to the **Bible**, and acceptance of Charles Darwin's theory of **evolution**. By way of challenging these developments, a number of conservative Protestant leaders convened a Bible Conference in Niagara, New York, in 1895, where they defined "Five Points of Fundamentalism," namely, "1) the plenary inspiration and inerrancy of Scripture; 2) the deity of **Jesus Christ**; 3) the virgin birth of Christ; 4) the substitutionary atonement of Christ on the **cross**; 5) the bodily **resurrection** and the personal and physical second coming of Christ on the earth." In the early years of the 20th century several volumes entitled *The Fundamentals: A Testimony to the Truth* appeared.

Jehovah's Witnesses reject the term *fundamentalism* as a self-description, partly because of its pejorative connotations. They also do not affirm all of the Five Points of Fundamentalism defined at Niagara: while affirming scriptural inerrancy and the virgin birth, they prefer to regard **Christ**'s atonement as a **ransom sacrifice**; they believe that Christ was resurrected "in the spirit" and expect his "appearance" (*parousia*) rather than a return in physical form.

FUNERALS. The purpose of funeral rites is to comfort the bereaved and reflect on the brevity of life and what lies beyond. A **Kingdom Hall** may be used for funerals of members or for their children, if they are minors.

Funerals are kept brief and simple, with few flowers. Outward signs and excessive expressions of mourning are discouraged. The service is conducted by someone in good standing, who is selected by the family. Although officiants make explicit reference to the deceased, they refrain from eulogizing them. The funeral service normally consists of a **song** or songs, a **Bible** talk, and a **prayer**. The talk normally addresses three main points: the reason for dying (the sin of **Adam**), the condition of the dead, and the hope for the dead. In the case of a deceased member who belongs to the **anointed class**, the nature of the heavenly hope of the **144,000** members is expanded upon. Whether one is cremated or buried is a matter of personal choice.

While it is permissible for **Jehovah's Witnesses** to attend funerals in mainstream churches out of courtesy, it is a matter of **conscience**, and the **Watch Tower Society** warns of the dangers of hearing false doctrines or being expected to participate in unacceptable practices, like making the sign of the cross. If a "worldly person" or **disfellow-shipped** member dies, it is a matter of conscience as to whether a brother conducts a funeral at a graveside, crematorium, or home. *See also* ASSOCIATIONS; DEATH.

– G –

GAMBLING. Although it is not explicitly mentioned in the **Bible**, **Je-hovah's Witnesses** believe that its results are invariably bad and that it is therefore to be avoided. Since the aim of gambling is the acquisition of unearned wealth, Witnesses believe that it encourages greed and is an attachment to money, which scripture condemns (1 Timothy 6:10). Gambling frequently leads to debt and addiction. Small-scale gambling, although seemingly less serious, is nonetheless proscribed, since there is the risk of its leading to gambling on a larger scale. Card games and board games are permitted, so long as they merely involve the keeping of scores rather than exchanges of money. In 1976, the **Watch Tower Society** ruled that no Witness could work in a gambling establishment and remain a member of a **congregation**.

The Bible teaches that all decisions should come from **Jehovah** (Proverbs 16:33), but in places it appears to sanction methods involving chance. For example, lots were used to select sacrificial goats for Jehovah and Azazel on the Day of Atonement (Leviticus 16:7–10), and the Urim and the Thummim, which were kept in the High Priest's robes (Exodus 28:30) are thought to have been lots to provide answers to questions of national importance. Lots were also used by **Jesus'** 11 remaining disciples to determine who should replace Judas Iscariot (Acts 1:26). However, lots do not appear to have been used to win material assets, and Witnesses note that there is no reference to the use of lots after **Pentecost** in 33 C.E.

Witnesses regard trust in Jehovah as being incompatible with belief in luck, and many avoid using expressions like "good luck" or "by a stroke of luck."

GANGAS, GEORGE D. (1896–1994). Member of the **Governing Body** from 1971 to 1994. Born in New Ephesus, Asia Minor, Gangas migrated to the United States in 1920, where he met **Bible** students and became baptized in 1921. In 1928 he entered the **Watch Tower Society**'s full-time preaching ministry and joined the Brooklyn **Bethel** staff as a translator. He was proficient in Greek, and it is speculated that he was a member of the **New World Translation** Committee.

GEHENNA. The valley of Hinnom (*Gei-Hinnom* in Hebrew) in west and southwest Jerusalem, Gehenna served as a refuse depository where a continually sulfurous fire burned the city's waste. The **Bible** employs the term as a metaphor for the destruction of **death** and the irredeemably wicked. Those who are in Hades after death can expect a **resurrection** during the **millennial rule of Christ**, with an opportunity for repentance afforded to those who accept true teachings. Those who refuse to do so will experience the "second death," symbolized by Gehenna, from which there is no awakening (**Revelation** 20:14). Some of the dead go directly to Gehenna, without any further opportunity for repentance. **Watch Tower** literature cites the unrepentant scribes and Pharisees of **Jesus'** time as examples. *See also* IMMORTALITY; SOUL.

GENERATION. The primary meaning of the word is "persons born at approximately the same time." This definition has typically been used to interpret **Jesus' prophecy**, "Truly I say to you, All these things will come upon this generation" (Matthew 23:26). The prophecy originally applied to the destruction of Jerusalem in 70 C.E., which was witnessed by many of Jesus' disciples. However, difficulties occur in connection with the prophecy's "greater fulfill-ment," which **C. T. Russell**, **J. F. Rutherford**, and subsequent **Jeho-vah's Witnesses** identified with the signs related to Christ's *parou-sia*, which was believed to have taken place in 1914. Some 20th-century Witnesses certainly experienced the "signs of Christ's presence," as defined in Matthew 24: **war**, earthquakes, pestilence, famine, and lawlessness and persecution, among others. However, they did not experience the commencement of **Armageddon**.

As late as 1984, the *Watchtower* stated, "Just as Jesus' prophecies re-garding Jerusalem were fulfilled within the life span of the **generation** of the year 33 C.E., so his prophecies regarding 'the time of the end' will be fulfilled within the life span of the generation of 1914" (*WT* 84 5/15: 4–7). As time progressed, this expectation became less plausible, until finally in 1995, the **Watch Tower Society** offered a revised interpreta-tion of the "generation," pointing out that it can be used to mean a class of people with a common set of characteristics and that it was used this way in the **Bible**. One example cited was Jesus' expression "a wicked and adulterous generation" as a description of the scribes and Pharisees (Matthew 12:39). Thus, the generation who will not pass away until all prophecies are fulfilled is to be identified with those who see the signs of **Christ**'s presence but refuse to repent.

GENTILE TIMES. Aka appointed times of the nations. The period in Israel's history from the **Babylonian** Exile onward, beginning with King Nebuchadnezzar's conquest of Jerusalem, which ended the monarchy in Judah (Judea) and hence **Jehovah**'s theocratic rule over his people. **C. T. Russell** ascribed the date of 607 B.C.E. to this event, which features significantly in the **Jehovah's Witnesses' end-time calculations**. From that date forward, national governments have been ruled by humans rather than God.

Through this understanding of biblical **prophecy**, Russell con-cluded that **1914** would mark the end of this period. Although other **Adventists** expected some remarkable supernatural event to occur, Russell and subsequent Witnesses regard the event that is believed to have happened as an invisible one, being **Christ**'s presence rather than his return. The occurrence is to be equated with the return of the "**faithful men of old**" on earth, the faithful being taken up to heaven, or Israel having a messianic king. The beginning of the theocratic rule is held to have taken place in heaven rather than on earth, when Christ began to assemble the **144,000** members of the **anointed class**, having cast **Satan** out of heaven.

Russell announced at the Brooklyn **Bethel** on 2 October 1914 that the Gentile times had ended. The outbreak of the **World War I** in August of that year was taken as confirmation that theocratic rule in heaven was beginning. *See also* ADVENTISM; DAY-FOR-A-YEAR RULE; THEOCRACY.

GILEAD SCHOOL OF MINISTRY. Aka Watch Tower Bible School of Gilead. On 9 February 1942, **Nathan H. Knorr** announced the offering of an advanced course in Theocratic Ministry at the Brooklyn **Bethel** for the purpose of training missionaries for foreign service. At an **assembly** the following year, local **congregations** were encouraged to train their members, and a booklet entitled *Course in Theocratic Ministry* was launched.

Originally called the Watch Tower Bible College of Gilead, the school was set up at Kingdom Farm in South Lansing, New York. Albert D. Schroeder was appointed as the first registrar and chairman of its organizing committee. The main purpose of the school was to train missionaries in public speaking and **Bible** research. In 1961, the school was relocated to the New York Brooklyn Bethel, where it remained until 1988. It was again relocated to Wallkill, New York, and subsequently to Patterson, New York, in 1995. *See also* THEOCRATIC MINISTRY SCHOOL (TMS).

GIVEN ONES. Aka Nethinim; Sons of the Servants of Solomon. The name derives from an ancient group of slaves who were promoted to become sacred officials in Solomon's Temple. From 1992, in the **Watch Tower Society,** the name Nethinim designates a class of male **Jehovah's Witnesses** belonging to the **great crowd**, who assume increased responsibilities on behalf of the dwindling **anointed class**, engaging in international travel, preparation of publications, and serving as members of **Branch** Committees. The term is used infrequently.

GOBITAS, WALTER. Father of Lillian and William Gobitas (aged 11 and 10, respectively), who were expelled from a Minersville School

District school in 1935 for refusing to salute the U.S. flag. Walter Gobitas attended the **Jehovah's Witnesses' convention** in Washington, D.C., in that year, when **J. F. Rutherford** counseled Witnesses against such declarations of nationalist allegiance. Gobitas first successfully challenged the school's decision in court, aided by the American Civil Liberties Union. The first court hearing was held in 1937 and, after the school appealed twice against favorable decisions to the Gobitas family, the case went to the Supreme Court in 1940, where Rutherford personally testified on their behalf in *Minersville District School vs. Gobitis* 310 U.S. 586 (1940). The school prevailed, but a subsequent Supreme Court decision in 1943 on a different case, *Murdock v. Commonwealth of Pennsylvania* 319 U.S. 105 (1943), forced the reappraisal of past court rulings, including that of Gobitas, on 14 June 1943. The landmark case *West Virginia State Board of Education v. Barnette* 319 U.S. 624 (1943) definitively reversed the *Gobitis* decision. (The court papers consistently listed the family's name incorrectly as Gobitis.)

GOG OF MAGOG. The prophet Ezekiel is commissioned by God to prophesy against Gog of Magog, informing him that God is against him and will place hooks in his jaws, bringing him forth together with his armies from all corners of the earth to attack Israel. Gog will be lured into Israel and face floods, fire, and pestilence; his followers will fight among themselves and face utter defeat. Gog and all his supporters will be buried in the Valley of Hamon-Gog—the Valley of Gog's crowd (Ezekiel 38:11–22). The **Watch Tower Society** identifies Gog as **Satan**, who is now on earth, having been cast out of heaven, and who will mount an earthwide attack on God's people, the "spiritual Israel," that is, the restored **remnant** of the **anointed class** who remain on earth. This attack, which will involve an army constituted of every world power, will be the final incident that provokes God to commence the Battle of **Armageddon**.

The Book of **Revelation** (20:8) refers to "Gog *and* Magog," who will mislead people of all nations after Satan's release. **Jehovah's Witnesses** hold that this passage makes a different allusion from Ezekiel's and refers to the period after the **millennial rule of Christ**, when Satan will be released from his abyss and will attempt to deceive humanity for a short time, until **Christ** assumes final control over **paradise earth**. *See also* PROPHECY.

GOVERNING BODY. Although the term is not used in the **Bible**, **Jehovah's Witnesses** believe that the early Church was governed by a group of 12 men, centered on Jerusalem, who were responsible for decision making and counseling on behalf of the churches elsewhere. The Governing Body is not a legally constituted body, unlike the directorate of the **Watch Tower Bible and Tract Society of Pennsylvania** (WTBTS), which is the society's legally incorporated institution, and hence an "earthly" body subject to Caesar's law. Unlike the WTBTS, members of the Governing Body are not elected; there are no officers, like a president, vice president, and treasurer; and the chairmanship of the body rotates annually according to alphabetical order of surname. The body is not regarded as the "head" of the Watch Tower organization since its government is theocratic, being ruled by God and **Christ**. The Governing Body is made up exclusively of the **anointed class** and is God's visible government on earth and part of his **faithful and discreet slave**.

The Governing Body meets weekly in Brooklyn, New York, and since 1976, its policies have been enacted through six committees: a Personnel Committee, Publishing Committee, Service Committee, Teaching Committee, Writing Committee, and Chairman's Committee. *See also* CAESAR'S RULE; THEOCRACY.

GREAT CLOUD OF WITNESSES. *See* GREAT CROWD.

GREAT CROWD. Aka great multitude; other sheep. The great crowd contrasts with those **Jehovah's Witnesses** who belong to the **144,000** members of the **anointed class**, the former being assured of eternal dwelling in **paradise earth** rather than eternal life in heaven.

In *Studies in the Scriptures* (principally volume 1—*The Divine Plan of the Ages*), **C. T. Russell** professes the existence of a secondary heavenly class who has not been completely overcome by worldly spirit and therefore will not be granted a throne or given a divine nature in the coming **kingdom**. This idea was initially supported by **J. F. Rutherford**, who states in *Light, Book 1* (1930) that followers who believe but have not done sufficient preaching belong to this inferior class. However, Rutherford says in *Millions Now Living Will Never Die* (1920) that there are associates who display zeal but do not entertain a heavenly hope. These came to be known as the **Jonadabs**, who were explicitly invited to the 1935 **Convention** in Washington, D.C., where Rutherford called on attendees to stand if they had an expectation of eternal life on earth. When the Jonadabs stood up, Rutherford declared that they constituted the great crowd, as mentioned in the Book of **Revelation** (Revelation 7:11).

Present-day teaching in the **Watch Tower Society** is that the great crowd are those who are faithful to **Jehovah** but are the "other sheep" whom **Jesus** mentioned (John 10:16), in contrast with the "little flock" (Luke 12:32), whom Witnesses identify with the anointed class. Unlike the 144,000, the number of the great crowd is unrestricted. They will be dedicated Christians drawn from all nations who will receive a favorable judgment from God and be brought "before the throne and before the Lamb" (Revelation 7:9). Unlike mainstream Christianity, this crowd is unified, without sects or denominations; its spirituality is not channeled through a priesthood or clergy. Those joining the Witnesses after 1935 are generally reckoned to belong to the great crowd rather than the anointed class. Witnesses see their numerical strength as corroboration of the appropriateness of the adjective *great*. See also PARADISE EARTH.

GREAT DISAPPOINTMENT. The failed expectation of **Adventist** preacher **William Miller** and some 50,000 followers, when Christ's return was initially expected on 21 March 1843. Miller's end-time prediction was based on Daniel 18:14: "Unto two thousand and three hundred days; then shall the sanctuary be cleansed." In common with a number of Adventists, Miller applied a "**day-for-a-year rule**," regarding these biblical days as years, beginning with the date of King Artaxerxes' decree permitting the **Jews** to rebuild Jerusalem after the **Babylonian** Exile. The presumed date for this event was 452 B.C.E.

When the 1843 expectations failed to materialize, some of Miller's associates recalculated the date, noting that Miller's calculations erroneously supposed the existence of a year 0 between B.C.E. and C.E. dates. Accordingly, they set the new date as 18 April 1844 and subsequently 22 October 1844. When the predicted event failed to materialize, many of his followers were disillusioned and abandoned the movement. Other Second Adventists recalculated dates, while Hiram Edson claimed to have received a **revelation** that the date referred to a heavenly rather than an earthly event. This insight was appropriated by Ellen G. White, the founder of Seventh-day Adventism, as well as by **C. T. Russell**. **Jehovah's Witnesses** have reset the date as **1914**, the year in which they believe **Christ** began his heavenly rule. *See also* END-TIME CALCULATIONS.

GREAT MULTITUDE. *See* GREAT CROWD.

GREAT PYRAMID. Aka Pyramid of Giza (Gizeh). The pyramid aroused scientific interest in the mid-19th century, and a Scotsman by the name of Robert Menzies (not a **Bible** student) claimed that it provided testimony to God and his plan for humankind. Interest in the Great Pyramid gained momentum in the **Adventist** movement with the publication of an article by Piazzi Smyth in the *Bible Examiner*, published by **George Storrs**. Storrs subsequently published a series on the topic.

The *Bible Examiner* articles probably aroused **C. T. Russell**'s interest, which he first expressed in an article in *Zion's Watch Tower* in June 1884. In his *Studies in the Scriptures* (principally volumes 1 and 3), Russell argues that the Great Pyramid of Giza is a "miracle in stone," its proportions offering confirmation of the biblical claims regarding end-time dates, including **1914**. He says that the pyramid also symbolizes the relationship between **Christ** and his followers, Christ being the capstone and the faithful being represented by the sections below, leaving a larger imperfect shape at the base, corresponding to fallen humanity. Russell contends that it was to be identified with the stone pillar mentioned in Isaiah 19:10–20.

This explanation was accepted by Bible students until 1928, when two substantial articles appeared in the *Watch Tower* refuting the claims. Although Russell had not asserted that the pyramid revealed any additional information to the Bible, the anonymous author—probably **J. F. Rutherford**—urged that the Bible alone should be used to establish the organization's teachings. Moreover, the author argued that Egypt symbolizes **Satan** (**Revelation** 11:18) being the Land of Ham, the grandfather of **Nimrod**. The pyramid and sphinx were therefore built by **pagans** and were graven images, prohibited by the second of the Ten Commandments, and the sphinx itself was a symbolic image of Satan, who had put the pyramid's measurements in place to deceive humanity.

While **Jehovah's Witnesses** acknowledge that Russell was wrong, they view such revisions of his teachings as evidence that light on God's word increases with the passage of time and that God is progressively purifying his organization. *See also* END-TIME CALCULATIONS; NEW LIGHT; PAGANISM.

GREAT TRIBULATION. The term is originally applied in the **Bible** to a period of calamities, which would be "cut short" (Matthew 24:15–22) culminating in the fall of Jerusalem in 70 C.E. The **Watch Tower Society** teaches that biblical apocalyptic writings also designate an antitypical period, corresponding to these events in the world's present times. In the ***Watch Tower*** on 1 May 1925, it was explained that the Great Tribulation was the final part of the last days, commencing in **1914** with the outbreak of **World War I**, which was "cut short" in **1918**, leaving a period of respite in which the **anointed** elect could proclaim God's message before the final Battle of **Armageddon**.

When it became apparent that the ensuing **World War II** did not culminate in Armageddon, the society revised its teaching, claiming that the period of 1914 to 1918 was "a beginning of pangs of distress," and that the Great Tribulation itself was to be anticipated. The same signs associated with the destruction of Jerusalem were expected: **wars**, food shortages, earthquakes, pestilence, lawlessness, persecution of the faithful, and the rise of messianic pretenders. The reference in the Book of **Revelation** to a "disgusting thing that causes desolation" is taken to refer to the **League of Nations**, which became the **United Nations**.

The exact date of the commencement and the duration of the Great Tribulation are unknown. Its extent precedes and encompasses Armageddon, and it will occur when the number of God's anointed **remnant** is complete. It will involve the destruction of the present political and religious system and all **false religion**, including **Christendom**. During this period, God's people are assured of being safeguarded physically and spiritually. *See also* END-TIME CALCULATIONS.

GREBER, JOHANNES (1876–1944). A Roman Catholic priest and spiritist, Greber produced *The New Testament: A New Translation Based on the Oldest Manuscripts* in 1937, having also authored *Communication with the Spirit World: Its Laws and Its Purpose* in 1932. His translation was unorthodox and controversial but in some aspects appeared supportive of **Jehovah's Witnesses'** teachings, for example his rendering of John 1:1, where the Word is described as "a god," in common with the Witnesses' **New World Translation**. Occasionally Greber was cited in support in **Watch Tower** publications.

Greber claimed that his translation was accomplished with the aid of spirits, who allegedly suggested translations and informed him of ways scribes had forged and altered the text. Although the Watch Tower organization possessed copies of his translation, the society's strong disapproval of spiritism caused it to cease using his work and to dissociate itself with his writings. Greber was last cited in 1976 in a copy of the **Watchtower**, and a 1983 edition states that, "The *Watchtower* has deemed it improper to make use of a translation that has such a close rapport with spiritism" (*WT* 83 4/1:31). *See also* OCCULTISM.

GRUSS, EDMOND C. (1933–). Brought up as a **Jehovah's Witness**, Gruss rejected the **Watch Tower Society**'s beliefs after becoming a student, when he converted to evangelical Protestant Christianity. In 1958, he studied for a master of theology degree and wrote his thesis on the Witnesses, completing it in 1961. Gruss became a prolific countercult writer. His best-known books include *Apostles of Denial* (1970), *The Jehovah's Witnesses and Prophetic Speculation* (1972), and *Cults and the Occult* (1974). The last of these deals with a variety of new religious movements, not merely the Witnesses.

– H –

HADES. Aka Sheol. Humanity's common grave, Hades is not to be conflated with **Christendom**'s concept of **hell**, which is a fiery place of eternal torment, or with the ancient Greek concept of a world of wraiths. The doctrine of eternal punishment has been consistently rejected by the **Adventist** tradition and by **C. T. Russell**. Hades is conceived as a place—described as a "grave" or "pit"—rather than a condition, although its inhabitants are in the state of oblivion but with their **souls** still alive, awaiting **resurrection**. **Jesus** is held to have descended into Hades during the period between his death and **resurrection**, and he holds its keys (1 Peter 3:19; **Revelation** 1:18). The inhabitants of Hades consist of both good and bad people, all of whom await resurrection, and also the members of the **great crowd** who are no longer alive, but not the **144,000** members. It is expected that Hades will give up its dead during the **millennial rule of Christ**, after which **death** and Hades will be destroyed (Revelation 20:14). *See also* ADVENTISM; GEHENNA; IMMORTALITY.

HEALING. The **Bible** recounts stories of miraculous healings in both the **Hebrew-Aramaic Scriptures** and **Christian Greek Scriptures**. However, it is noted that healing within the early Church was only carried out by **Jesus** and his apostles. Those who attempted to imitate the apostles' powers were unsuccessful (Acts 8:9–24). The gift of healing was merely a mark of the Church's infancy, and it died out with the early apostles. It is mentioned as a gift in early Christian congregations (Acts 12:27) but is regarded as having a secondary status and it is not listed among the gifts of the **holy spirit** (1 Corinthians 12:7–11). The principal emphases of **Jehovah's Witnesses** are therefore defined as preaching, witnessing, and teaching.

Accordingly, Witnesses do not practice faith healing or pray for miraculous cures of illnesses, and they condemn faith healers as fraudsters. Cures can only be effected through medical treatment, healthy living, and the human body's own restorative powers. *See also* HEALTH; MIRACLES.

HEALTH. Jehovah's Witnesses are recommended to pursue both physical and spiritual health. They are encouraged to lead a healthy lifestyle with regard to behavior, home environment, standards of hygiene, and adequate health care. **Smoking** and recreational drug use is forbidden, moderate **alcohol** consumption is permitted, and overeating should be avoided. Physical sickness can be associated with such undesirable emotions as fear, envy, and hatred, and it is reckoned that approximately half of human illnesses are attributable to one's emotions. Although the **Bible** sometimes portrays God or

Satan as directly causing disease (2 Chronicles 21:16–19; Job 2:4–8), illness and disability are not regarded as punishments for **sin**.

Although a number of articles in the *Golden Age* in the 1930s were opposed to orthodox medicine and recommended alternative methods of health care and remedies, present-day Witnesses typically use allopathic medicine, although a significant number are open-minded about alternative forms of therapy, when appropriate. The **Watch Tower Society** warns against health fads, noting that some advertising of health products can be exploitative, and counsels that, although visiting health resorts can be beneficial, clients run the risk of harmful **associations**.

Spiritual **healing** is held to be more important than physical healing, and the present world is reckoned to be sick. **Jesus**, being the great healer, offers a solution to humanity's predicament, often suggesting that physical and spiritual health are interlinked. Physical and spiritual sickness can be expected to continue since perfect health is impossible until the arrival of **Jehovah**'s new system. In **paradise earth** all illness and disabilities will disappear. *See also* WOODWORTH, CLAYTON J.

HEBREW-ARAMAIC SCRIPTURES. The term used by **Jehovah's Witnesses** to refer to the first 39 books of the **Bible**, constituting its first major section. These are the pre-Christian writings, from Genesis to Malachi, to which **Christendom** refers as the "Old Testament." Witnesses consider this term to be a misnomer since "testament" is more properly rendered as "**covenant**" and since scripture forms a unity. Witnesses therefore prefer to make a distinction between the two parts of scripture on the basis of the respective languages in which they were written, the second section being known as the **Christian Greek Scriptures**. The Hebrew-Aramaic Scriptures are regarded as having authority, being quoted by **Jesus** and other writers in the Christian Greek Scriptures and containing prophecies relating to Jesus **Christ** and humanity's present time. They are part of the canon of scripture, which they believe was formally defined by Ezra in the 5th century B.C.E. (Ezra 7:1–11). Witnesses accept the traditional threefold division of the Jewish scriptures into the Law, the Prophets, and the Writings. However, although they accept that these writings are divinely inspired, they do not believe that all of the commandments remain applicable, since Jesus Christ is held to have offered humanity a "new covenant." *See also* NEW WORLD TRANSLATION (NWT); PROPHECY.

HELL. Aka **Gehenna**; **Hades**; Sheol; Tartarus. In common with many Second **Adventists**, the **Watch Tower Society** has consistently denied the existence of eternal torment as a punishment for **sin**, and it was one of the main difficulties that **C. T. Russell** found with mainstream Christian doctrine. Russell published a booklet entitled *What Say the Scriptures About Hell?* (1896). **Bible** students and **Jehovah's Witnesses** have endorsed Russell's exegesis and have maintained his position throughout the organization's history. Witnesses contend that the Bible does not support the notion of eternal punishment since it states that **death** is an unconscious state (Ecclesiastes 9:5). Watch Tower publications argue that the synonymous term *Sheol* means "grave" or "pit" and that "Gehenna" means "Valley of Hinnom," which was a refuse depository where constant burning occurred. **Jesus'** statement about undying fire (Mark 9:47–48) is an allusion to Isaiah 66:24, where the prophet describes the extinction of God's enemies. References to a lake of fire are found exclusively in the Book of **Revelation** (20:10) and describe "the second death," which is to be distinguished from the death that humanity inherits from **Adam**'s sin. This is the state of oblivion that will face those who are unrepentant after being raised from the dead during the **millennial rule of Christ**.

The notion of hell as a fiery place, inhabited by demons, and involving eternal torment stems from the medieval Church and presupposes the existence of a **soul** that is distinct from the body and survives bodily death. Witnesses reject this view and contend that it is a feature of apostate **religion**. *See also* APOSTASY; RESURRECTION.

HENSCHEL, MILTON G. (1920–2003). Fourth **president** of the **Watch Tower Bible and Tract Society**, Henschel was born into a family of **Bible** students and moved to Brooklyn, New York, in 1934, when his father, Herman George Henschel was asked to assist with construction projects at the **Bethel**. He embarked on administrative work in 1939, becoming secretary to **Nathan H. Knorr**, who was then **overseer** at the Brooklyn printery. When Knorr became **president** in 1942,

Henschel was appointed as his assistant. Henschel undertook much travel on behalf of the society, visiting more than 150 countries, at times at the risk of personal safety. He was appointed to the **Governing Body** in 1976, and in 1992, he succeeded **Frederick W. Franz** as president. During his period of office, the society saw important changes, notably the uncoupling of the Governing Body from the **Board of Directors** of the Watch Tower Bible and Tract Society of Pennsylvania in 2000. At the Annual General Meeting of the Society on 7 October 2000, Henschel resigned his presidency, and, together with the six other members of the Governing Body who constituted the directors, was replaced. He was succeeded as president by **Don Alden Adams** but continued to serve on the Governing Body until his death.

HIGHER POWERS. This expression is found in the King James Version of the **Bible**, rendered in the **New World Translation** as "Let every **soul** be in subjection to the superior authorities, for there is no authority except by God; the existing authorities stand placed in their relative positions by God" (Romans 13:1). This was initially taken as an instruction to obey civil authorities. In *The New Creation*, **C. T. Russell** taught that one should obey the law of the land, except where it conflicts with God's law. **World War I** and the ensuing formation of the **League of Nations** caused Bible students to reconsider whether civil authorities were really divinely ordained, and from 1928 onward the **Watch Tower Society** revised its thinking, arguing that God and **Christ** were the supreme authorities, since there could be no higher powers than these. The society has criticized the Christian churches for their support of worldly rulers, for example, their compliance with the Nazi regime during the 1930s and 1940s. Despite the reinterpretation of "higher powers," the society continues to advocate compliance with civil law, unless it conflicts with divine law. *See also* CAESAR'S RULE; NEW LIGHT.

HOLOCAUST. Although the term is sometimes taken exclusively to designate the genocide of **Jews** under Adolf Hitler's Third Reich in Germany, **Jehovah's Witnesses**—known in Germany as the **Bibelforscher**—also suffered persecution, incarceration, and death during the 1930s and 1940s. When Hitler was appointed chancellor in 1933, **J. F. Rutherford** composed a statement called the "**Decla-**

ration of Facts," which has been construed as condoning Nazi ideals, and which was adopted at the Bibelforscher's Berlin-Wilmersdorf Convention that year. The declaration had no effect, and the Bibelforscher were held "ideologically unfit" in contrast to Germany's Jewish population, who were reckoned to be genetically unfit. The accusation related to the Witnesses' refusal to participate in national festivals, salute the flag and use the greeting "Heil Hitler," and further the **war** effort. As a consequence, they were banned from assembling, distributing literature, and engaging in **house-to-house ministry**. The Bibelforscher's refusal to comply resulted in their houses being raided, dismissals from government employment, boycotts of business, and withdrawal of state benefits. They were subjected to beatings and arrests, and children who persistently refused to give the salutation "Heil Hitler" were removed from school.

Persistent noncompliance was punished with incarceration in prisons and concentration camps. Witnesses were one of the first groups to be sent to these camps, and they were unique in being the only Christian group to be given their own distinctive symbol, the **purple triangle**. Unlike other groups, Witnesses were given the opportunity to be released, provided that they signed a declaration renouncing their faith.

At the start of **World War II** in 1939, there were approximately 6,000 Witnesses being held in concentration camps. Around 13,400 were consigned to camps and prisons during the Third Reich; around 2,000 died, 270 of whom were executed. Approximately 500 children were removed from their homes.

HOLY SPIRIT. The holy spirit (always spelled by the **Watch Tower Society** in lower casing) is regarded as God's active force or agenda. It is not a person, and *a fortiori* not part of any **trinity** of gods and not to be worshipped. **Jehovah's Witnesses** claim that **Christendom**'s attribution of personality to the holy spirit is unbiblical and was not part of the 1st-century Church's teaching. Witnesses acknowledge the role of the holy spirit in the **baptism** of **Jesus** (Matthew 3:7.16) and its coming to the early disciples at **Pentecost** (Acts 2:4). They point out, however, that the concept of baptism of the holy spirit is juxtaposed to water baptism and fire baptism, and that it is therefore reasonable to support that it is inanimate, like water and fire. They further argue that a being cannot be "poured out" on a group of disciples. The holy spirit is not given a distinctive name in scripture, unlike **Jehovah** and Jesus, and it is not seen in visions recounted in scripture.

The society teaches that "spirit" has seven distinct senses in the **Bible**: 1) It is applied to God himself, for example, at **creation**. 2) It is connected with Jesus **Christ** ("Christ's spirit"). 3) **Angels** are described as spirits. 4) "Spirit" refers to the life force, for example, when **Adam** was created. 5) It denotes a mental disposition ("spirit of wisdom"). 6) It can mean an inspired utterance or **prophecy**. 7) It can refer to the impersonal holy spirit that pertains to God. The holy spirit, in this final sense, is creative; it inspired the ancient prophets and caused early Christians to perform signs and wonders. It is also the divine energy that enables God's messengers to proclaim his truth, as well as the power that anoints and commissions his proclaimers. Although powerful, the holy spirit always remains under God's control, thus preventing unpredictable or undesirable actions by those who possess it.

HOMOSEXUALITY. Homosexuality is held to include not only sodomy but any activity that sexually arouses a member of the same **sex**, male or female. It is an example of "disgraceful sexual appetites" (Romans 1:26), regarded as sinful, and defined as one of the "practices that God hates." **Jehovah's Witnesses** do not believe that it is hereditary, but that it is chosen and can be encouraged by autoerotic practices, as well as by increasingly permissive public attitudes and legislation. Witnesses particularly deplore the liberal attitudes that are frequently found in mainstream churches, especially when they are endorsed by members of the **clergy**.

The **Watch Tower Society** maintains that homosexuality can be "cured" and that the remedy lies in following the biblical instruction to "abstain from fornication" (1 Thessalonians 4:3). Homosexuals are recommended to repent, fight against their tendencies, and seek forgiveness.

HOSPITAL LIAISON COMMITTEES. Jehovah's Witnesses are proactive in endeavoring to secure medical treatment that is consistent with their beliefs. The **Watch Tower** organization has set up several Hospital Liaison Committees both countrywide and internationally. These committees consist of specially elected **elders** who visit hospitals in their locality disseminating information about their beliefs and practices to hospital staff and negotiating appropriate courses of treatment for members, particularly in the light of their beliefs regarding **blood**. All elders in a **congregation** have a list of Hospital Liaison Committee members who can be contacted in an emergency. Special consent forms for hospital treatment, dictating what is and is not permitted, are prepared by and available from the organization, and Witnesses have worked to ensure that hospitals have these on file. *See also* HEALTH.

HOUSE-TO-HOUSE MINISTRY. Aka door-to-door ministry; public witnessing. The method of evangelizing for which **Jehovah's Witnesses** are best known, this work is justified as a practice of the 1st-century Church. The **Bible** states that **Jesus** commissioned his disciples to preach and convert all nations (Matthew 28:19) and describes the disciples proclaiming their message from house to house immediately after **Pentecost** in 33 C.E. (Acts 5:42). It is stated that Paul adopted a similar practice (Acts 20:20).

The **Watch Tower Society** established the practice of distributing literature in 1881 with itinerant **colporteurs**, of which there were 625 worldwide by 1909. In 1919, **J. F. Rutherford** introduced the house-to-house visitation with which the public are familiar, making it an expectation for **elders** in 1927. House-to-house work grew progressively after that time. **Publishers** are assigned a part of their **congregation**'s area, which they usually cover in pairs. The **Governing Body** provides guidance about ways to initiate conversation, and publishers endeavor to engage householders in discussion of spiritual matters and to get them to accept literature—usually copies of the *Watchtower* and *Awake!* or a brochure that the society has recently produced. Where interest is expressed, the initial visit can be followed up by a series of home Bible studies, often based on one of the society's latest booklets. Publishers report back on their work, completing forms that indicate the time spent on house-to-house work and other **field service** data.

As well as being scriptural, Witnesses believe that house-to-house work is effective and that it encourages such Christian virtues as humility and endurance in the face of apathy and, at times, hostility. *See also* PIONEER.

– I –

IMMORTALITY. Jehovah's Witnesses believe that the doctrine of the innate **immortality** of the **soul** is unbiblical and that it entered Judaism, **Christendom**, and Islam through the influence of Greek philosophy. The idea is therefore **pagan** and should be rejected. It is noted that the word *immortality* (*athanasia*) occurs three times in the **Bible** (1 Corinthians 15:53, 54; 1 Timothy 6:16), but it is not juxtaposed to "soul." The word refers to the eternal and incorruptible nature of God and **Christ** and of the **144,000** members of the **anointed class** who will rule with them in heaven. The term does not apply to the **great crowd**, who will experience eternal life in **paradise earth** at the end of the **millennium**. *See also* CONDITIONAL IMMORTALITY; DEATH.

INTERFAITH MOVEMENT. A movement aimed at fostering dialogue and understanding among representatives of the world's various **religions**. Interfaith activity gained considerable momentum through the World's Parliament of Religions, held in Chicago in 1893, attracting some 7,000 attendees. **C. T. Russell**'s **Bible** students held a **convention** in Chicago in the same year, and *Zion's Watch Tower* printed scathing comments about the Parliament, as well as a report on the **Watch Tower Society**'s own convention.

    Jehovah's Witnesses believe that interfaith activity is "utterly condemned" by **Jehovah**, whom the Bible describes as a "jealous god" (Exodus 34:14). It is a misguided attempt to promote harmony and understanding among the world's **faiths**, compromising the **truth** and causing its supporters to be "unevenly yoked with unbelievers" (2 Corinthians 6:14). The **Hebrew-Aramaic Scriptures** demonstrate Jehovah's emphatic disapproval of the Israelites' appropriation of elements of Canaanite worship. Witnesses deny that different world faiths are evolving toward the same goal or locating the same source of wisdom: there is only one truth, and all other forms of worship constitute **false religion**.

Witnesses may neither participate in interfaith activities nor belong to other organizations that support them, such as the Young Men's Christian Association (YMCA). Witnesses cannot share premises with other faiths, although it is permissible for them to purchase premises from them for their own use, provided that all evidence of false religion is subsequently removed.

INTERNATIONAL BIBLE STUDENTS ASSOCIATION (IBSA). Incorporated in 1914 in London, England, the IBSA worked with the **Watch Tower Bible and Tract Society of Pennsylvania** disseminating publications and meeting to pray and study the **Bible**. When the **Jehovah's Witnesses** were formed on 26 July 1931, IBSA members decided to adopt the name "Jehovah's Witnesses."

Beginning in the United States in 1910, some of **C. T. Russell**'s followers had used the name, but after **1914** they became known as Associated Bible Students to avoid confusion with the British organization.

INTERNET. From the time of the Internet's inception, **Jehovah's Witnesses** have been cautious regarding its use, warning that it could lead to harmful **associations.** In particular, their concerns include access to pornography, the risk of addiction, and misuse of one's time. The anonymity and possible pseudonymity of much of the World Wide Web's material makes its accuracy difficult to evaluate. The Internet is therefore capable of becoming one of **Satan**'s tools. Although it might potentially be used for such spiritual purposes as the preparation of **Bible** talks, Witnesses emphasize that illustrations for talks should be one's own, and the Watch **Tower Society**'s own literature and CDs guarantee the authenticity of the material. Although information from the Internet may assist the society's evangelism, it cannot be a substitute for **house-to-house ministry**, which was the method used by the early Church to further the **kingdom**.

In 1997, the society launched its official website at www.watchtower.org and subsequently a domain for public information at www.jw-media.org. The former contains selected tracts and *Watchtower* and *Awake!* articles but no material that cannot be found in other Watch Tower sources. Material exists in more than 300 languages. Facilities for e-mail contact are limited: there are no bulletin boards; seekers are only provided with a form for requesting a Bible study, and the media are given telephone contacts and **branch** addresses. A few Witnesses have created their own unofficial websites, some of which permit blogging.

INVISIBLE PRESENCE. *See PAROUSIA.*

– J –

JEHOVAH. The personal name for God used by **Jehovah's Witnesses** when addressing him is their transliteration of the tetragrammaton (יהוה), and it is used throughout the **New World Translation**, both in the **Hebrew-Aramaic Scriptures** and **Christian Greek Scriptures**. This form of the divine name occurs more than 7,000 times in the **Bible**. In Jewish and mainstream Christian scholarship, the transliteration is normally "Yahweh" (or "Jahweh"), but the divine name is not pronounced by **Jews**, who will substitute *adhonai*, normally rendered in English as "Lord," when reading scripture. The **Watch Tower Society** holds that the name was originally used by patriarchs like Abraham and Moses, but that a Jewish superstition arose, which caused them to omit the word in the Septuagint (the Greek rendering of Hebrew scriptures), substituting an abbreviated version of *kurios* ("Lord").

Witnesses believe in the importance of using a personal name to address God rather than a generic one, like "God" or "Lord," since this enables a closer, more personal relationship with him. Although Jewish and Christian scholars have maintained that the original divine name is "Yahweh" and that "Jehovah" is a corruption introduced in the Latin Vulgate, Witnesses claim that this cannot be proved, particularly since the divine name remained unpronounced for the greater part of Jewish history. In any case, the importance of using the name "Jehovah" does not lie in attempting to reconstruct authentic ancient pronunciation: they do not teach that **Jesus** should be called "Jeshua." Its significance lies in its being regarded as a personal name, and it is acknowledged that the exact pronunciation varies in different countries (for example, "Gehova" in Italian).

Jehovah is regarded as the one true God, not a **trinity**, whose attributes are love and justice, and who is the creator of heaven and earth and the Father of Jesus **Christ**. Etymologically, the society teaches that the name derives from the Hebrew *ha-wah* ("he causes to become"), thus indicating that God becomes whatever is necessary to accomplish his purposes.

JEHOVAH'S WITNESSES. Formerly known as **Bible** students, they received the name "Jehovah's Witnesses" from **J. F. Rutherford** at the **convention** in Columbus, Ohio, in 1931. They continue to use this name, by which they are best known. It alludes to Isaiah 43:10: "'You are my witnesses,' is the utterance of **Jehovah**, 'even my servant whom I have chosen.'" The name served to distinguish those Bible students who continued in the **Watch Tower** organization with Rutherford as **president** from a number of schismatical groups that had been unable to accept Rutherford's authority. The name does not designate a legal organization but is simply a name, and the 1931 decision made no difference to the status of the **Watch Tower Bible and Tract Societies of Pennsylvania and New York**. The fact that it simply names the body of people who witness to Jehovah was formerly indicated by the use of the lower case on "witness," but this was changed in 1976, when the *Watchtower* magazine used initial capitals on both words.

A Witness is one who is "in the truth" and willing to proclaim it. Jehovah's witnesses in this sense are held to have existed since **creation**. During most of **Christendom**'s history, however, they virtually died out until the late 19th century, when the Watch Tower Society emerged as Jehovah's organization. One becomes a Witness through accepting the **truth** and undergoing **baptism** once a **congregation**'s **elders** are satisfied that one is sufficiently acquainted with the **faith** and lives an appropriate lifestyle. Baptism is not a precondition of **publishing**, however. There are two types of Witness: those who belong to the **anointed class** and those who belong to the **great crowd** or earthly class. The former expect to rule with **Jesus Christ** in heaven after **death**, while the latter look forward to life in **paradise earth**. The number of anointed ones is fixed at **144,000**, and this number consists of the faithful members of the early Christian Church before its **apostasy** and those in recent times who belong to

Jehovah's organization. Only a very small number of converts joining after 1935 claim to belong to the anointed class.

JESUS. Aka Christ; Jesus Christ; Jesus the Nazarene; Messiah; Son of Man. The founder of the Christian faith, he was born, according to the **Watch Tower Society**, in 2 B.C.E., having previously existed as a spirit, sometimes referred to as **Michael**. Jesus is regarded as having unique deity in the sense of being the only Son of God, but **Jehovah's Witnesses** deny that he is God himself. He is not regarded as consubstantial or coeternal with God the Father, and he is not part of any divine **trinity**. Witnesses hold that Jesus, being born of a virgin, had no human father, just as **Adam** had no father, and Jesus is described as the "last Adam." The Witnesses' Christology is a form of adoptionism since they claim that Jesus was anointed by God at his **baptism**, when he was ordained to preach the good news of God's **kingdom**. Witnesses regard the four canonical gospels as an accurate record of Jesus' birth, teachings, and sinless life, accepting that he was a teacher, a worker of **miracles**, and the world's savior.

Jesus' teaching aroused opposition from the **Jewish** authorities, who handed him over to the Romans, who then put him to **death**. Witnesses hold that Jesus' death was on a "torture stake," not a **cross**. His death is regarded as the **ransom sacrifice** for human sin. He rose from the dead "in spirit form," materializing a physical body to make **resurrection** appearances to his disciples. Paul refers to his resurrection as the "first fruits" of the resurrection of the dead (1 Corinthians 15:20), indicating that others will participate in everlasting life under his rule. This rule is held to have begun in **1914**, when **Satan** was cast down from heaven, which is currently populated by the **144,000** members of the **anointed class** who will rule with Christ. When this number is complete, Christ will lead the heavenly armies in the Battle of **Armageddon** to restore the earth from Satan's rule. The **millennial rule of Christ** will then follow, in the course of which the dead who have accepted the truth will be raised to life on **Paradise earth**.

JESUS CHRIST. *See* JESUS; CHRIST.

JEWS. The ancient Jews were God's chosen people, with whom he entered into a **covenant** relationship, which included the giving of the Law to Moses at Mount Sinai. The term was subsequently applied to members of the tribe of Judah, the southern **kingdom**, who were taken into captivity in **Babylon** by King Nebuchadnezzar. According to **Jehovah's Witnesses**, this event occurred in 607 B.C.E. and marked the end of the Jewish times, in which the Jews enjoyed God's special favor. The ensuing **Gentile times** are held to have lasted until **1914**. According to **J. F. Rutherford**, the return of the Jews to God's favor was evidenced by the 1917 Balfour Declaration, which supported plans for a Jewish return to Palestine, and which Rutherford believed, provided supportive evidence for his end-time chronology.

Witnesses do not believe that Jews continue to have special privileges with respect to **salvation**. They point out that Judaism became tainted with **pagan** Hellenistic influences, that it prohibited the use of **Jehovah**'s personal name, and that the Jews failed to acknowledge **Jesus** as the messiah. Witnesses use the phrase "spiritual Israel" to refer to the people of God who can experience God's new covenant and whose existence began at **Pentecost** in 33 C.E. Membership in this new Israel is open to both Jews and Gentiles. *See also* END-TIME CALCULATIONS; PAGANISM.

JOHNSON, PAUL S. L. (1873–1950). Born a Jew, Johnson subsequently became a Lutheran **minister**. His study of the **Bible** brought him to question the doctrines of the **Trinity**, the **immortality of the soul**, and eternal punishment in **hell**. He joined the **Watch Tower** organization, becoming a close associate of **C. T. Russell**, who sent him to London in 1916 to resolve problems there. Following controversy in London, he was recalled by **J. F. Rutherford**, who had assumed control of the organization. Upon returning to the Brooklyn **Bethel**, Johnson objected to the publication of *The Finished Mystery* (1917) and was finally ordered to leave on 27 July 1917. His name was proposed as a candidate for elections to the **Board of Directors** in 1918, but he withdrew, and with the aid of Raymond G. Jolly, he founded the **Layman's Home Missionary Society** in 1919, where he remained a director from 1920 until his death.

JONADABS. Aka earthly class; **great crowd**; great multitude; Jehonadabs; other sheep; people of good will. The term, now obsolete, designated those who had an earthly hope rather a heavenly one. The idea was introduced by **J. F. Rutherford** in *Vindication—Book 3* (1932), and it originates from the biblical story of Jonadab (or Jehonadab), who, despite being non-Jewish, was invited by King Jehu to mount his chariot and assist in his work slaughtering the priests of Baal (2 Kings 10:15–16). In the 1930s, a group of people expressed support for the **Jehovah's Witnesses** but had not formally joined. Rutherford suggested that they were the antitype of Jonadab, being favorably disposed to the organization and opposed to **Satan**. They thus came to be identified with the **great crowd** mentioned in the Book of **Revelation** (Revelation 7), in contrast with the **144,000** members of the **anointed class**, who would experience eternal life in heaven.

In a 1934 edition of the *Watchtower*, they were encouraged to undergo **baptism**, and the following year a **convention** was called in Washington, D.C., bearing the title "Convention of Jehovah's Witnesses and Jonadabs." In 1937, they were given positions of responsibility in **congregations**, including offices in their service committees, and the following year they were invited to attend the annual **Memorial** service "as companions of the **remnant**." Since the aspirations of the Jonadabs were earthly rather than heavenly, it was speculated that they would be more drawn to earthly affairs than the anointed class, for example, by having a love of nature. The term appears to have fallen into disuse in the early 1950s. *See also* PARADISE EARTH.

JUDGMENT DAY. The **Bible** teaches that **Jehovah** is the judge of all and that no one can escape his judgment. Although he has set a "day" on which humankind will be judged (Acts 17:31), there have been past occasions on which God has exercised his judgment. Thus, the antediluvians of Noah's time were judged by God and died in the great flood; Sodom and Gomorra were destroyed (Genesis 19:24); the conquest of **Babylon** by the Medes and Persians was a divine judgment; and **Jehovah's Witnesses** believe that the destruction of Jerusalem by the Romans was God's judgment on the **Jews** of that time. God's judgment does not entail eternal punishment; however, these people will not experience **resurrection** but rather nonexistence. Judgment is not invariably condemnatory: the **144,000** members of the **anointed class** have received God's favorable judgment, and, from 1919, began to assume their places in heaven, where they reign with God and **Christ** and will play their part in the final judgment of humanity.

Where nations, groups, or individuals have already been judged by God, they will not have to face a future judgment. The rest of humanity—the living and the dead—awaits a time in which their eternal fate will be determined. Those who are irredeemably wicked and have died will not experience resurrection, and the wicked who are alive when the Battle of **Armageddon** commences will be destroyed. During the ensuing **millennial rule of Christ**, the remainder of the dead will be raised, and they will be judged together with the living; people will not be judged by their past deeds but by what they do during this judgment period. Those who continue to perform evil deeds will be destroyed either during or at the end of the **millennium**, while those who do good will experience **paradise earth**. The **remnant**, or anointed class, will rule with Christ in heaven. *See also* DEATH; HELL.

– K –

KINGDOM. The principal theme of **Jesus**' preaching, and the focal point of **Jehovah's Witnesses**' teaching, the proclamation of the kingdom was particularly emphasized under **J. F. Rutherford**'s presidency and thereafter. Seeking the kingdom and preaching is regarded as Witnesses' first priority. **Jehovah**'s heavenly kingdom is believed to have come into existence already, as a result of **Christ**'s entering into the heavenly sanctuary in **1914** and casting out **Satan**. Starting in 1919, the kingdom has become populated with the **144,000** members of the **anointed class** who have died. The members of the **great crowd** await the coming of Jehovah's kingdom on earth, which was promised in God's **covenant** to King David (2 Samuel 7:16) and which will be brought fully into its perfected state at the end of the **millennial rule of Christ**.

This **paradise earth** will involve a restoration of the state enjoyed by **Adam** and Eve in the Garden of Eden. It will be everlasting and will mark the end of **sin, death,** sickness and disability, **war** and violence, natural disasters, and the confusion of languages that occurred at Babel. There will be an abundance of food, ample shelter, and fulfilling work. The Witnesses reject the views of some mainstream Christians that the kingdom is merely a condition of one's heart, that it can be achieved by political means, or that it simply refers to God's present sovereignty over the world. *See also* 1918; BABYLON; CLEANSING OF THE SANCTUARY.

KINGDOM HALL. The meeting place for individual **congregations,** the name was first suggested by **J. F. Rutherford** in 1935. The first of these was built in Honolulu, Hawaii, during that year. The Kingdom Hall is the center of worship, and serves as a symbol of **Jehovah**'s coming **kingdom.** It is simple in design. The main auditorium seats between 100 and 300 people and consists of seats and a raised platform: there is no altar and there are no images, except sometimes a picture of **Jesus.** Other features of a Kingdom Hall often include a library, counters from which literature can be obtained, and washroom and cloakroom facilities. There may be smaller rooms for purposes like training.

Congregations generally build their own Kingdom Halls, drawing on the skills of their members and help from nearby congregations. Construction moves as quickly as possible so as not to detract from the congregation's preaching and **publishing** work. Witnesses aim to finance the work themselves, collecting monies in advance and, where necessary, taking out a loan from the **Watch Tower Society.** A Kingdom Hall fund was set up in 1983 offering loans for the construction of new Kingdom Halls.

Two or more congregations may share one Kingdom Hall, arranging their meetings so as not to coincide. *See also* QUICK BUILD.

KINGDOM SUPPORT SERVICES, INC. Formed as a consequence of the organizational restructuring that took place during the year 2000, this arm of the **Watch Tower Society** attends to the design, engineering, and maintenance of its buildings. It owns its vehicles and holds the titles of its property. *See also* ADAMS, DON ALDEN; CHRISTIAN CONGREGATION OF JEHOVAH'S WITNESSES; RELIGIOUS ORDER OF JEHOVAH'S WITNESSES.

KNORR, NATHAN H. (1905–1977). Successor to **J. F. Rutherford** as president, in 1942. Knorr was born in Bethlehem, Pennsylvania, and at the age of 16 he joined the Allentown Congregation of **Bible** students. His attendance at the Cedar Point **Convention** in 1922 persuaded him to resign his membership of the Reformed Church. He was baptized the following year and became a member of the Brooklyn **Bethel**. Knorr was appointed by Rutherford as a copartner in the publication the *Golden Age* in 1928. In 1934 he was elected director of the **Peoples Pulpit Association**, which became the **Watchtower Bible and Tract Society of New York**, and he became vice president of the association the following year. In 1940, he became a director and vice president of the **Watch Tower Bible and Tract Society of Pennsylvania**, and he was president of both societies in 1942.

Knorr did much to increase the organization's membership and was particularly active in foreign work, traveling widely. When he assumed office, **Jehovah's Witnesses** had a presence in 54 countries; by 1961, this had increased to 186. Knorr strongly believed in the importance of training Witnesses for their work. Accordingly, he established the Watch Tower Bible School of Gilead in Lansing, New York, and subsequently **Theocratic Ministry Schools** in all **congregations**. Under his presidency, publication work continued with textbooks on the **Bible**, witnessing, and history of the organization. Knorr established the principle that Watch Tower authors should write anonymously to ensure that God rather than humans received appropriate credit. Knorr was succeeded by **Frederick W. Franz**. *See also* GILEAD SCHOOL OF MINISTRY.

– L –

LARSON, MAX H. (1915–). President of the **Watchtower Bible and Tract Society of New York**, Larson was born in Montana to Lutheran parents. He became a **Jehovah's Witness** in 1938 and was baptized by **William van Amburgh**. He immediately became a **pioneer** and soon a special pioneer before joining the Brooklyn **Bethel** staff in 1939. In 1942, he became the factory **overseer** and worked closely with President **Nathan H. Knorr**, with whom he subsequently traveled internationally. He continued to work at the society's printery until it closed in 2004. He was a director of the Watchtower Bible and Tract Society of New York before becoming president following the resignation of **Milton G. Henschel** in 2000.

LAYMAN'S HOME MISSIONARY SOCIETY. Founded in 1919 by **Paul S. L. Johnson**, this organization was a breakaway group following the 1917 schism between Johnson's supporters and those of **J. F. Rutherford**. Johnson's supporters sought a return to **C. T. Russell**'s teachings and published his six-volume *Studies in the Scriptures*, together with Johnson's multivolume *Epiphany Studies in the Scriptures*. The society published two regular magazines: *The Bible Standard* and *The Present Truth*. Johnson was director from 1920 until his death in 1950, when he was succeeded by Raymond G. Jolly. There were further schisms after that date.

LEAGUE OF NATIONS. An international organization founded in 1919 after the Paris Peace Conference ending **World War I**. Its aims were disarmament, the prevention of **war**, settlement of disputes between nations, and the improvement of global welfare. While most major countries were members, the United States was not, despite the fact that the original impetus came from U.S. President Woodrow Wilson.

From the time of its inception, the **Watch Tower Society** voiced its vehement disapproval of the league. In a talk in Cedar Point, Ohio, on 13 September 1922, **J. F. Rutherford** denounced the organization, and the *Watchtower* identified it with the scarlet-colored wild **beast** mentioned in the Book of **Revelation** (Revelation 17:3), predicting its demise. It was also identified with the "disgusting thing that causes desolation" (Daniel 11:31). With the outbreak of **World War II**, the league failed to meet, and it became clear that it was unable to fulfill its objectives. **Nathan H. Knorr** declared in 1942 that "the wild beast . . . is not," but predicted that another international peace organization would emerge. The **Jehovah's Witnesses**' disapproval of the League of Nations arises from their conviction that only God's **kingdom** can bring peace over a world that is ruled by **Satan**. They strongly disapproved of the churches' acclamation of the League as "the political expression of the Kingdom of God on earth," perceiving this as further confirmation of **Christendom**'s **apostasy**. *See also* UNITED NATIONS (UN).

LIFESTYLE. Jehovah's Witnesses do not clearly fit into scholars' categories of "world-affirming" and "world-renouncing" religions since they emphasize **Jesus**' teaching that they are "no part of the world" (John 15:19), despite living in it. With the exception of full-time **Bethel** staff, Witnesses do not live in distinctive communities but rather reside among other citizens. Although the **anointed class** has a "heavenly hope," the vast majority of present-day Witnesses look forward to **paradise earth**, which is expected to follow the **millennial rule of Christ**.

Witnesses' lifestyle tends to be simple but not austere. Their **publishing** work is judged to be more important than amassing material wealth, and many Witnesses prefer to enter trades rather than professions. Higher **education** is not given a particularly high priority, although Witness **children** attend state schools and are encouraged to maximize the benefits that they can obtain from them. Active Witnesses and their children devote a substantial part of their time to attending **congregation** meetings and doing **house-to-house ministry**.

High priority is given to **health**, and Witnesses are encouraged to eat healthful foods but not in excess. Physical exercise is encouraged. **Smoking** and **drugs** are prohibited; **alcohol** is permitted but only in moderate amounts. There are no dietary restrictions, apart from the prohibition of **blood**: Witnesses avoid foods like blood sausage. Medical help should be sought when needed, but blood transfusion is disallowed.

Witnesses are willing to enjoy pleasures that are compatible with doing **Jehovah**'s will, which can include public entertainment, holidays, **music**, dancing, and celebrating weddings and wedding anniversaries. A high value is attached to family and **congregational** life, and Witnesses tend to commemorate celebrations and enjoy entertainment as families or communities, and they draw their friends from their circles rather than risk potentially harmful **associations** with unbelievers. Care must be exercised in deciding to attend a dance, concert, or film, so as to avoid entertainment that might be sexually suggestive, **occultist**, or violent. The **Watch Tower Society** offers guidance rather than precise rules on such matters, on which individual members must exercise their **conscience**.

Sexual relationships may only take place within **marriage**. It is expected that one will marry another believer, and, until the wedding ceremony takes place, the courting couple will always be chaperoned by a relative or friend. Same-sex relationships are totally prohibited, since an important function of marriage is procreation. Neither marriage nor the bearing of children is an obligation, however, and couples should exercise conscience regarding contraception.

Witnesses do not celebrate such festivals as **Christmas**, New Year, **Easter**, Halloween, or **birthdays**, which they believe to pertain to **pagan** religions. The annual **Memorial** is the only religious celebration in their calendar; however, they may celebrate wedding anniversaries, and some families hold "present days," on which gifts are exchanged. Weddings and **funerals** are celebrated in **Kingdom Halls**; both events are kept modest, although wedding celebrations are nonetheless joyful.

Witnesses emphasize the need to follow Jehovah's ways, obey his laws, and behave with honesty and integrity. Such a lifestyle is not regarded as burdensome since the **Bible** states that "The orders from Jehovah are upright, causing the heart to rejoice" (Psalm 19:8). *See also* MARRIAGE; SEX.

LITTLE FLOCK. *See* 144,000; ANOINTED CLASS.

LORD'S EVENING MEAL. *See* MEMORIAL.

LORD'S PRAYER. *See* PRAYER.

LUCIFER. Not to be identified with **Satan**, the name Lucifer has only one occurrence in the **Bible** (Isaiah 14:12–16). The name means *shining one*; it refers to the fallen **Babylonian** dynasty. The **New World Translation** removes the explicit reference to Lucifer: "O how you have fallen from heaven, you shining one, son of the dawn!," and it is explained that this is a taunt, prophetically foretelling Babylon's destruction.

– M –

MACMILLAN, ALEXANDER HUGH (1877–1966). A prominent **Watch Tower** leader during the presidencies of **C. T. Russell**, **J. F. Rutherford**, and **Nathan H. Knorr**, Macmillan met Russell in 1900 and was baptized by him. He was subsequently invited to the Bible House in Allegheny, Pennsylvania, and from 1905 onward, he participated as a speaker in **convention** tours. He met Rutherford on one such tour in 1906 and baptized him. Following the Watch Tower Society's move to New York in 1909, he became a **director** of the **Peoples Pulpit Association** and was placed in charge of the Brooklyn **Bethel**.

Upon Russell's death in 1916, he assumed interim responsibility for the organization but did not wish to become its second **president**, preferring to support Rutherford. He was imprisoned with Rutherford in 1918–1919 for the circulation of Russell's posthumous *The Finished Mystery* (1917). Macmillan continued his role as a director and convention speaker under Rutherford and Knorr's presidencies. He is particularly well known for his autobiographical *Faith on the March* (1957).

MARK OF THE BEAST. This is given as 666 in the **Bible** (**Revelation** 13:18), and the number six is explained as falling short of seven, the number signifying perfection. It is noted that the reference to wearing it on one's forehead and arms is an allusion to the Jewish practice of wearing tefillin—the divine mark reminding **Jews** of the obligation to obey God's law. The **beast** is **Satan**, and his mark is "a man's number," hence his followers are those who subject themselves to human governments and conform to such worldly standards as materialism, dishonesty, celebrating **pagan** holidays, and following **false religion**. The statement that those who do not wear the mark will be unable to buy and sell (Revelation13:17) is not only a reference to materialistic standards but to the persecution of **Jehovah's Witnesses**, for example their being disallowed to buy property in certain countries. *See also* CAESAR'S RULE.

MARRIAGE. Jehovah's Witnesses regard the institution of marriage as going back to **Adam** and Eve, who are said be "one flesh" (Genesis

2:24) as husband and wife. Marriage must be entered into in accordance with biblical teaching. A Witness should only marry a partner who belongs to the organization: "Marry only in the Lord" (1 Corinthians 7:39). It is observed that in biblical times religious officials such as priests did not preside over the ceremony, and marriages conducted in **Kingdom Halls** are relatively simple ceremonies, over which an authorized **elder** presides. At the wedding in Cana, it is noted that **Jesus** was a guest, not the officiant. The ceremony consists of **songs**, **prayer**, a **Bible** reading, and a short talk. A ring is not essential, and it is a matter of **conscience** as to whether rings are given or exchanged.

Since Witnesses take pains to ensure that they comply with civil authorities, any civil ceremony or civil registration must be undertaken. In countries where compliance with civil law is inconvenient, a "Declaration of Marriage" can be performed at the appropriate Kingdom Hall, after which the couple are held to be formally married in a religious sense and permitted to have sexual relations. Premarital **sex** and trial marriages are not permitted. Consensual and common law marriages are regarded as legally valid but incomplete, and a couple who are related in this way must formalize their marriage before seeking **baptism**. If a couple has only undergone a civil marriage before seeking baptism, there is no additional religious requirement.

Although marriage is regarded as a permanent bond, divorce is permitted on the grounds of adultery. Incompatibility is not a reason for divorce; an incompatible couple may separate, but each partner is required to observe complete chastity. Separation from a nonbelieving partner is permissible, but remarriage is disallowed.

MEETINGS. Jehovah's Witnesses are expected to attend five meetings a week, each lasting approximately an hour. On Sundays, a public meeting is followed by a *Watchtower* study, and Tuesday is normally reserved for **congregation book study**. On Thursdays, there are two additional meetings: **Theocratic Ministry School** and a **Kingdom** Service Meeting. The first Sunday meeting is open to the public, and it is the principal worship service, consisting of **songs**, **prayer**, and a talk. The *Watchtower* study centers on a passage in a recent edition of the *Watchtower* introduced by an **elder**, after which comments from the **congregation** are invited.

The Theocratic Ministry School prepares members for public speaking and to some extent for **house-to-house ministry**. Members are afforded the opportunity to give short sample talks and receive a critique. The Kingdom Service Meeting focuses on house-to-house work, as well as how to welcome attendees to **Kingdom Hall** meetings and how to interest them in the organization.

Members are also encouraged to attend **conventions** and **assemblies** and make every effort to attend the annual **Memorial**. The justification of meetings is based on the **Bible**'s instruction that God's people should assemble (Deuteronomy 31:12–13; Hebrews 10:25) and **Jesus**' promise of his presence where even a small group of people gather (Matthew 18:20). Men, **women**, and **children** are encouraged to attend and are all expected to participate actively.

MEMORIAL. Aka Lord's Evening Meal. This service commemorating **Jesus**' last evening meal with his disciples is the only festival celebrated by **Jehovah's Witnesses**. It takes place annually after dusk on the 14th day of the Jewish month of Nisan. The first celebration was in Pittsburgh, Pennsylvania, around 1876 and was originally a gathering of all **Bible** students until the **Watch Tower Society** grew too large for this to be feasible. Witnesses now gather in their individual **congregations**. In 1938, members of the **great crowd** were invited to attend for the first time, and the service is now open to the public. Only those who belong to the **anointed class** may consume the **emblems**; the rest of the congregation merely handle them and pass them on. The Memorial consists of a talk by an **elder** based on the **Bible**, followed by **prayer** and the distribution of the "emblems" of unleavened bread and wine. The wine must be red and unfortified.

Although attendance is not necessary to gain everlasting life, members are encouraged to make every effort to be a part of the service. There is no miracle, like transubstantiation, associated with the event; the service is a reminder of **Jehovah**'s new covenant and Jesus' **ransom sacrifice**, and it is enacted in obedience to his words "Keep doing this in remembrance of me" (1 Corinthians 11:23).

MESSENGERS. *The Finished Mystery* (1917) identifies seven men: Paul, John, Arius, Waldo, Wycliffe, Martin Luther, and **C. T. Russell**.

In early **Watch Tower** teaching, these individuals were regarded as special messengers who made important attempts to bring **Christendom** back to its original authentic state. However, **Jehovah's Witnesses** no longer name specific human messengers in Christian history. **Angels** are regarded as God's supernatural messengers.

MESSIAH. *See* CHRIST.

MICHAEL. Although seldom mentioned in the **Bible**, **Jehovah's Witnesses** hold that Michael is **Jesus Christ** in his prehuman and posthuman forms. In Jewish thought, Michael is the protector of Israel and commander of the heavenly hosts, and he is described by Daniel as a prince and heavenly son of God who defends Daniel's people in a time of distress (Daniel 12:1). In the Book of **Revelation**, Michael casts **Satan** out of heaven and down to earth and leads the heavenly armies against him to conquer the earth.

It is reasoned that the role ascribed to Michael in the **Bible** is identical to that of Jesus and that someone distinct from Jesus could hardly be a prince superior to him. The meaning of the name Michael is "Who is like God," which again is held to confirm the identification. Michael is further described in Jude as "the archangel" (Jude 9), and it is noted that the word "archangel" is singular, there being no other references to any other archangel in scripture. Again, this is believed to point to an identification of Michael and Jesus.

Mary is instructed to give the name Jesus to her son to remove any hint on earth of Jesus' previous identity. It is believed that Jesus resumed the name Michael on his return to heaven in **1914**, establishing the connection with his prehuman existence. *See also* ANGELS.

***MILLENNIAL DAWN.** See STUDIES IN THE SCRIPTURES.*

MILLENNIAL RULE OF CHRIST. After the Battle of **Armageddon**, Christ will establish his **kingdom** on earth for a 1,000-year period, after **Satan** has been defeated and condemned to the abyss. There will be a **resurrection** of the dead, who will be judged. Those who are declared worthy of participating in **paradise earth** will not yet be perfected but will require to be taught the ways of righteousness. The new kingdom will mark the end of earthly governments and national divisions, and its rule will be theocratic instead of Satanic. The kingdom will not become immediately perfect: hard work is expected on the part of its inhabitants to bring it to perfection and repair the damage caused by Satan and his followers. There will be no **sin** and no more **death**.

At the end of this **millennium**, Satan and his demons will be released from the abyss and will once again attempt to deceive humanity. This event will enable those who have been resurrected to demonstrate whether they have chosen **Christ** or Satan. God's followers will experience no enduring harm during this time, but some will be deceived and destroyed eternally as a consequence. This is the "second death" (Revelation 20:7–15). The earth will have been restored to perfection, with a total absence of disease and pollution and with its rulership uncontested. *See also* RESURRECTION; THEOCRACY.

MILLENNIALISM. Aka chiliasm. A sociological and theological term designating a belief in an imminent utopian age, it may refer either to an exact 1,000-year period or a future of unspecified length. In Christianity, its literal meaning relates to the belief that **Christ** will defeat **Satan** in the Battle of **Armageddon** and rule for a 1,000-year period, when Satan will be bound and consigned to an abyss, after which he will be released for a short time and allowed to deceive the nations until his final destruction, after which the final judgment will take place (**Revelation** 20).

There have existed three broad types of millennialism within Christianity: premillennialism, postmillennialism, and amillennialism. Premillennialism holds that humanity is currently living before this 1,000-year period, while postmillennialism teaches that the 1,000-year period has already elapsed or is about to do so. Amillennialism treats millennialist beliefs symbolically or metaphorically, denying that the ideas of the Book of Revelation set out a literal calendar of end-time events.

In terms of this typology of millennialism, **Jehovah's Witnesses** are premillennialist, believing that the **millennial rule of Christ** is expected in the future. In common with other premillennialists, Witnesses believe in the return ("second presence") of Christ, which heralds the transformation of the earth into its former paradisiacal state with the return of the saints, destruction of evil powers, and resurrection of those in **Hades**, culminating in a final judgment. Witnesses differ from many premillennialists, since they look forward to Christ's invisible rule from heaven rather than expect him to return physically to earth. The term *millennialism* itself, however, is little used among Witnesses. *See also* END-TIME CALCULATIONS; FAITHFUL MEN OF OLD; MILLENNIUM.

MILLENNIUM. A period of 1,000 years. The term is used principally to refer to the 1,000-year rule of **Christ** after **Satan** is bound. The word can be used more widely to designate any 1,000-year period. For example, **Jehovah's Witnesses** assert that the third millennium after **Jesus'** birth commenced in 1999. The earth is reckoned to have existed for six millennia after God's **creation** of the world was complete. This was some time after the creation of **Adam** in 4026 B.C.E., but the exact date is unspecified. Hence, although the **millennial rule of Christ** is believed to be imminent, its exact start-date cannot be precisely determined. *See also* END-TIME CALCULATIONS; MILLENNIALISM.

MILLER, WILLIAM (1782–1849). Born in Pittsfield, Massachusetts, Miller is generally regarded as the founder of the **Adventist** movement. After moving to Poultney, Vermont, in 1803, he took up a career in local government and then in the army, attaining the rank of captain in 1814. By that time he had lost his **faith** and become a deist, but in 1814 he fought in the Battle of Plattsburgh and believed that his life had been miraculously preserved. He rejoined the Baptist Church and was particularly interested in questions relating to **death** and the afterlife. He also believed that **Christ**'s return was imminent and foretold in biblical **prophecy**.

In 1831 Miller began his career as a preacher, and in 1832 he submitted a number of articles to the *Vermont Telegraph*, a Baptist publication. By 1840 he was nationally known. Miller's teachings are summarized in his *Evidence from Scripture and History of the Second Coming of Christ, about the Year 1843: Exhibited in a Course of Lectures* (1842). Based on calculations relating to Daniel 18:14, "Unto two thousand and three hundred days; then shall the sanctuary be cleansed"), he concluded that the Second Coming would occur in 1843. When this failed to happen, he recalculated the date to 1844.

His followers were disillusioned, and the event became known as the Great Disappointment.

The Millerites who remained faithful to their leader either recalculated the date or claimed that it referred to a supernatural rather than a natural event. Miller's movement gave rise to Seventh-day **Adventism** and the Advent Christians, with whom many of **C. T. Russell**'s **Bible** students associated. *See also* CLEANSING OF THE SANCTUARY.

MILLIONS CAMPAIGN. On 24 February 1918, **J. F. Rutherford** gave a lecture in Los Angeles, California, entitled *The World Has Ended—Millions Now Living May Never Die*. This formed the basis for Rutherford's short book published in 1920, with the slightly amended title *Millions Now Living Will Never Die*. The "millions campaign," which centered on the book, began on 25 September 1920 with a public talk by Rutherford and was followed by further public speeches and wide distribution of copies of the book at US$.25 per copy. The campaign was advertised in newspapers and on billboards and spread worldwide. *See also* FAITHFUL MEN OF OLD; GENERATION.

MINISTER. Aka ordained minister. Literally "one who serves," the term applies widely to God's servants, including **angels**, the Levites (the Israelite priestly class), prophets, and **Jesus Christ**. A government can be said to be God's "minister" when it metes out justice. **Jehovah's Witnesses** apply the term to any baptized member of the **Watch Tower Society** regarding the water of **baptism** as the symbol of ordination. The qualifications for being a minister in this sense are a strong sense of **faith**, study of the **Bible**, and **associations** with other Christians. Witnesses note that the term is also used to refer to Protestant clergy, whom they regard as false ministers, being servants of **Satan** rather than God. Witnesses have typically argued that their status as ministers exempts them from military service.

MINISTERIAL SERVANT. A **congregation**'s **elders** are assisted by ministerial servants, who must be baptized male members, normally younger than the elders. They are responsible for the accounts and literature distribution and are variously designated as accounts servants, literature servants, and magazine-territory servants. It is expected that, in time, ministerial servants will aspire to become elders, but meanwhile their designated tasks are largely to keep records. They may be allowed to lead book studies, and, if an insufficient number of elders are available, they may be invited to teach from the platform in a **Kingdom Hall**. Occasionally one of them may be given a role normally assigned to an elder, for example oversight of the **Theocratic Ministry School**, but only if no elder is available. Such assignation would not qualify him to be an elder.

MINISTERIAL TRAINING SCHOOL. *See* GILEAD SCHOOL OF MINISTRY.

MIRACLE WHEAT. In March 1908, *Zion's Watch Tower* featured an article on "miracle wheat" with an unusually high yield, produced by a Virginia farmer named K. B. Stoner. The article suggested that this might be a fulfillment of biblical **prophecy** that "the earth shall yield her increase" (Ezekiel 34:27). In 1911, **Brother** J. A. Bohnet wrote to *Zion's Watch Tower* stating that he had purchased some of the wheat and wished to donate his profit of 100 dollars. He also offered to sell the wheat at one dollar a pound, promising the proceeds to the **Watch Tower Society**. Meanwhile, Stoner (who was not a brother) dropped his price, and the Brooklyn newspaper *The Eagle* accused **C. T. Russell** of profiteering. Russell sued for defamation but lost the case. The society subsequently wrote to all its customers, offering a refund if any of them were dissatisfied, but no one took the organization up on the offer.

MIRACLES. The **Watch Tower Society** accepts the definition of a miracle as an extraordinary event that lies outside human or natural powers, and is therefore attributable to supernatural agency. However, since humanity's understanding of the world remains partial, one cannot be certain that a remarkable occurrence is miraculous. The world's creation is held to be a miracle, and thus a God who is capable of creating the universe and the laws that govern it possesses unlimited might. Nevertheless, God does not arbitrarily violate his own laws, and the Bible records occasions on which he has used natural events, such as floods and earthquakes, to further his purposes.

Miracles were characteristic of Jesus' ministry and of the early Church. Their principal purpose was to demonstrate that human beings could receive power to accomplish Jehovah's work. However, the power to work miracles is one of the gifts that were expected to pass away, as the first generation of Christ's followers died out (1 Corinthians 13:8). Such powers are no longer deemed to be necessary, since everything that is necessary for salvation has now been made available to humankind. Jehovah's Witnesses therefore attach no credence to claims of present-day miracles or apparitions.

MONEY. Jehovah's Witnesses' standards of living tend to be modest but not austere. "Treasure in heaven" is regarded as preferable to earthly riches, and wealth creation could interfere with a Witness' **kingdom** ministry. Some Witnesses sacrifice personal wealth by working part-time rather than full-time so they can serve as **publishers** or **pioneers**. Witnesses tend not to practice generosity by giving to secular charities and certainly do not give to those of **Christendom**, but they will provide financial support to needy **congregations** in other parts of the world.

Witnesses are encouraged to be prudent, avoid debt, have a personal budget, and save. Saving 5 percent of one's income is recommended. There is no objection to paying or receiving interest, so long as this does not involve exploitation. No mention is made of ethical investment. Such issues are matters of **conscience**. Witnesses are obliged to pay their taxes to the state, since Jesus taught that one should "pay back Caesar's things to Caesar, but God's things to God" (Mark 12:17). Tax declarations should be honest, and Witnesses do not withhold proportions that are used for military or other undesirable purposes. Such gestures would be unduly political (Romans 13:7).

Congregations receive money through direct giving on the part of members. Since its inception, the **Watch Tower Society** has deliberately avoided the mainstream churches' practice of passing a collection plate. **C. T. Russell** promoted his organization as "the church without a collection," where seats were free. Witnesses do not raise money by means of fêtes or concerts. They are, however, encouraged to take full advantage of the benefits available within the law, like tax relief for charitable giving. Their buildings, like the **Kingdom Hall** and **Assembly Hall**, are kept simple for financial as well as religious reasons, and the accommodations are built, as much as possible, by voluntary work carried out by members.

MOYLE, OLIN R. An attorney, Moyle moved in to the Brooklyn **Bethel** in 1935 as a legal counsel to work alongside **J. F. Rutherford**. On 21 July 1939, he departed, leaving a letter accusing Rutherford of ill-treatment of workers, displays of temper, vulgar language, encouraging excessive consumption of **alcohol**, and generally condoning low moral standards at the Bethel. Rutherford called a joint meeting of the **Boards of Directors** of both the **Watch Tower Bible and Tract Society of Pennsylvania** and the **Watchtower Bible and Tract Society of New York**, at which they passed a resolution condemning and **disfellowshipping** Moyle, the full text of which was published in the *Watchtower* on 15 October 1939. Moyle sued for libel: he was initially awarded $100,000 for two alleged defamatory *Watchtower* articles, but this was later reduced to $30,000 when the **Watch Tower Society**'s appeal reached the Supreme Court on 10 May 1943.

MUSIC. According to the **Bible**, the first musician was Jubal, who is credited with the organization of a band of players, and the use of music is referred to at various points in both sections of scripture. King David is credited with the composition of the psalms, some of which were used in connection with worship in the Jerusalem Temple. Music is thus a divine gift, and in the coming **kingdom**, the **anointed class** is described as singing a "new song" in heaven (**Revelation** 5:9). However, music can also be used by **Satan**. **Watch Tower** literature cites the story of the golden calf (Exodus 32:18), whom the Israelites worshipped with singing and dancing while Moses was on top of Mount Sinai. Music was also associated with Canaanite fertility cults, as well as the worship of the **Babylonian** goddess Ishtar.

Jehovah's Witnesses have no inherent objection to classical music, little of which, they contend, is scripturally objectionable, and it is acceptable to listen to such music, even though its sources may be secular. Present-day popular music is to be regarded with great caution, however. The Watch Tower Society has expressed concern regarding the amount of time young people spend listening to it, as well as its connotations. Rap music extols rebellion, while heavy metal encourages violence and has links to suicide and **drugs**. Much popular music has sexual innuendo and at times alludes to the **occult**. People should be aware of the potentially harmful effects of loud music. There is no inherent objection to loudness. The Bible refers to 120 trumpets being sounded simultaneously at the Temple (2 Chronicles 5:12), but prolonged listening to loud music can discourage conversation and even cause deafness. Rock concerts are often linked with the abuse of **sex**, drugs, and **alcohol**. One must exercise **conscience** as to whether to attend such events, bearing in mind the potential harmful **associations** that might result. *See also* SONGS.

– N –

NATIONAL GOVERNMENT. *See* CAESAR'S RULE.

NETHINIM. *See* GIVEN ONES.

NEW LIGHT. Jehovah's Witnesses teach that understanding of the **Bible** is progressive; hence their teachings on a number of important issues have changed over time. Particular examples are the identity of the **great crowd** and their **end-time calculations**. The **Watch Tower** organization sometimes refers to doctrinal changes as "adjustments in view."

NEW WORLD SOCIETY. The phrase was first introduced by **Nathan H. Knorr** at an international **convention** in New York in 1950. It designates **Jehovah**'s society on earth and was devised to establish clear continuity between the present-day **Watch Tower** organization and the renewed earth that will appear during **the millennial rule of Christ**. The latter new earth will include the resurrected dead—the **faithful men of old** or "princes." Some previous Watch Tower literature asserts that there could be no modern princes or worthies (*WT* 20 1/15), but Knorr argued that modern **Jehovah's Witnesses** had the advantage of having accepted **Christ** in faith rather than merely looked forward to him, like the ancient patriarchs. **J. F.**

Rutherford's identification of the **great crowd** in 1935 enabled this shift in the Watch Tower Society's teaching. In anticipation of the new order, Knorr urged the importance of transforming the society's standards and form of government to that of the new world. Government should therefore be theocratic, members should live righteous lives in harmony with each other, and personal integrity should be given great importance. The belief in the continuity between the Watch Tower organization and **paradise earth** entails that the New World Society is eternal, not merely temporal. *See also* DEATH; RESURRECTION; THEOCRACY.

NEW WORLD TRANSLATION (NWT). The **Jehovah's Witnesses'** translation of the **Bible**, rendered from the original Hebrew and Greek texts and superseding the King James Version, which English-speaking members previously used. The **Governing Body** announced in 1949 that a translation committee had been appointed, although the individual names of translators was never divulged, in line with the **Watch Tower Society**'s policy of author anonymity. The translation was launched on 2 August 1950 at a **convention** in Yankee Stadium in New York. It was released progressively in six volumes from 1950 to 1960 and underwent revisions in 1961, 1970, and 1971.

The distinctive features of the translation were its use of modern language, its removal of trinitarian references that appeared in the King James Version, and, most especially, the use of the name "**Jehovah**" as a translation of the Hebrew tetragrammaton. The NWT also dropped the terms *Old Testament* and *New Testament* on the grounds that the latter was not a revision of the former. Instead they substituted the expressions "**Hebrew-Aramaic Scriptures**" and "**Christian Greek Scriptures.**"

In 2004, the society reported that the complete NWT had been translated into 32 languages, with two Braille editions, and that the Christian Greek Scriptures had been translated into a further 18 languages and one more Braille edition. The NWT has been much criticized, particularly by Protestant evangelicals. Although it is the preferred translation by the Witnesses, they remain willing to use other translations in **house-to-house ministry** and in countries where a NWT has not yet been published. *See also* EMPHATIC DIAGLOTT; TRINITY.

NIMROD. The great-grandson of Noah, Nimrod is described as "in op-position to **Jehovah**" (Genesis 10:9) and reckoned to be the source of worldwide religious **apostasy**. According to the **Bible**, he travelled to Babel (**Babylon**), where he established his "**kingdom**." He is thus the first person in scripture—and, **Jehovah's Witnesses** believe, in hu-man history—to be called a king and to have established a form of civil government, as opposed to **theocracy**. Witnesses speculate that the Tower of Babel was one of the first ziggurats—towers used for religious purposes in ancient Babylonian **religion**. The account of these early practitioners of this religion being scattered abroad entails that **false religion** became propagated throughout the world.

From the study of the extant evidence, Witnesses conclude that Semiramis was the first **woman** to be deified. Her name literally means "branch bearer" or "dove"—the name and symbol of the Babylonian goddess by that name. Nimrod and Semiramis were both deified and came to be regarded as husband and wife, as well as son and mother. Nimrod was thus his own father and son, and so, it is rea-soned, a **trinity** of deities emerges: father, mother, and son. After his death, Semiramis taught that he had become a tree-spirit and that overnight a dead stump blossomed into an evergreen tree, represent-ing Nimrod redivivus. She instructed that on his **birthday** on 25 De-cember, offerings should be left at this tree. The stump and tree are believed to be the origins of the yule log and **Christmas** tree, thus as-sociating Christmas with **pagan** celebrations.

The organization's account of Nimrod draws substantially on Alexander Hislop's *The Two Babylons* (1858).

– O –

OCCULTISM. All forms of occultism and interest in the paranormal re-ceive strong disapprobation by **Jehovah's Witnesses**, who point out that they are consistently condemned in the **Bible** and thwarted by God's true followers. Witnesses do not deny the possibility of certain paranormal occurrences but regard them as the work of **Satan**, evil spirits, and demons. They are particularly counseled to avoid any **as-sociation** with astrology, conjuring, predicting the future, (for exam-ple, by divination or horoscopes), and any form of magic or sorcery.

These are all believed to be stepping-stones to contact with Satan and his demons.

Some of these practices are associated with **pagan**, especially **Babylonian** religion, which purported to effect contact between the living and the dead. Witnesses argue that such phenomena cannot be authentic since there is no disembodied **soul** that survives **death** and since the dead are in a state of sleep awaiting **resurrection**. Necromancers are therefore practicing "lying divination" (Ezekiel 13:6–7), and participation in popular Western practices like the celebration of Halloween are forbidden.

Witnesses deplore recent media interest in the **occult**, like television programs and films relating to witchcraft, exorcism, and vampirism. Interest in unidentified flying objects (UFOs) and extraterrestrials is also judged to belong to the occult and is strongly discouraged.

ORDAINED MINISTER. *See* MINISTER.

ORGAN TRANSPLANTATION. Since transplant surgery was not available in ancient times, the **Bible** contains no explicit directives. In a 1961 article, the *Watchtower* states that any decision to donate one's body parts upon **death** for scientific purposes was a matter of individual **conscience** (*WT* 61 8/1). A later 1967 issue declares that the acceptance of parts of another person's body amounted to "cannibalism" (*WT* 67 11/15) and was therefore unacceptable. In 1980, organ donations and transplantations were once again said to be matters of conscience, and the **Watch Tower Society** acknowledged that tissue and bone were not the same as **blood**, from which the believer must abstain. Bone marrow constituted a borderline case since it was debatable whether or not it was "flesh," hence it is a matter for individual conscience. In any transplant surgery, blood transfusion is prohibited. The individual's conscience must take into account the possibility that a donor's life may be shortened in the process, whether the amount of vehicular blood involved is significant, and whether artificial body parts might be used instead. **Jehovah's Witnesses** have no objection to the removal of body parts in autopsies.

OTHER SHEEP. *See* GREAT CROWD.

OVERSEER. Sometimes used synonymously with "**elder**," but since the term literally means "one who presides," it is used to designate anyone who has been assigned oversight of a specific task in the organization. Thus a "**presiding overseer**" is the chairman of a **congregation**'s elders. **District** and **circuit** overseers—formerly called district and circuit servants—are appointed to take responsibility for districts and circuits and travel to them to support and further establish the congregations. The system of overseers was first announced in 1894. In 1956, the **Watch Tower Society** recognized the need for overseers to develop international work and divided the world into 10 **zone**s for this purpose. Each zone has its zone servant—now renamed "zone overseer"—and traveling overseers are sent to parts of the world where there are special needs to assist in and encourage the work of the elders and congregations.

– P –

PAGANISM. Although generally synonymous with **false religion**, the term is principally used to refer to forms of **religion** that have tainted Christianity, causing its **apostasy**. These are principally forms of Egyptian, **Babylonian**, and Greco-Roman religion, which are believed to have introduced such false doctrines as the **immortality** of the **soul** and the **Trinity**, as well as celebrations like **Christmas**, **Easter**, and Halloween. False religion is held to have originated in Babylon and spread worldwide from there, affecting both Judaism and Christianity. The **Bible** students and subsequent **Jehovah's Witnesses** claim to practice a restored form of the Christian faith that has shed its pagan accretions. *See also* NIMROD; OCCULTISM.

PARABLE OF THE PENNY (DENARIUS). This parable of **Jesus** (Matthew 20:1–16) tells of a steward who hired workers in a vineyard at various times during a day but paid them all the same wage of one penny (Roman term *denarius*), causing resentment on the part of those who had worked the longest. **C. T. Russell** regarded parables as symbolic **prophecies** and contended that the penny represented the "**kingdom** honors" to be conferred on the faithful, whom God had commissioned to complete his work. Later thinking, however, came to associate the parable with affairs on earth, specifically the controversies surrounding the leadership after Russell's death in 1916 and the publication of *The Finished Mystery* the following year. **Clayton J. Woodworth** delivered a sermon supporting Russell's interpretation, subsequently published as a five-page pamphlet entitled *The Parable of the Penny* (1917), which compared *The Finished Mystery* with the penny in the parable and the dissenting **Watch Tower** leaders with the disgruntled workers who complained about their pay. Meanwhile, **Paul S. L. Johnson**, who was ousted by Rutherford, contended that the "day" in the parable represented the 40 years of Russell's ministry and that he (Johnson) was the steward and hence had the right of succession.

Later Watch Tower interpretations abandoned the 1917 controversies. In *Jehovah* (1934), Rutherford explained that the "penny" was the divine name "**Jehovah**" that God had given his people. Since this benefit did not accrue solely to **Jehovah's Witnesses**, the parable was later reinterpreted once more. A 1967 *Watchtower* article explains that it has two fulfillments, the first of which was at the first **Pentecost**, where the disciples—"hired" later than the Jewish religious authorities—received the gift of belonging to the "spiritual Israel." The second and final fulfillment began in **1914**, when **Christ**'s heavenly rule offered the reward of being "anointed ambassadors" of his kingdom. The clergy, whom Witnesses accused of their persecution, were in existence before the Watch Tower organization and hence are represented by the disgruntled workers in the parable.

PARADISE EARTH. The final hope of **Jehovah's Witnesses**, it is the state to which the earth will be restored during the **millennial rule of Christ** following the Battle of **Armageddon**. The earth will be restored to its primordial paradisiacal state before **Adam**'s fall; the former **Satanic** rule will be abolished, and it will be ruled by **Christ** and the **144,000** members of the **anointed class**.

The restored paradise earth will be enjoyed by the **great crowd**, consisting of Witnesses, together with the "ransomed dead," who will be resurrected during the **millennium**. In this paradise, there will be no **death**, pain or sickness, or sorrow. Those with disabilities will become able-bodied. There will be plenty of food, with a climate conducive to agriculture, and work will be satisfying. **War**, violence, and crime will have died out, and there will be harmony between humans and **animals**.

To enjoy everlasting life in paradise earth, four conditions must be satisfied: one must know God by his true name (**Jehovah**), obey God's laws, be associated with God's organization (the Jehovah's Witnesses), and faithfully proclaim God's message to others.

PAROUSIA. Literally "second presence," the word refers to the manner of **Christ**'s return. **C. T. Russell** and the **Watch Tower** organization have pointed out that the Greek word *parousia* does not mean "second coming," which they regard as a frequent mistranslation in Christian **Bibles**. Rather, it means "being alongside" and hence does not refer to a literal return of **Jesus** on the clouds to "rapture" his followers, as is expected in many forms of mainstream Christian **fundamentalism**. The second presence is regarded as an extended period of time rather than an episodic happening—a spiritual and invisible global phenomenon.

The *parousia* is believed to have begun in **1914**, at the end of the **Gentile times**, when Christ assumed his heavenly rule, where he is present with his **anointed class**. While the Bible's references to a return on a cloud might appear to indicate dramatic supernatural intervention, **Jehovah's Witnesses** point out that the promise at Jesus' ascension is that he will return "in the same manner" (Acts 1:11) and that Jesus did not ride a cloud to return to heaven. The "manner" of Christ's return will be invisible, like a thief in the night (Matthew 24:43–44). Biblical references to clouds are taken to indicate invisibility, and "seeing" in connection with Christ's second appearance is regarded as figurative. In the **Hebrew-Aramaic Scriptures**, a cloud symbolizes God's presence, leading his people and delivering the law at Mount Sinai.

Witnesses therefore do not expect an imminent "rapture" but rather the "conclusion of the system of things," which is a sign of Christ's presence (Matthew 24:3). Such a conclusion of the present system will involve the **resurrection** of the dead, the gathering of Christ's followers, the defeat of **Satan**, the destruction of the unredeemed, and the **millennial rule of Christ**. *See also* MILLENNIALISM; MILLENNIUM.

PASTORAL BIBLE INSTITUTE (PBI). Established in 1918, by R. H. Hirsh, I. F. Hoskins, A. I. Ritchie, J. D. Wright, and 50 others, dissociating itself from **J. F. Rutherford.** They opposed the publication of **C. T. Russell**'s posthumous *The Finished Mystery* (1917), believing that some of its ideas were unscriptural, and objected to Rutherford's attempts to control the **Watch Tower Society** after Russell's death. The PBI is the largest of the Watch Tower splinter groups and the most conservative in supporting Russell's ideas and ensuring that his writings remain in print. They produced a **creedlike** statement, affirming that a number of their doctrines accord with the **Bible**; however, they are free in the sense of commending ideas of those outside the organization for study. Teachings laid emphasis on the year 1938, in which they hoped for the "glorification of saints." The writings of Percy L. Reed (d. 1983) are also of significance to the organization.

The PBI's organization is through a number of autonomous **ecclesias**, who come together for an annual assembly. The Institute is headed by seven board members and an editorial committee of five. The editorial committee was originally headed by R. E. Streeter, who inaugurated the periodical *The Herald of Christ's Kingdom*, established in 1918. Estimates of circulation figures vary widely: Melton suggests that 3,000 were distributed in the United States and Canada and a further 1,000 overseas, while Bergman reckons that its circulation was as high as 30,000. The organization enjoys links with the British **Bible Students** (Bible Fellowship Union) and the **Berean Bible Institute** in Australia.

The organization is small and nonproselytizing and has experienced its own splits; many of its splinter groups have died out. It has been in decline since 1918.

PATON, JOHN H. (1843–1922). An early associate of **C. T. Russell** and **Nathan H. Barbour** for a short period around 1879 to 1881. Born in Ayrshire, Scotland, Paton's family emigrated to Michigan in 1852, where he was baptized into Almont Baptist Church. He received an Exhorter's License from the Methodists in 1867 and returned to the Almont Baptists in 1870 as their ordained minister. Paton's views were considered unorthodox, and he was tried for heresy in 1872 on the grounds that he denied the natural **immortality** of the

soul, regarded **death** as sleep until the **resurrection**, and did not accept the final destruction of the wicked. He subsequently organized his own Church of Christ, which became united with the Michigan **Adventist** Christ Conference, and made the acquaintance of Barbour.

Paton wrote a number of theological works. His *Day Dawn, or The Gospel in Type and Prophecy* (1880) was promoted by **Zion's Watch Tower Tract Society**. Other works include *Moses and Christ* (c. 1896), *The Perfect Day* (1882), and *The Atonement* (1895). In 1882, he established the monthly journal *The World's Hope*, which was printed for three years. In 1879, *Zion's Watch Tower* identified him as a regular contributor, although he appears to have contributed one article in 1880, entitled "The Pre-Existence of Christ." He seems to have had no further association with the **Watch Tower Society** after 1881, and in 1915 his autobiography makes no mention of Russell, Barbour, or Zion's Watch Tower Tract Society.

PENTECOST. Originally a Jewish celebration commemorating the first fruits of harvest and the giving of the Law to Moses on Mount Sinai, the festival had an anti-typical fulfillment in **Jesus'** sending of the **holy spirit** to 120 disciples who had assembled in an upper room in Jerusalem in 33 C.E., 40 days after his ascension into **heaven**. The event was reckoned to be a fulfillment of Jewish **prophecy** (Joel 2:28–32) and was marked by the disciples' ability to speak in unknown languages. Jesus' principal disciple, Peter, preached boldly to a Jewish audience who had come to Jerusalem to celebrate the festival, inviting them to call upon God's true name and be baptized. The event is therefore held to be the first example of Christian **baptism** and marks the inception of the new Christian **congregation**. The association of Pentecost with the giving of the covenantal Law is judged to be significant since this highlights the new covenant that Jesus **Christ** brought into existence. **Jehovah's Witnesses** believe that the miraculous phenomena associated with Pentecost died out with the first **generation** of Christians (1 Corinthians 13:8) but that the practices of baptism and proclaiming **Jehovah**'s **kingdom** remain of paramount importance.

The prophecy relating to Pentecost is believed to have a "second fulfillment" in modern times, beginning in 1919. In that year **J. F. Rutherford** inspired delegates at the Cedar Point **Convention** in

Cedar Point, Ohio, where in 1922, he urged his sympathizers to "Advertise, advertise, advertise, the kingdom." *See also* MIRACLES.

PEOPLES PULPIT ASSOCIATION. Following the **Watch Tower Society**'s move to Brooklyn in 1909, the Peoples Pulpit Association was set up as the society's New York corporation to meet legal requirements. In 1939, its name was changed to the Watchtower Bible and Tract Society, Inc. and subsequently the **Watchtower Bible and Tract Society of New York, Inc.**, in 1956.

PHOTO-DRAMA OF CREATION. In 1912, **C. T. Russell** commenced working on a project that culminated with the screening of this motion picture on 4 January 1914 at the Temple in New York City. It was attended by 5,000 members of the public, with many people having to be turned away. Cinematic production was in its early stages at the time, and the four-part presentation consisted of motion picture, slides, and musical and sound recordings. It lasted for eight hours. The subject matter encompasses the **creation** of the world, as recounted in the Book of Genesis; the story of the **Jews** from **Adam** to the time of Daniel; the life and ministry of **Jesus**; and the early years of the Christian Church to the present. During **1914**, the production was screened at various locations in North America, Europe, Australia, and New Zealand. *See also* BIBLE.

PILGRIM. The name given to a traveling representative of the **Watch Tower Society** from between 1897 and 1927. The term is now obsolete. In 1894 the society introduced the role of Tower Tract Society representative, who was provided with a testimonial from the organization and sent on a traveling ministry outside his region. The term *pilgrim* became the accepted name for such a role, until 1928, when it was replaced by "regional service director," and beginning in 1936, "regional servant." Their itineraries were published in *Zion's Watch Tower* and subsequently the *Watch Tower*, and their role was to preach and to strengthen the **congregations** they visited. Congregations could request visits if the society had not arranged them.

This role was suspended during much of the **war** years, and, when it was revived in 1946, these officers became **district** servants. They are now known as district **overseers**.

PIONEER. Aka pioneer publisher. A **Jehovah's Witness** who wishes to make a greater time commitment than the average **publisher** can apply to become a pioneer, of which there are three categories: auxiliary, regular, and special. A regular pioneer spends 90 hours a month or 1,000 hours a year evangelizing. Such work may be undertaken at home or overseas. Since the time commitment involved is considerable, pioneers are usually unable to combine this work with full-time employment and typically live a simple lifestyle, devising ways of reducing their expenses. Pioneers used to be eligible for special rates on **Watch Tower** literature in the days when charges were imposed. Pioneering is voluntary, and is not regarded as essential for gaining eternal life.

The category of "special pioneer" was created in 1937. It involves devoting 140 hours a month to evangelization, and special pioneers are required to be available for service anywhere in the country. Modest expenses are paid, and until 2004 a small stipend was available. Auxiliary pioneers are those who assist the Watch Tower Society's pioneering work but often do so on a temporary basis to sample the pioneer's lifestyle. Such pioneers are asked to devote 50 hours a month to proclaiming the **kingdom**.

Pioneers carry out normal **house-to-house ministry** and also conduct **Bible** studies in people's homes. They may be asked to undertake work in more remote areas that cannot reasonably be covered by normal publishers. They are sometimes assigned to areas where there is no **congregation** or to congregations that are in need of help.

PIONEER PUBLISHER. *See* PIONEER.

POLITICS. Jehovah's Witnesses eschew political activity since earthly government is one of the principal aspects of **Babylon** the Great. They therefore do not join political parties, seek governmental office, campaign for political causes, or incorporate any political messages into talks given to **congregations**, **assemblies**, or **conventions**. Even attempts to "clean up" politics are avoided. Since Witnesses regard themselves as belonging to **Jehovah**'s **kingdom**, and hence "no part of the world" (John 15:19), participation in politics would imply a friendship with the world, which would be at odds with the **Watch Tower Society**'s goals. Politics are viewed as unduly divisive and have resulted in military conflicts, in which Witnesses will not participate. They believe that the present system of worldly affairs is under **Satan**'s rule and is doomed; it will be destroyed in the Battle of **Armageddon**.

In the **Hebrew-Aramaic Scriptures, Nimrod** is identified as the first earthly king who established his earthly government and **false religion** in Babylon, incurring God's disapproval (Genesis 10:8–10). Witnesses note that, by contrast, **Jesus** declined to be made an earthly ruler (John 6:15) and that the early Christians did not participate in earthly government, being at odds with the Roman Empire. At a later stage, "nominal Christians" came to compromise with civil governments, commencing with Constantine in 312 C.E. From that time forward, **Christendom** wrongly influenced affairs of the state, and the state exerted undue interference in matters of religion. Witnesses deplore the way in which mainstream Christianity has preached political messages, the holding of political offices by some clergy, and the use of churches for political purposes, like polling stations during elections.

Witnesses advocate neutrality in political matters, although **voting** in elections is a matter of **conscience**. Jehovah's coming kingdom will be an everlasting kingdom, a **theocracy** in which Jehovah and **Christ**, together with the **144,000** members of the **anointed class** in heaven, will rule over **paradise earth.** This cannot be achieved through political means, but by Christ's defeat of Satan in the last days.

PRAISE, PRAYER, AND TESTIMONY MEETINGS. *See* DAWN CIRCLES FOR BIBLE STUDY.

PRAYER. Jehovah's Witnesses emphasize the importance of private and public prayer. Prayers invariably feature in congregational meetings and **conventions** and are led by **elders** or **ministerial servants**. Members of the **congregation** are at liberty to add "Amen" at the close, but they are not obliged to do so. Prayer must come from the heart and thus should be spontaneous, not previously prepared or from a prayer book. To maintain a close relationship with God, prayer is to be addressed to **Jehovah**, through **Jesus Christ**, and not to intermediaries such as saints or the Virgin Mary. The prayers of apostates, **pagans**, and hypocrites are believed to be disregarded by God. Prayer is not to be used to effect **miracles**, including **healing**. Its purpose is to obtain consolation and develop virtues like wisdom, the strength to perform one's tasks, or the patience to deal with one's concerns.

Jesus' "model prayer"—known as "The Lord's Prayer" in mainstream Christianity—is not to be recited, since Jesus instructed, "when praying, do not say the same things over and over again" (Matthew 6:7). However, it highlights the features that make prayer acceptable, including acknowledging God's sovereignty, sanctifying his name, and seeking his **kingdom** in heaven and on earth.

PREDESTINATION. This doctrine, held by some Christian theologians, notably Augustine of Hippo and John Calvin, claims that, before the moment of **creation**, God foreknew and hence willed all human and other earthly affairs, as well as the respective eternal destinies of all human beings. **C. T. Russell** found this doctrine unacceptable, and subsequent **Bible** students and **Jehovah's Witnesses** have consistently rejected it. Witnesses hold that this doctrine was not taught by the early Church and that it came into existence after its **apostasy**.

Witnesses make several objections to the doctrine, arguing that assigning men and women to **hell** in advance of their actions is contrary to God's love and justice. Predestination, they believe, is incompatible with human free will and renders God's appeals pointless, when he urges humanity to repent and accept Christ's **ransom sacrifice**. Further, the doctrine makes God the author of **sin**, which contradicts the Bible's teaching that sin is hateful to him (Proverbs 15:9).

The **Watch Tower Society** argues that when the Bible uses expressions like "foreknown before the founding of the world" (1 Peter 1:20), the Greek word *katabolē* connotes the sowing of seeds. God lays the foundations but does not predetermine their outcome. Denial of predestination does not preclude God's knowledge of the future or the certainty of coming events on earth. As believers in biblical **prophecy**, Witnesses acknowledge the Bible's predictions of the messiah's coming, sufferings, and **resurrection** and of end-time events like **Armageddon**. The reference in the Book of **Revelation** to a Book of Life (Revelation 3:15) does not indicate a fixed future of individuals, since its entries can be "blotted out."

PRESIDENT. The principal officer of the legal corporation of the **Watch Tower Society** on earth. The first president when **Zion's Watch Tower Tract Society** was organized in 1881 was **William H. Conley**, before the presidency was passed to **C. T. Russell**, who was president when the society became incorporated in Pennsylvania in 1884. In the United States, there have been two incorporated Watch Tower organizations, now legally incorporated as the **Watch Tower Bible and Tract Society of Pennsylvania, Inc.**, and the **Watchtower Bible and Tract Society of New York, Inc.**, the latter being called the **Peoples Pulpit Association** until 1939. Since Russell was president of both the Watch Tower Bible and Tract Society of Pennsylvania and the Peoples Pulpit Association, the presidency of both societies fell vacant simultaneously, and, until the year 2000, the same leader presided over both organizations. Since the society's incorporation, there have been five presidents: C. T. Russell, **J. F. Rutherford**, **Nathan H. Knorr**, **Frederick W. Franz**, and **Milton G. Henschel**. All have belonged to the **anointed class** and have been members of the **Governing Body**, to which they have belonged as equal members with the others, notwithstanding their presidential status.

Following the resignations in 2000 of Henschel and the other members of the **Board of Directors** of both societies, different presidents were appointed for each organization, neither of whom belongs to the **144,000** members of the **anointed class**, and hence neither has a place on the Governing Body. *See also* ADAMS, DON ALDEN; LARSON, MAX H.

PRESIDING OVERSEER (P.O.). Aka congregation servant. Each **congregation** was led by a presiding **overseer** whose appointment was permanent, until 1972, when congregational government was changed. At that time, the **congregation** servant became one of a body of **elders** who governed the congregation. He retained the title, but only for a year, after which the office was rotated. In 1983, the position of P.O. became a permanent one. His role is to chair the body of elders and perform an elder's duties.

PROPHECY. Jehovah's Witnesses do not claim to have any special revelation and hence have no designated prophetic office and do not recognize new prophecies that occur outside the **Bible**. Biblical prophecy is not regarded exclusively as predictive: it "tells forth" as well as foretells. It takes various forms, including direct statement, dramatic incidents with prophetic import, (for example, Sarah and Hagar in Genesis 16 prefiguring the Gospel and the Law), and prophetic characters (like Jonah prefiguring **Christ**—Matthew 12:40). Much written prophecy employs figurative and symbolic language, which requires appropriate explanation. Prophecy is found in both the **Hebrew-Aramaic Scriptures** and the **Christian Greek Scriptures**. The latter casts **Jesus** as a prophet, notes that the early disciples prophesied at **Pentecost**, and states that the 1st-century Church appointed prophets (1 Corinthians 12:11–14, 27–19), including **women**, who could foretell coming events. Witnesses believe that the Bible foretold the dying out of prophecy (1 Corinthians 13:8); hence they believe that it is to be studied rather than added to.

Witnesses subscribe to a "multiple fulfillment" view of prophecy. It can have a lesser and a greater fulfillment: in the case of ancient Hebrew prophecy, it can point forward to imminent events in the prophet's time, as well as to Jesus **Christ.** Importantly, prophecy in both parts of scripture is held to predict end-time events and can enable readers to apprehend the signs of the last days. Much work has been done within the **Watch Tower** organization to identify and understand key events from King Nebuchadnezzar's destruction of Jerusalem—presumed to have occurred in 607 B.C.E.—to the present. *See also* END-TIME CALCULATIONS; GENTILE TIMES.

PUBLIC WITNESSING. *See* HOUSE-TO-HOUSE MINISTRY.

PUBLISHER. One who engages in "publishing salvation" (Isaiah 52:7), meaning one who proclaims the message of God's **kingdom** outside the **Watch Tower** organization. This is principally done by **house-to-house ministry**, which is an expectation of those who have undergone **baptism**, although it can also be carried out by those who are unbaptized but seek to display commitment to the Watch Tower Society's work. Unbaptized members may undertake publishing if they wish, but, if they lapse morally or spiritually, they can be removed from the work, although they are not subject to **disfellow-shipping**.

The practice was introduced by **J. F. Rutherford** in 1919. **Bible** students were initially slow to undertake house-to-house work, until 1926, when the society expressed the expectation that a part of Sunday should be spent doing tract and book distribution. The following year, **elders** became ineligible for office if they would not publicly witness, and by 1928, there was a substantial increase in publishing. From 1933 until the 1940s, "testimony cards" were employed: these were cards with a brief message that could be left with a resident after a brief verbal message had been provided. During the 1930s and 1940s, use was made of the phonograph, which enabled recordings by the society, lasting around four and a half minutes, to be played on gramophone records. The 1940s also saw outdoor publishing, with **Jehovah's Witnesses** distributing copies of the *Watchtower* and *Consolation*, the precursor of *Awake!* In 1942, **Nathan H. Knorr** announced the inception of **Theocratic Ministry Schools**, which provided training for publishers.

The **elders** of a **congregation** decide when someone is ready to publish, and their decision is announced to the congregation. The congregation is also informed if a publisher withdraws. Publishers are issued a publisher record card, on which they return information itemizing the time spent on this work. If they change districts, the card is passed on to the receiving congregation. The practice of keeping records of house-to-house visits commenced in 1938, and publishers note where they have visited and the response they received. *See also* PIONEER.

PURPLE TRIANGLE. A triangular purple badge worn by the **Bibelforscher** during their imprisonment in Nazi concentration camps during **World War II**. Approximately 250,000 members of the **Watch Tower** organization wore such badges. Apart from the **Jews**, who were forced to display a Star of David on their prison uniforms, the **Jehovah's Witnesses** were the only religious group who were formally identified as such.

PYRAMID OF GIZA (GIZEH). *See* GREAT PYRAMID.

– Q –

QUICK BUILD. Aka quickly built. The preferred method of constructing **Kingdom Halls**, the method was introduced in the United States in 1970s. To cope with the increasing numbers of **congregations**, additional building on a large scale proved necessary. The "quick build" method, by which a new Kingdom Hall can be erected from a flat site in as little as two days, was devised to ensure minimal interruption to the congregation's preaching work. The **Watch Tower Society** makes architectural plans available, and members offer unpaid labor, often with the help of skilled workers from neighboring congregations. Materials and other expenses are provided by donations from the congregation, and, if necessary, loans can be given by other congregations or from the Society Kingdom Hall Fund. Work at a quick build is interspersed with devotion, including **prayer**s and readings, and it affords an opportunity for unity, cooperation, and dedication. The first quick build was completed in Carterville, Missouri, in the early 1970s. The main framework and part of the roof were completed in two days. The first European structure was built in Northampton, England, in 1983.

QUICKLY BUILT. *See* QUICK BUILD.

– R –

RANSOM SACRIFICE. This theory of atonement has been held by **Jehovah's Witnesses** and **Bible** students since the time of **C. T. Russell**, who claimed biblical support for it (Mark 10:45). Some of Russell's early associates, notably **Nathan H. Barbour** and A. D. Jones, disputed the doctrine, and this proved to be grounds for a schism.

According to the ransom sacrifice theory, because of **Adam**'s **sin**, the possibility of a perfect life was lost, and no human life was of sufficient value to redeem humanity from **death**. Accordingly, God sent a "spirit son"—**Jesus**—who underwent a virgin birth and was born in human form. The Bible describes him as the "last Adam," who sacrificed his life on 14 Nisan, 33 C.E., and whose spirit God raised back to life. Ransom theories of atonement in mainstream Christianity have sometimes suggested that Christ's ransom was paid to **Satan**, but Witnesses do not accept this and hold that the ransom was required solely by God.

Witnesses regard Christ's ransom sacrifice as benefiting them by offering forgiveness for sins, providing them with hope of escape from Satan's rule and affording proof of God's love. It is through Christ's blood that the **great crowd** is said to wash their robes and make them white (Revelation 7:9, 14).

REGIONAL SERVANT. *See* PILGRIM.

REGIONAL SERVICE DIRECTOR. *See* PILGRIM.

RELIGION. In J. F. Rutherford's writings, the term is equated with "**false religion**." Rutherford's book *Religion* (1940) argues that religion was created by **Satan**, stemming from **Nimrod**'s early **kingdom** in **Babylon**. Christianity, as practiced by the churches, consisted of **pagan** and demonic elements, having renounced the doctrines and standards of **Jesus**' time. Rutherford's followers were noted for their "information marches," in which they displayed placards with the slogan "Religion is a snare and a racket." For a short time after Rutherford's death, this view of religion prevailed. A booklet entitled *Religion Reaps the Whirlwind* (1944) equates religion with the religion of the churches, criticizing it for its apostate beliefs and involvement in politics, describing it as "a betrayer and a fraud." The author concedes, however, that there is a true Christianity that contrasts with its apostate version.

Beginning in the 1950s, the **Watch Tower Society** was more inclined to use the term *religion* to cover both its "true" and "false" varieties. True religion, it teaches, existed before Adam's fall and continued to be practiced by Noah and Shem after Nimrod's emigration to Babylon. True religion was practiced by Abraham and the patriarchs and other ancient Hebrew worthies, as well as by Jesus and the early Church. True religion is characterized by its eternal nature, its use of God's true name **Jehovah**, and its followers' adherence to God's standards. The society has produced information on aspects of "false religion," for example, in *Mankind's Search for God* (1990), which describes a number of the world's major religions, but this does not diminish their dissocation from their beliefs and practices. *See also* APOSTASY; CHRISTENDOM; FAITHFUL MEN OF OLD; OCCULTISM.

RELIGIOUS ORDER OF JEHOVAH'S WITNESSES. Created as a result of the 2000 organizational restructuring of the **Watch Tower Society**, this arm of the society supervises its religious and educational work, especially its preaching and **conventions**. *See also* ADAMS, DON ALDEN; CHRISTIAN CONGREGATION OF JEHOVAH'S WITNESSES; KINGDOM SUPPORT SERVICES, INC.

REMNANT. The word is used in the **Hebrew-Aramaic Scriptures** to designate those who have been spared by God and who will be brought back to their land—in particular, the **Jews** who returned from **Babylon** to reestablish true worship in the Jerusalem Temple. The term was subsequently applied by Paul to those Jews who accepted the new **covenant** by acknowledging **Jesus Christ** as messiah (Romans 11:5).

The **Watch Tower Society** holds that the Babylonian captivity has its antitype in 20th-century events and is paralleled by the escape of God's faithful ones from apostate Christianity, which is identified with Babylon the Great. The date given for this "release" is 1919, since **Bible** students regarded **World War I** as causing hostility to the organization.

The remnant is identified with the **anointed class**, the **144,000** members who will experience eternal life under **Christ**'s heavenly rule, thus avoiding the **Great Tribulation**. They will come from all nations, having repented for their **sin**s and been cleansed; they are faithful to **Jehovah**, know him, and worship him in a true manner. Not being destined for eternal life in **paradise earth**, they are unattached to worldly values.

The doctrine of the remnant was defined before the notion of the "other sheep" eternally inheriting the earth; hence the remnant now contrasts with the **great crowd** who will experience eternal life, but not in heaven. The term now designates those of the anointed class who still remain alive on earth—now merely a few thousand.

RESURRECTION. Since **death** was introduced into the world by **Adam**'s sin, death and **resurrection** were not originally part of God's plan. Eternal life is possible through **Jesus Christ**'s **ransom sacrifice**, which bought humanity back from **Satan**'s power. Before the time of the ransom sacrifice, resurrection could occasionally be performed miraculously, for example, by Elijah and Elisha. However, those who were brought back to life, having died before the payment of this sacrifice, died without the prospect of eternal life in heaven.

After **Pentecost**, **Jehovah's Witnesses** teach, resurrection became more widely available to those who repented and had faith in Christ. Members of the early Church were eligible for heavenly resurrection, but such hope was lost when **apostasy** occurred. A few remained loyal, and those who have remained faithful between Pentecost and the present day can hope for eternal life. The **Bible** declares Christ to be the "first fruits" of those who are asleep in death (1 Corinthians 15:20), hence Christ is regarded as the first to have experienced resurrection. After **1914**, those who believed in him "during his presence" were raised up to heaven to begin the gathering of the **144,000** members of the **anointed class**. Upon death, the anointed ones go immediately to heaven without having to wait in a state of sleep. They have already been judged and their eligibility established. These people have participated in the "first resurrection."

Those who are eligible for eternal life on earth are believed to be asleep in death, awaiting the **millennial rule of Christ** before the "second resurrection" can take place. The **faithful men of old**—the faithful who lived before Christ—will be raised first, followed by the **great crowd**. The unrighteous, who remain in **Hades**, will be the last to rise and await judgment according to their deeds. Witnesses hold that not all of humanity is ransomed: in particular, those who have deliberately sinned and are unrepentant, those who have sinned against the **holy spirit**, and those who have accepted the **truth** but fallen away will not participate in the resurrection.

Witnesses believe that it is the **soul** that is raised, not one's physical earthly body, since Paul taught that "flesh and blood cannot inherit God's kingdom" (1 Corinthians 15:50). Hence, the resurrection is not a rejoining of the soul and body; instead the soul will be provided with a "spiritual body" that is appropriate to the environment of either heaven or earth.

REVELATION, BOOK OF. Part of the **Christian Greek Scriptures** and the last of the 66 books of the **Bible**, the Book of Revelation is believed to have been written in 96 C.E. by the Apostle John on the island of Patmos toward the end of the Roman emperor Domitian's reign. In common with the second half of the Book of Daniel, Revelation is apocalyptic, consisting of a series of 16 visions described in dramatic symbolism. **Jehovah's Witnesses** hold that this book portrays a future that is far distant from John's time, referring to end-time events in humanity's present era. It describes the rise and fall of seven world empires, the last of which is Anglo-America, symbolized by a two-headed **beast**. The book tells of **Christ**'s entry into the heavenly sanctuary, the casting out of **Satan**, the **Great Tribulation**, the Battle of **Armageddon**, God's judgment on **Babylon**, the marriage of the Lamb, the **millennial rule of Christ**, and the establishment of the New Jerusalem, affording everlasting happiness to God's people—for the **144,000** members of the **anointed class** in heaven and the **great crowd** on **paradise earth**. *See also* 1914; CLEANSING OF THE SANCTUARY; END-TIME CALCULATIONS; HELL; LEAGUE OF NATIONS; MARK OF THE BEAST; MICHAEL; PROPHECY; RESURRECTION; TRUMPETS; UNITED NATIONS (UN); WAR.

RUSSELL, CHARLES TAZE (C. T.) (1852–1916). Founder-leader of the **International Bible Students Association**, the precursor of the **Jehovah's Witnesses**. Born in Allegheny, Pennsylvania, on 16 February 1852, Russell was raised a Presbyterian but became a Congregationalist in his youth. Having become disenchanted with organized Christianity, in 1869 he listened to a lecture by **Jonas Wendell**, an **Adventist**, and was inspired to start his own group of sympathizers to study the **Bible**. The group requested that he become their "pastor," hence he is often referred to as "Pastor Russell," despite the fact that the Bible students and Witnesses always remained lay movements.

Russell established **Zion's Watch Tower Tract Society** in 1874, and the first copy of *Zion's Watch Tower and Herald of God's Presence* appeared in 1879. Russell inaugurated the institutional structures of the **Watch Tower** organization, establishing its headquarters at the Bible House in Allegheny, which was transferred to Brooklyn, New York, in 1909.

Russell's first book, *The Object and Manner of Our Lord's Return* (1877), was principally concerned with end-time events, a theme which featured largely in his subsequent writings. Russell gave many public lectures and wrote six volumes entitled *Millennial Dawn*, subsequently renamed *Studies in the Scriptures*. These works addressed the themes of biblical **prophecy**, Christ's Second Advent, atonement, and expectations of life after **death**. His first volume, *Divine Plan of the Ages* (1886), introduced mathematical calculations yielding a program of end-time events, arguing that the **Gentile times** would come to a close in 1914. Russell subscribed to a doctrine of **conditional immortality**, and he firmly advocated a "ransom" theory of **Christ**'s atonement, rejecting a "penal substitutionary" one. He was critical of mainstream Christianity, casting Roman Catholicism as the "harlot" to whom the Book of **Revelation** refers. His critique of mainstream religion also encompassed Protestantism: he was unable to accept their doctrines of **predestination**, **hell**, and the **Trinity**.

Russell was also famed for his *Photo-Drama of Creation*, an audiovisual presentation released in 1914. His final work, *The Finished Mystery*, remained in note form upon his death in 1916 and was completed under **J. F. Rutherford**'s supervision in 1917. *See also* CHRISTENDOM; END-TIME CALCULATIONS; RANSOM SACRIFICE.

RUSSELL, MARIA (1850–1938). Born Maria Frances Ackley, she married **C. T. Russell** in 1879 and was on the original **Board of Directors** of **Zion's Watch Tower Tract Society**. She became associate editor of *Zion's Watch Tower*, contributed regularly to the journal, and undertook speaking tours on her husband's behalf. Tensions arose between the couple, however, causing Maria to leave Russell in 1897. Their problems related to her desire for greater editorial control of the journal and her ideas concerning **women**'s rights. In 1903 Maria outlined their disagreements in a tract, which Charles claimed was a gross misrepresentation of the facts. She filed for legal separation, and on 4 March 1908 a decree "In Divorce" was granted. It was in effect a legal separation rather than an absolute **divorce**.

Maria authored two books, *The Twain One* and *A Cup of Cold Water for a Thirsty Soul*, both published in 1906 and both of which express her views on the role of women, whom she believed should be equal to men and have a teaching role in **congregations**. In the same year, her husband published an extended article in *Zion's Watch Tower*, making public their marital problems. Notwithstanding their acrimonious relationship, Maria attended her husband's **funeral** in 1916 and laid a wreath on his coffin, which bore the words "To my beloved husband."

RUSSELLITES. A nickname given to **C. T. Russell**'s **Bible** students, it continued to be used after Russell's death in popular parlance and by the media. Other nicknames included "Millennial Dawners," "nohellers," "soul sleepers," and—during **J. F. Rutherford**'s era—"Rutherfordites." The term appears to have fallen into disuse after the adoption of the name "**Jehovah's Witnesses**" in 1931. *See also* HELL; IMMORTALITY; SOUL; *STUDIES IN THE SCRIPTURES.*

RUTHERFORD, JOSEPH FRANKLIN (J. F.) (1869–1941). Sometimes known as "Judge Rutherford," on account of the attorney's license he obtained in 1892, Rutherford succeeded **C. T. Russell** as the leader of the **Watch Tower** organization in 1916. Rutherford centralized the association, transforming it from a confederation of autonomous **eccelesia**s to a centrally governed organization. He introduced the name "**Jehovah's Witnesses**" at the **convention** in Columbus, Ohio, in 1931. He was responsible for the more distinctive and radical elements that are now typically associated with the organization, including its **house-to-house ministry** and theocratic form of government. His antiwar stance during **World War I** brought him into conflict with the government and clergy, causing him to introduce the organization's distinctive anticlericalism and dissociate the society from mainstream Christianity. While Rutherford was in office, the celebration of **Christmas** and **birthdays** was abolished.

Rutherford was a prolific writer. His *Millions Now Living Will Never Die* (1920) is renowned for its **end-time calculations**. Beginning in 1921, he averaged writing almost a book a year until his death.

– S –

SALVATION. The state of release from **sin** and **Satan**'s control requiring repentance and acceptance of the **truth**, it is frequently mentioned in the **Bible** as the ideal state of attainment and is available to the pre-Christian as well as the Christian faithful. There are two levels at which salvation can be attained. The "greater salvation" is in heaven, where the **144,000** members of the **anointed class** live eternally under **Jesus Christ**'s heavenly rule. The **great crowd**, who do not belong to this class, will experience salvation as **paradise earth**, after the Battle of **Armageddon**. Everlasting life in heaven was made possible by Christ's **ransom sacrifice** to atone for sin and by his casting out of Satan from heaven, which is believed to have occurred in **1914**. Beginning in 1919, the 144,000 members have progressively been brought to heaven. Although belief in God and Jesus Christ are prerequisites for salvation, **faith** must be accompanied by **works**, and the importance of endurance is emphasized. Salvation is therefore not universal, although it is not reserved for a predestined elect, and it is also possible to forfeit one's salvation through **apostasy**. *See also* DISFELLOWSHIPPING; FAITHFUL MEN OF OLD; PREDESTINATION.

SATAN. Aka Beelzebub; the Devil. **Jehovah's Witnesses** believe in the reality of Satan as a personal corporeal spirit being and reject the view that the term simply personifies evil. Originally created by God as an **angel**, Satan rebelled against God, together with other angels who became demons and could enter the earth with materialized human bodies (Genesis 6:1–4). Satan deceived Eve in the Garden of Eden, using a serpent as his mouthpiece, thus causing **sin** to enter the world. He controls the entire earth, in association with the "wild **beast**" (**Revelation** 20:10) and the "false prophet" (Revelation 16:3). The former is the worldwide political system, which **Nimrod** began in ancient times in **Babylon**, and the latter is the Anglo-American world power, also described as a two-horned beast (Revelation 13:11). Satan is responsible for the corruption of the world's political and religious systems. He opposed **Jesus** at various points in his ministry and continues to oppose Christians.

As described in the Book of Revelation, Satan was cast out of heaven, and Witnesses believe this event to have occurred in **1914**.

Satan continues to rule the earth and will continue to do so until his defeat at the impending Battle of **Armageddon**. He will then be thrown into an abyss and bound for 1,000 years, after which he will be released for a short period, when he will make a last attempt at deceiving the nations. He and his angels will subsequently be cast into a lake of fire and sulfur and experience everlasting destruction.

Witnesses do not believe that **Lucifer** is to be identified with Satan. *See also* MILLENNIAL RULE OF CHRIST.

SEX. Jehovah's Witnesses teach that sexual relationships may only occur within the context of **marriage**. Adultery and premarital sex are strictly prohibited, as are homosexual relationships and masturbation. While the **Watch Tower Society** notes that sexual misdeeds can result in unwanted pregnancies and sexually transmitted diseases, attitudes toward sex must be governed by biblical standards. At creation, **Jehovah** deliberately created two sexes—male and female—and instructed them to procreate. However, the society has no objection to sex being used for pleasure; hence contraceptive measures are permitted, although their use is a matter of **conscience**. Sexual relationships can be either "natural" or "contrary to nature." Oral and anal sex fall into the latter category, while sexual relationships during the woman's period of menstruation fall into a gray area; hence this is also a matter of individual conscience. Some types of sexual misdeeds are so depraved as to constitute *porneia*, for example, bestiality. Sexual impropriety can be a ground for **disfellowshipping**.

Sex **education** is thought to be desirable, but it should be taught within the context of family life. The society believes that most sex education, as taught in schools, is purely biological, offering no moral guidance, and it deplores the over-explicitness of some of the material that is used. The society also condemns over-liberal attitudes of mainstream Christianity, in which premarital sex is often condoned and where homosexual and lesbian **clergy** are allowed ordination. *See also* BIRTH CONTROL; HOMOSEXUALITY.

SHAREHOLDERS. In its early years, under **C. T. Russell**'s presidency, shares in the **Watch Tower Society** could be purchased by any member, for the sum of US$10, with no limit to the number of shares that any one individual could hold. The society's charter empowered shareholders to elect office bearers—a **president**, vice president, and secretary-treasurer—to the **Board of Directors**, whose term of office was for life. The majority of the shares were held by Russell.

J. F. Rutherford, having assumed the role of legal adviser after Russell's death in 1916, challenged the legality of this arrangement and successfully persuaded the society to hold annual elections for its Board of Directors. This system prevailed until 1944, when a Special Service and Business **Assembly** convened from 30 September to 2 October, and the decision was made to limit the number of shareholders to a maximum of 500. These shareholders were "to be chosen on the basis of their active service to **Jehovah**" and were empowered to elect the board and its officers. This change to the charter was ratified by law in 1945.

By 1971, it became apparent that the shareholders who belonged to the **anointed class** had become a minority, and it seemed inappropriate that the **Governing Body**, which was identical to the Board of Directors of the **Watch Tower Bible and Tract Society of Pennsylvania**, should be subject to election by the **great crowd**. Hence, these two bodies became distinct, the Governing Body no longer being subject to election.

The system of shareholders has served merely as a means of ensuring that the society operates in accordance with the law of the land, and in 1944 the desire was expressed to devise an organizational system that was "as near to theocratic arrangement as the law of the land permits." *See also* THEOCRACY.

SHUNNING. The term is frequently used outside the **Watch Tower** organization to refer to the consequences of **disfellowshipping**—in particular the **Jehovah's Witnesses**' avoidance of **associations** with the expelled member. Witnesses themselves rarely employ the term with this meaning but use it simply to mean "avoiding," as in their injunctions to "shun" gambling, apostate material, **blood**, or participation in **pagan** practices like celebrating **Christmas**. *See also* APOSTASY.

SIN. A universal condition contrary to God's will, it consists of actions or thoughts against God, other beings, or one's own body. Sin first occurred in the spiritual realm, with **Satan**'s rebellion, and subsequently on earth when **Adam** and Eve disobeyed God. **Jehovah's Witnesses** believe that humanity's original sin consisted of disobedience rather than sexual sin, and they note that the **woman** was the first to sin. Adam's sin was transmitted to subsequent generations, thus humanity is universally sinful by nature. The consequences of sin are guilt and shame, but most especially **death**, including its associated maladies of sickness, pain, and aging. It is to be noted that the **Bible** identifies death as sin's punishment, not eternal damnation (Romans 8:23).

Sin requires redemption, which is achieved by **Jesus Christ**'s **ransom sacrifice**. Redemption is available to all, not a predestined elect. The only unforgivable sin is blasphemy against God's **holy spirit** (Matthew 8:32), which is interpreted the deliberate rejection of true worship of **Jehovah**. *See also* ASSOCIATIONS; DISFELLOW-SHIPPING; PREDESTINATION; SEX.

SISTER. A female member of a **congregation** who has undergone **baptism**. *See also* BROTHER; WOMEN.

SMOKING. Since the 1890s, the **Watch Tower Society** has expressed disapproval of smoking and issued warnings against it. Although the **Bible** does not explicitly forbid it, **Jehovah's Witnesses** have viewed it as a violation of the first of the Ten Commandments ("love **Jehovah** with all your strength"), arguing that one's strength is diminished by the health hazards associated with smoking. It is also believed to be a violation of the commandment to love one's neighbor. Numerous editions of the *Watchtower* and *Awake!* itemize the dangers of smoking, which include such smoking-related diseases such as heart and lung conditions, the effects of passive smoking, unpleasant and harmful effects on the workplace, and the effects on children. Witnesses also deplore the expensiveness of tobacco, in particular its addictive effect, which makes the smoker a "slave."

In the past, some Witnesses have been smokers, despite the society's disapprobation. In 1973, however, the **Governing Body** pronounced that all Witnesses must quit the habit. Since then, one must be a nonsmoker to be regarded as "an acceptable member of a **congregation**," and to be eligible for **baptism**. Witnesses may not engage in work for the tobacco industry.

SON OF MAN. *See* JESUS.

SONGS. The **Jehovah's Witnesses** preferred term for "hymns." **Bible** students initially used hymns that were shared with mainstream Christianity, but they progressively came to ensure that the words were consistent with their distinctive teachings. As they came to dissociate themselves with **Christendom**, they wished to rid themselves of musical settings that came from an apostate church, and consequently their current hymnody consists entirely of words and **music** composed by members of the **Watch Tower** organization.

The first collection of hymns was *Songs of the Bride*, published by **C. T. Russell** in 1879, all of which were written by Bible students. A small collection entitled *Zion's Glad Songs of the Morning* is featured in the 1896 edition of *Zion's Watch Tower*. Other song books include *Hymns of the Millennial Dawn* (1905), *Songs of Praise to Jehovah* (1928), *Kingdom Service Songbook* (1944), *Singing and Accompanying Yourselves with Music in Your Hearts* (1966), and *Sing Praises to Jehovah* (1984). This last book is exclusively compiled by Witnesses, with contributions from composers and writers in the United States, Canada, Europe, Latin America, and Australia.

Songs are used at **Kingdom Hall** meetings, **assemblies**, and **conventions**, weddings, and **funerals**. The precise songs for any given Sunday are the same throughout the world, and, where technology permits, a recorded CD piano accompaniment is used. *See also* MARRIAGE.

SONS OF THE SERVANTS OF SOLOMON. *See* GIVEN ONES.

SOUL. Jehovah's Witnesses do not accept that the soul is an immaterial substance or ethic body distinct from body and which survives its **death**. **Watch Tower Society** literature explains that the Hebrew word *nephesh*, translated as "soul," literally means "one who breathes." The word refers to the visible, living creature itself—human and animal—thus "my soul" is synonymous with "I." Apart from **Adam** and Eve, whom God specially created, human souls are subject to birth and death. With regard to Adam, the **Bible** mentions that he "came to be a living soul" from his previous dustlike state (Genesis 2:7), hence a human soul consists of a physical body imbued with a life force provided by God's spirit. Souls, in this sense, are mortal and destructible: **Jesus** stated that it was possible to "kill a soul" (Mark 3:4). *See also* CONDITIONAL IMMORTALITY; IMMORTALITY.

SOUL SLEEP. *See* CONDITIONAL IMMORTALITY.

SPIRIT-ANOINTED CHRISTIANS. *See* ANOINTED CLASS.

SPIRITISM. *See* OCCULTISM.

SPIRITUAL ISRAEL OF GOD. *See* 144,000; ANOINTED CLASS.

STAND FAST BIBLE STUDENTS. Aka Stand Fasters; Standfasters. Founded in Portland, Oregon, by Charles E. Heard and others on 1 December 1918, these **Bible** students asserted the need to stand fast to **C. T. Russell**'s principles rather than those of the new president **J. F. Rutherford**. In particular, they objected to Rutherford's purchase of **war** bonds on behalf of the **Watch Tower** organization, insisting that all forms of support of military service, including noncombatant service, should be avoided. The organization's magazine was called *Old Corn Gems*—an allusion to Joshua 5:11–12, where reference is made to the manna from heaven ceasing to be delivered to Moses and the Israelites. They accepted Watch Tower teachings until Easter 1918, although they also accepted *The Finished Mystery* (1917). The Standfasters held that the harvest was over and that public witnessing was of no avail, since God's people had already been gathered.

Members of the organization moved westward in 1920, owing to a prevalent belief that God's people would be translated into heaven from a particular area in Oregon. Following failed expectations, the group set up a commune in Stookie Harbor, British Columbia, in 1924, which disintegrated by 1927. The Stand Fast movement is now defunct.

STETSON, GEORGE (1814–1879). A teacher, medical doctor, and minister in the Second Advent Church, Stetson met **C. T. Russell** in 1872, when the latter attended his church in Pittsburgh, Pennsylvania. He worked collaboratively with **Jonas Wendell** in churches in Pennsylvania and Ohio. The doctrines of Stetson's church in Pittsburgh included the **millennial rule of Christ, death** as sleep until the **resurrection**, a second opportunity for those who are unavoidably ignorant of the gospel, and death as extinction for the wicked. These were not compulsory tests of **faith**, but it was expected that members would regard the **Bible** as the supreme standard of authority and that they be recognizable by their good character. In collaboration with **George Storrs**, he edited the magazine *The Herald of Life and the Coming Kingdom* (1862–1882).

STORRS, GEORGE (1796–1879). Born in Lebanon, New Hampshire, Storrs became a Methodist minister but came to question his beliefs after finding a pamphlet on a train in 1837, probably written by Henry Grew. He left the Methodist Church, moving to Albany, New York, in 1840. Storrs became an itinerant preacher in the **Adventist** tradition, and in 1842, he delivered six lectures entitled *An Inquiry—Are the Wicked Immortal?* The lectures were subsequently published, with a circulation of 200,000 copies in the United States and Britain.

Storrs subscribed to the doctrine of **conditional immortality**, while questioning ancient Greek philosophical notions of the **soul**, teaching that some would experience eternal life on earth. He held that the doctrines of an immortal immaterial soul and the destiny of eternal **hell** for the wicked were unacceptable. Those who died in ignorance would be restored to life at the Second Coming, to be given a second opportunity to accept **Christ**'s **ransom sacrifice**. In his later years, after 1870, Storrs concluded that there were two classes of people who died in ignorance: those who had conclusively rejected the gospel and those who had merely failed to hear it. Only the former would be **resurrected**. He also taught that the Lord's Evening Meal was to be celebrated on Nisan 14.

Storrs published the journal *The Bible Examiner*, with which **C. T. Russell** became familiar. Articles included a contribution by Piazzi Smith on the **Great Pyramid**, which was followed by a series on the topic. *See also* MEMORIAL.

STUDIES IN THE SCRIPTURES. Originally published as *Millennial Dawn*, these six volumes of **C. T. Russell**'s writings, composed between 1886 and 1904, contain his main teachings, mainly relating to biblical prophecy, biblical and end-time chronology, and atonement. The first volume, *The Divine Plan of the Ages* (1886), divides history into three "dispensations": the first being the period ending with the great flood, the second being "the present evil world" from the Old Testament patriarchs to modern times, and the third commencing with the "harvesting" period, which heralded the **millennial rule of Christ**. Volume 2, *The Time Is at Hand* (1889) deals largely with **end-time calculations**, while Volume 3, *Thy Kingdom Come* (1890), interprets the prophecy of Daniel, relating it to **Christ**'s invisible presence, the date of which is reckoned to have been **1874**. This third volume was later to prove controversial on account of its detailed analysis of the **Great Pyramid** of Giza, which Russell believed lent support to his theories. The fourth volume, *The Battle of Armageddon*, was written in 1886, but not published until 1897: this work interprets the Book of **Revelation**, and discusses the fall of **Babylon**. Fifth in the series is *The Atonement between God and Man* (1899), which sets out Russell's belief in Christ's **ransom sacrifice**. The last in the series, *The New Creation* (1904), deals with the characteristics and expectations of those who have received the "heavenly calling." This final volume argues against Darwin's theory of **evolution**, supporting human chronology as set out in the Bible, and deals with the hope of **resurrection**, rejecting the doctrine of **predestination**. Also mentioned is the rite of **baptism**, and the **Memorial**.

During his lifetime, Russell made notes for a seventh volume, which **J. F. Rutherford** later published as *The Finished Mystery* (1917). However, many of Russell's followers believed that this posthumous publication did not reflect Russell's true intentions. *See also* ARMAGEDDON; *PAROUSIA*.

– T –

TARTARUS. *See* HADES.

THEOCRACY. Government by God. Theocratic government was the initial system at the beginning of the world, when God created **Adam**

and Eve, who were placed in a paradise under instruction to submit to his commandments. Their disobedience placed them under **Satanic** rule, with characteristics of disobedience to and rebellion against God. God again established his rule over ancient Israel by entering into a **covenant** with Abraham and giving his laws to his people through the patriarchs, and subsequently Moses. In the time of Moses, the Ark of the Covenant was made the central meeting place of the Israelites, when God was invisibly present. While the establishment of a monarchy over Israel was against God's will, the king was an earthly ruler whose kingship depended on God. The Davidic **kingdom**, being the pinnacle of Israel's prosperity, is viewed as a "type," prefiguring the coming messianic kingdom. Theocratic rule over Israel ended with the **Babylonian** Exile, which marks the beginning of the **Gentile times**.

Christ's messianic rule began 10 days after his ascension into heaven, with the coming of the **holy spirit** at **Pentecost** (33 C.E.), giving rise to the birth of the Church. From this time onward, there were men and **women** on earth who became subject to theocratic rule under God and **Christ**. Christ's task was to cleanse the heavenly sanctuary from Satan and his demonic **angels**, and this is believed to finally have been accomplished in **1914,** when Satan was hurled out of heaven down to earth. Satan's imminent defeat at the Battle of **Armageddon** will once again secure theocratic rule on earth. The key feature of theocracy is headship: it is not dictatorship, since God wishes to secure willing obedience from his subjects, motivated by love.

God's visible organization on earth, the **Jehovah's Witnesses**, endeavors to organize their affairs on theocratic lines, regarding God and Christ as the head, with the **anointed class** as his **faithful and discreet slave** and the **Governing Body** as a subgroup, responsible for their members' spiritual well-being. Witnesses teach that there can only be one theocracy, not several, since God will rule the entirety of heaven and earth. *See also* CLEANSING OF THE SANCTUARY; CREATION.

THEOCRATIC MINISTRY SCHOOL (TMS). Established by **Nathan H. Knorr** in 1943, the TMS aims to prepare its **publisher**s for teaching by public speaking and **house-to-house ministry**. TMS meets weekly and provides guidance on studying, reading, and researching one's material; analyzing and organizing; conversing by listening and answering questions; and writing and delivering talks. Students are given opportunities to practice giving talks and door-to-door exchanges, and are counseled on their progress. Use is made of the **Watch Tower Society**'s publication *Course in Theocratic Ministry* (2002).

THOUSAND-YEAR REIGN OF CHRIST. *See* MILLENNIAL RULE OF CHRIST.

TOBACCO. *See* SMOKING.

TRAVELING MINISTER. *See* PILGRIM.

TRINITY. A central doctrine of mainstream Christianity that is utterly rejected by **Jehovah's Witnesses**. According to mainstream Christian teaching, God exists in triune form as Father, Son, and **Holy Spirit** (or Holy Ghost), and these three "persons" are equal, separate, eternal, none preceding another, almighty, omniscient, and wholly divine, yet not three separate gods. Witnesses point out that this doctrine is nowhere mentioned or implied in the **Bible** and does not form part of **Jesus**' teaching or that of early Christianity.

Much **Watch Tower** literature traces the development of the doctrine of the Trinity, demonstrating that it originated from disputes about whether **Christ** was of one substance or merely of like substance with the Father, leading to the formulation of the **Creed** of Nicea in 325 C.E. The creed was subsequently expanded at various ecumenical councils: in 381 C.E., the Council of Constantinople affirmed that the Holy Spirit was worthy of worship. The Watch Tower Society notes that the *Tome of Damascus* (382 C.E.) condemned trinitarian doctrine. The exact origins of trinitarianism are unknown. The Athanasian Creed, which makes clear reference to the doctrine, is pseudonymous and probably originated in France during the 5th century. Witnesses believe that the doctrine originated in **Babylon**, where **Nimrod** introduced **false religion**. Trinity doctrine is associated with other forms of "false religion," such as Hinduism (the triad Brahma, Vishnu, and Shiva) and ancient Egyptian religion (Osiris,

Isis, and Horus). The concepts used in expounding the Trinity, like "substance," belong to Greek philosophy, indicating **pagan** corruption of the primordial Christian **faith**.

Witnesses therefore object to trinitarian doctrine on the grounds that it is unbiblical and that it imports pagan corruptions into Christianity. They further claim that it blurs the relationship between God the Father and Jesus the Son, since **Christendom** holds that they are coeternal. Finally, the doctrine makes God a mystery, thus preventing the believer from drawing close to him and using his personal name **Jehovah**, which is not employed in trinitarian teaching.

TRUMPETS. The seven trumpets described in the Book of **Revelation** are regarded as significant. **C. T. Russell** claimed that the references to trumpets were symbolic, rather than literal eschatological events. The sounding of the seventh and final trumpet was the call in October **1874** when **Christ** was believed to begin his heavenly rule. In the second volume of his *Studies in the Scriptures* (*The Time Is at Hand*, 1889) Russell states that he would explain elsewhere the significance of the preceding six trumpet calls. This explanation awaited the posthumous *The Finished Mystery* (1917), which interpreted them as a series of attempts in **Christendom**'s history to restore it from its **apostasy**, particularly from its Roman Catholic form. These included Martin Luther's reformation, the Anglican movement, Calvinism, the rise of the Baptist churches, John Wesley and Methodism, and the Evangelical Alliance of 1846. The seventh trumpet was the antitypical trumpet of the Jubilees (Leviticus 23:23).

Under **J. F. Rutherford**'s leadership, this interpretation was revised, and the seven trumpets were held to represent proclamations of God's judgments associated with seven **convention**s held between 1922 and 1928, the first of which culminated in Rutherford's injunction "Advertise, advertise, advertise the **kingdom**!" This interpretation continues to be favored by **Jehovah's Witnesses**. *See also* PROPHECY.

TRUTH. When spelled with an initial capital, the expression "the Truth" refers to the full body of teaching regarding God, **Jesus Christ**, and the world, and which can only be found in God's Word, as taught by the **Watch Tower** organization. This entails being destined to obtain a place in **Jehovah**'s **kingdom**, over which God and Christ rule. Christ is also regarded as personified truth, having stated himself to be "the way, the truth and the life" (John 14:6), and the **Holy Spirit** is God's power to mediate the truth. **Congregation**s are regarded as the pillars that support the Truth. "Being in the truth" is an expression frequently used by **Jehovah's Witnesses** to designate acceptance of the Watch Tower Society's teachings. *See also* BIBLE.

– U –

UNITED NATIONS (UN). International organization founded in 1945 when 51 countries signed the United Nations Charter. It replaced the **League of Nations** and aims at fostering cooperation in international security and economic development. **Jehovah's Witnesses** regard the UN as no more than a reconstituted form of the former League of Nations. It is the eighth world power referred to in the Book of **Revelation** (17:10), represented by the eighth head that springs from the seven-headed scarlet wild **beast**. Although the *Watchtower* acknowledges that it has some earthly achievements, it is doomed to destruction and is a "blasphemous counterfeit of God's Messianic **kingdom**," which can only be a theocratic one. *See also* THEOCRACY.

– V –

VACCINATION. Articles in the *Golden Age* in 1929 and 1931, under the editorship of **Clayton J. Woodworth**, strongly opposed vaccination on both medical and religious grounds. Since it was believed that the practice involved ingesting animal **blood**, it was argued that it was a violation of God's **covenant** with Noah (Genesis 9:4), as well as an illicit intermarriage of species (Genesis 6:1-4). **Bible** students were taught that the procedure was ineffective and that it significantly increased the risk of diseases, including "syphilis, cancers, eczema, erysipelas, scrofula, consumption, even leprosy and many other loathsome affections" (*GA* 5-1-29). In 1935, the *Golden Age* printed a standard form for parents to use to refuse vaccination for their children.

In the early 1950s, a number of *Watchtower* articles reversed this position, arguing that the practice was not unscriptural and that any decision regarding vaccination was a matter of **conscience**. More recent *Watchtower* articles have recommended vaccination, pointing to the number of lives that it has saved and hailing it as one of the principal successes of modern medical science.

VAN AMBURGH, WILLIAM (1864?–1947). Secretary-treasurer of the **Watch Tower Bible and Tract Society** under the leadership of **C. T. Russell**, Van Amburgh was a supporter of **J. F. Rutherford** when he came to office in 1916 and was imprisoned with him in the Atlanta Penitentiary in 1917–1918 following the publication of *The Finished Mystery* (1917) after Russell's death. A contributor to early editions of *Zion's Watch Tower*, he engaged in many speaking tours and **conventions** and served at the Brooklyn **Bethel**.

VOTING. Since **Jesus** taught his disciples that they are "no part of the world" (John 15:19), they belong to **Jehovah**'s **kingdom** and look forward to an end to the present system of affairs on earth. Hence, human **politics** does not afford a solution to humanity's present state. **Jehovah's Witnesses**, therefore, do not seek political office and do not engage in any political campaigning. Voting in political elections is disapproved of, although not totally prohibited: it is said to be a matter of individual **conscience**. In some countries, voting may be compulsory, in which case each individual Witness must decide how to cope with this state of affairs. A nonbelieving husband may demand that his wife votes, and the biblical injunction for wives to be in subjection to their husbands remains an obligation (Colossians 3:19). Again, it is a matter of conscience as to how such a situation is handled.

Witnesses have several objections to voting. The **Bible** describes **Christ**'s followers as his "ambassadors"; this ambassadorial role makes them citizens of another country, and voting in earthly politics is therefore tantamount to interfering with another country's affairs. Further, God's kingdom is a unity, and politics tend to be divisive; Witnesses believe that they will find themselves in a better position to preach about God's kingdom if they exercise neutrality with regard to earthly politics. Witnesses are also reminded that they are responsible for the outcome their actions; hence if they were to vote a politician into office, they would bear a share of responsibility for his or her subsequent actions.

Witnesses also disapprove of elections in schools that mimic the political electoral process, for example, where children campaign for election as class president or if a "mock election" is organized. There is normally no objection to voting in nonpolitical contexts, however, for example, if one is on a company board and a vote on a proposed policy is needed.

Jehovah's kingdom is based on **theocracy**, not democracy, therefore office bearers are not voted into their positions. Historically, the **Watch Tower Society** used ballots to elect directors and congregational elders, but **J. F. Rutherford** abolished such practices. Only the **Board of Directors** is elected into office, but through a maximum of 500 shareholders and not the organization as a whole. Because of the structural changes in 2000, the **Governing Body** is now separate from this board, hence no longer subject to any election.

Since **assemblies** and **conventions** do not decide matters of policy, no votes are taken at such events. However, a **congregation** may take a show of hands to decide minor domestic affairs, like the timing of a meeting.

– W –

WAR. C. T. Russell stated that war could be a necessary evil, but **J. F. Rutherford** led the organization to a firm antiwar stance, which was expressed in his completion of Russell's *The Finished Mystery* (1917). From that time onward, **Jehovah's Witnesses** have consistently refused to participate in military conflict and other activities associated with war, like the manufacture of armaments or serving in the army medical corps. The Witnesses' stance on war has led to unpopularity, persecution, and imprisonment of members. Rutherford declared his neutrality in matters relating to war, and Witnesses hold that earthly wars are fought for political and material gain and thus are contrary to **Jehovah**'s purposes for humankind.

Witnesses acknowledge that wars were fought by the Israelites and recorded in the **Hebrew-Aramaic Scriptures** with approval. Such military conflicts are believed to be legitimate on the grounds that they were commanded by Jehovah, for the furtherance of his theocratic rule. Witnesses are therefore not strictly pacifist, although they deny that such a justification can be invoked now, hence they typically register as conscientious objectors during modern wars.

Witnesses deplore the stance of mainstream churches on war, including the "just war" theory and the involvement of **clergy** in military situations. They also disapprove of war toys and games, as well as violence on cinema and television, which sanction armed conflict. They claim to engage in spiritual warfare, representing God's law against "**sin**'s law." This conflict between God and **Satan** will culminate in the Battle of **Armageddon**, when Satan will be defeated and war finally abolished in the ensuing **paradise earth**. *See also* WORLD WAR I; WORLD WAR II.

WATCH TOWER BIBLE AND TRACT SOCIETY OF PENNSYL-VANIA, INC. Originally chartered in Pennsylvania in 1884 as **Zion's Watch Tower Tract Society**, it became legally registered under its present name in 1896, although the name was previously unofficially used. The society was initially set up for the distribution of tracts. Before 1896, it did not publish **Bibles** but rather provided information about various translations and sold the King James Version (KJV) at a subsidized price. In 1896, the society obtained the rights to publish Joseph B. Rotherham's 12th edition of the New Testament, and in 1901 it brought out its own edition of the *Holman Linear Bible*, with the society's own explanatory notes. In 1902, it acquired the rights to print the **Emphatic Diaglott** and in 1907 produced its own "Bible Students' Edition" of the KJV. The society continues to produce and distribute tracts, booklets, short books, and Bibles, and it is the primary legal institution representing the **Jehovah's Witnesses**.

WATCH TOWER BIBLE SCHOOL OF GILEAD. *See* GILEAD SCHOOL OF MINISTRY.

WATCH TOWER SOCIETY. The abbreviated name for the **Watch Tower Bible and Tract Society of Pennsylvania, Inc.**, which determines and coordinates the international affairs of **Jehovah's Wit-**

nesses. It has been described as "the legal instrument of the anointed **remnant**." The "Watchtower Society"—with "Watchtower" as a single word—is the abbreviated name for the totality of legally incorporated instruments worldwide, which comprises the Witnesses. These abbreviated names do not have legal status. *See also* ANOINTED CLASS.

WATCHTOWER. The principal magazine circulated by **Jehovah's Witnesses**. Its title relates to the Book of Isaiah: "I stand continually upon the watchtower in the daytime" (Isaiah 21:8). The name was not original to the **Bible** students: **George Storrs** had written *The Watch Tower: Or, Man in Death; and the Hope for a Future Life* (1850), and various other religious publications had already used the phrase. **C. T. Russell** devised the journal to proclaim **Christ**'s "**ransom sacrifice**" and draw attention to the end-times in which he believed humanity to be living.

First published in 1879, the magazine's original name was *Zion's Watch Tower and Herald of Christ's Presence*, and it ran to eight pages. In 1891, the size was doubled, and in 1892, it became a semi-monthly publication. In 1901, it was renamed *The Watch Tower and Herald of Christ's Presence* to emphasize Christ's heavenly rule. The magazine had previously been aimed at the "little flock," but from 1935 onward, **J. F. Rutherford** used it to target the **Jonadabs**, who had associated themselves with the organization. In 1939, the title was modified, becoming *The Watchtower: Announcing Jehovah's Kingdom* in attempt to underline the imminence of the coming end of the present system and place emphasis on the name **Jehovah**.

Translation of the *Watchtower* has been undertaken since 1883, when a sample copy was translated into Swedish for use as a tract. In 1886, translation into German began, and by 1916, the magazine was available in seven different languages. At the time of writing, it is translated into 161 different tongues and published twice monthly. Its current circulation is approximately 16.5 million copies. Production is carried out at the various **Watch Tower Society Bethels** throughout the world, and care is taken to ensure worldwide standardization, with minor adaptations to accommodate different cultural expectations. The *Watchtower* is read faithfully by Witnesses, and it forms the basis of the weekly Bible study meeting at **Kingdom Halls** and is distributed in the Witnesses' **house-to-house ministry**. Its function is to provide "spiritual food" for the faithful, disseminate the society's teachings, and interpret scripture. Its importance is second only to the Bible in proclaiming Jehovah's message.

WATCHTOWER BIBLE AND TRACT SOCIETY OF NEW YORK, INC. Formerly the **Peoples Pulpit Association**, the organization was formed when the **Watch Tower Society** moved to New York in 1909 and was subsequently renamed **The Watch Tower Bible and Tract Society, Inc.**, until 1956, when it assumed its present name. It is a nonprofit corporation of the Watch Tower Society. Based in Patterson, New York, it supervises the society's ministry work in the United States and undertakes the publishing of books, booklets, and pamphlets, together with the printing of the *Watchtower* and *Awake!* for distribution across the country. Its premises include a 13-story adapted factory warehouse with a nearby **Bethel**. Its charter defines its aims as being for "charitable, benevolent, scientific, historical, literary and religious purposes."

WATER BAPTISM. *See* BAPTISM.

WBBR. The code name of the radio station used by the **Watch Tower** organization from 1924 until 1957. **J. F. Rutherford** delivered his first radio broadcast on 26 February 1922 from California, and the following year work began on the construction of the Watch Tower Society's own station in Staten Island, New York. The first broadcast was given by Rutherford on 24 February 1924, entitled "Radio and Divine Prophecy." The Watch Tower's message was proclaimed over the air for two hours each evening and on Sunday afternoons. Rutherford was the principal speaker, and there was singing and musical accompaniment from the society's own orchestra. **Frederick W. Franz** sang some of the solos. Radio work expanded in the 1920s and early 1930s. In 1927, Rutherford was able to speak from Toronto, Canada, over a 53-station network. At its peak in 1933, the society was able to use 408 networked stations, reaching all six continents.

In 1957, WBBR was sold. During its period of use, the society regarded it as a powerful instrument, which was able to reach people of all nationalities as well as powerful political leaders. However, it was not sufficiently strong to reach all lands, and in the meantime membership in New York had grown from a single **congregation** in 1922 to 62 congregations in New York City alone, enabling more than 7,000 **publishers** and 322 **pioneers** to proclaim their message. Rutherford himself had found that the demands of radio broadcasting were restricting his ability to travel, and in his later years, he made use of recorded rather than live talks. While recognizing the power of broadcasting and other forms of mass communication, like the Internet, **Jehovah's Witnesses** continue to hold that house-to-house work is the authentically biblical way of proclaiming the **kingdom**, and they emphasize the value of personal contact in their publishing work.

WENDELL, JONAS (1815–1873). Born in Edenboro, Pennsylvania, Wendell was a Second **Adventist** preacher, having been a follower of **William Miller**. Disillusioned by the **Great Disappointment** of 1844, he recovered his **faith** through studying biblical chronology and applying it to his own times. Based on his interpretation of the books of Daniel and **Revelation**, he concluded that the present system would end in 1873. He preached in Ohio, Pennsylvania, Virginia, and New England and authored a booklet entitled *The Present Truth, or Meat in Due Season* (1870). **C. T. Russell** attended one of his talks in Allegheny, Pennsylvania, in 1870 and was inspired by his ideas.

WILMERSDORF DECLARATION. *See* DECLARATION OF FACTS.

WITHDRAWAL LETTERS. In 1900, the **Watch Tower Society** prepared standard letters on Watch Tower stationery, which new members were asked to sign and send to their former churches, resigning their membership. This practice lasted for some 30 years and was understandably unpopular with mainstream **clergy**.

WOMEN. The **Bible** teaches that man came into being before woman, who was created as a helper and complement. **Jehovah's Witnesses** accept Paul's teaching that men should have authority over women, with **Christ** having authority over men (1 Corinthians 11:13). The woman's role is to support her husband, respect him, look after household affairs, and raise their children in the **faith**. Witnesses regard this as an important role, for which they should be respected.

Women may not hold office in the **congregation**, since biblical teachings regarding office bearers are held to presuppose that they are male. However, they are expected to be present at congregational meetings, since the Bible records that women were present at Joshua's reading of the law (Joshua 8:35), ministered to **Jesus**, listened to his teaching, and were the first witnesses of the **resurrection**. They are expected to undertake **house-to-house ministry** and are eligible for **pioneer** work and **Bethel** service. They may be assigned roles in dramatizations at **assemblies** but may not directly address a congregation, except when no baptized male member is there to do so. Notwithstanding Paul's remarks on a woman's obligation to wear a head covering, women are not obliged to cover their head at meetings: Witnesses interpret Paul's requirement as applying exclusively to situations where women were prophesying or praying publicly. Women, as well as men, are included in the **144,000** members of the **anointed class**.

Witnesses do not subscribe to the ideals of the feminist movement, since it advocates an unbiblical role demarcation of the sexes. They suggest that it may contribute to societal problems, such as the break-up of families. However, they accept that women have been oppressed in some societies and at certain periods in human history and agree that women should not be treated as **sex** objects or used in sexist ways, for example, in pornography or prostitution. Witnesses hold that biblical gender demarcation leads to the fulfillment of God's word, and to peace and harmony. *See also* PRAYER; PROPHECY.

WOODWORTH, CLAYTON J. (1870?–1951). An early **Watch Tower** leader, he completed **C. T. Russell**'s posthumous *The Finished Mystery* (1917), together with **George H. Fisher**. Following the controversy the work aroused, he was imprisoned with **J. F. Rutherford** and others from 1918 to 1919. In 1919, Woodworth was appointed editor of the *Golden Age*, subsequently *Consolation*, in which he promoted his opposition to many ideas of the orthodox medical profession. In particular, the magazine opposed

vaccination and theories about germs, and highlighted presumed dangers relating to aluminum cooking utensils. Woodworth may well have been influential in the **Jehovah's Witnesses**' opposition to **blood** transfusion.

WORKS. The **Bible** teaches that **creation** is the result of God's work; hence work is commended by **Jehovah's Witnesses**. Although **salvation** is attained through **Jesus Christ**'s **ransom sacrifice**, it is not gained through **faith** alone, since true faith can only be demonstrated through the performance of proper works and the avoidance of improper ones. Witnesses point out that Jesus preaches the necessity of good works and that the Epistle of James asserts that works are a necessary corollary of faith. Although prescribed in the Bible, sacrificial offerings, purification rites, and circumcision are not requirements, since these belong to the old **covenant**.

Witnesses are expected to avoid sexual misconduct, **occult** practices, theft, **gambling**, lying, drunkenness, violence, unclean habits, and unnecessary risks. They should engage in family life, respecting the relationships between husband and wife, children and parents. **Animal** life and **blood** should also be respected. They should observe the law of the land, except where it conflicts with God's law. *See also* CAESAR'S RULE; DISFELLOWSHIPPING; SEX.

WORLD WAR I. This war, which began in August 1914, had a number of effects on **C. T. Russell**'s **Bible** students, who viewed it as partial fulfillment of biblical **prophecy**. The scale of the war caused the **Watch Tower Society** to view it as one of the signs of the end, heralding the Battle of **Armageddon**. Russell had previously stated that the autumn of 1914 would mark the end of the **Gentile times**, and the outbreak of war was seen as corroboration of this interpretation of the Bible.

Russell did not advocate complete opposition to **war**, arguing that although peace was desirable, war was sometimes a necessity. However, with regard to World War I, he recommended that Bible students take a neutral stance. They were urged to follow their **consciences** if drafted for military service but recommended to undertake hospital service or work in supplies departments rather than engage in direct combat. Any Bible students who found themselves in the firing lines were advised against shooting to kill.

Russell died during the war, and his successor, **J. F. Rutherford**, commissioned the publication of *The Finished Mystery* (1917) based on notes left by Russell. This volume, which appeared in 1917, proved enormously controversial on account of its more radical antiwar stance and opposition to patriotism, and it led to the arrest and imprisonment of Rutherford and other Watch Tower leaders.

Although the **League of Nations** was formed in 1919 to prevent war and settle controversies between nations, the Watch Tower Society condemned it and predicted its demise, claiming that it was the wild **beast** described in the Book of **Revelation**. Bible students and subsequent **Jehovah's Witnesses** have characteristically maintained that everlasting peace is unachievable through such political means and only through the establishment of God's theocratically ruled **kingdom**. *See also* THEOCRACY; WORLD WAR II.

WORLD WAR II. The outbreak of this war in 1939 confirmed the **Jehovah's Witnesses'** belief that the **League of Nations** could not effectively achieve peace. The Witnesses' position on **war** was more radical in 1939 than during **World War I**: Witnesses were urged to refuse conscription and to decline taking part in any activity that would assist the war effort on either side of the conflict, including offering medical assistance. The Witnesses' commitment to neutrality entailed the refusal to make such patriotic gestures as saluting national flags, or, in Germany, using the greeting, "Heil Hitler." Witnesses in several countries underwent imprisonment and in some cases execution for maintaining their stance. The **Watch Tower** organization deplores the complicity of mainstream Christianity in sanctioning war and does not regard the **United Nations** as providing a solution to human conflict, believing that lasting peace will only be achieved through God's theocratic rule.

The more widespread availability of **blood** transfusion during World War II caused Witnesses to define their stance on the practice, which was first stated in the *Watchtower* in 1944. *See also* FLAG SALUTE; THEOCRACY.

– Y –

YEARTEXT. A short verse from the **Bible** is selected annually by the **Watch Tower Society** for prominent display in **Kingdom Halls**, usually at the front or on a side wall, provided that it is practical to do so. This text serves as inspiration and encouragement to members and can be referred to, when appropriate, in talks. The design of the plaque is assigned to a member of the **congregation**.

– Z –

ZION'S WATCH TOWER TRACT SOCIETY. The precursor of the **Watch Tower Bible and Tract Society of Pennsylvania**, Zion's Watch Tower Tract Society was established on 16 February 1881, with **William H. Conley** as president and **C. T. Russell** as treasurer and secretary. Its headquarters were in Allegheny, Pennsylvania. The society was legally incorporated in 1884, with Russell as president, its aim being "the dissemination of **Bible** truths in various languages." Within the first four months, it distributed more than 1.2 million tracts and booklets. In 1896, the organization was renamed the Watch Tower Bible and Tract Society of Pennsylvania. Russell transferred by donating the assets of the Tower Publishing Company, which he owned, in 1898.

ZIONISM. A Jewish political movement in support of the return of the **Jews** to Palestine. The movement originated in the late 19th century in Europe, and its leader, Theodore Herzl, convened the first Zionist Congress in Basel, Switzerland, in 1895. **C. T. Russell** expressed sympathy for the Zionist cause as a political movement, while **J. F. Rutherford** expressed less politicized support, regarding the Balfour Declaration of 1917 and the subsequent return of the Jews as a fulfillment of biblical **prophecy**.

   Jehovah's Witnesses came to reappraise Russell's and Rutherford's positions, holding that God's will cannot be achieved through political means. While regarding affairs in the Middle East, particularly the **war** and violence that has entailed, as signs of the end-times, prophecies relating to the Jewish people and Jerusalem are now regarded as referring to the **remnant**—the **anointed class**—and the "New Jerusalem," which is **Jehovah**'s **kingdom** in heaven. *See also* POLITICS.

ZONE. One of 10 regions in the world defined in 1956 for the purpose of overseeing the development of the **Watch Tower Society**'s international work. Zone servants—now designated "zone **overseers**"—were drawn from qualified Brooklyn **Bethel** staff and experienced **branch** overseers. They were personally trained by **Nathan H. Knorr**.

Bibliography

CONTENTS

I. INTRODUCTION

There are literally thousands of publications about or by the Watch Tower organization, and any attempt at a comprehensive bibliography would be impossible. This bibliography includes the primary texts relating to the Watch Tower Bible and Tract Society, from its inception to the present. Devising a typology of the ensuing secondary sources has proved difficult. Such categories as "academic," "ex-member," and "critical" tend to overlap. Some former members have become academics, some academics are critical, and not all the "critical" literature necessarily presents negative evaluation of the Jehovah's Witnesses. Which authors can be counted as academics might also be disputed: whether one should count a member of the Christian denomination who has undertaken postgraduate study or a teacher in a Bible college as an academic are moot points, and academics do not always write as academically as one might hope, particularly when controversial religious organizations are involved.

While the reader may not always agree with the classification, an extended bibliography has to be organized in some manner. Identification of primary source material is relatively unproblematic. For the purpose of this dictionary, primary sources are those that are officially published by the Watch Tower organization. Since these are so numerous, it would use unnecessary space to list the publisher, and it should therefore be assumed, unless otherwise stated, that the publisher is the Watchtower Bible and Tract Society of New York, Inc. A further issue relates to the classification of the works of early leaders who subsequently left the society. A section on schism is included, containing both primary and secondary material. Some writers, like William J. Schnell, although quite hostile to the society, nonetheless provide valuable first hand testimony about life and conditions within the organization. Although these might be construed as primary sources, it is important to distinguish such testimony from the society's own material, hence a section has been created for accounts of former members.

In deciding what constitutes an "academic" piece of writing, this bibliography is compiled from the view that academic publications are characterized by their purpose and their genre. A piece of academic writing aspires to be objective, and to inform and explain, rather than to criticize or encourage apostasy. Again, some judgment has been exercised in this regard. M. James Penton, for example, is a disfellowshipped Jehovah's Witness, but he is unarguably an academic, and academic debate involves arguing one's case and taking controversial stances. Both of his books listed are solid, seek to inform, and are well argued, even if they are at times polemical; they are certainly vastly different from the countercult literature of the Protestant evangelicals. Although it is the policy of the Watch Tower organization not to divulge the identity of its own authors, there are a few Jehovah's Witnesses who have written independently, disclosing their identity. Some of these authors can be considered academic, most notably Rolf Furuli, who holds a university post, and Greg Stafford. The decision to list them as unofficial Jehovah's Witness authors rather than academic ones is no reflection on the quality of their work but is done to enable the reader to identify their distinctive stance. The genre of their writings certainly differs from that of Marley Cole, who was a journalist, although Cole's work is invaluable in a different way.

Countercult material is incorporated under the somewhat broader heading "Critiques of Jehovah's Witnesses." Although most of the material in this section gives a negative evaluation of the Watch Tower Bible and Tract Society, critiques are not necessarily unsupportive, and Helmut-Dieter Hartmann's *Jehovah's Witnesses: A Challenge* is one such exception. The section on critiques could have been expanded considerably. However, their content tends to be repetitious and frequently has little inherent merit; indeed, one colleague has described them as "hate mail." Jehovah's Witnesses will no doubt be disappointed to note their inclusion, but opposition is part of the phenomenon of emergent minority religious groups, and it therefore seems important to point the reader toward the areas of conflict between mainstream Christendom and the society. In selecting this material, the most frequently quoted and most accessible titles have been chosen. Further literature belonging to this genre can easily be located using Internet search engines.

The number of journal and newspaper articles on Jehovah's Witnesses is vast. A large amount of the literature in periodicals is medical, relating to blood. The section on journal articles below, of necessity, had to be selective. Only a sampling of the available material on blood has been included to allow a range of topics to be covered. Newspaper reports relating to Jehovah's Witnesses have been omitted; important topics of media interest can generally be accessed through Web links. Finally, the websites listed are, in the main, those that offer primary source material, some of which is difficult to obtain in traditional format, or sites that offer good hyperlinks to such material. Of the many websites that oppose Jehovah's Witnesses' teachings and practices, three of the most prominent and articulate are featured to illustrate some of the grounds of opposition to the society. Those who wish to further pursue this phenomenon can find more than a million sites using search engines, but most of them add little to understanding the organization.

II. PRIMARY SOURCES

A. Writings of C. T. Russell

The Atonement between God and Man. Vol. 5 of *Millennial Dawn* (later renamed *Studies in the Scriptures*), 1899.

The Battle of Armageddon. Vol. 4 of *Millennial Dawn* (later renamed *Studies in the Scriptures*), 1897.

"Christian Duty and the War." *The Watch Tower and Herald of Christ's Presence* XXXVI, no. 17 (September 1915): 5754–55.

The Divine Plan of the Ages. Vol. 1. of *Millennial Dawn* (later renamed *Studies in the Scriptures*), 1886.

The Finished Mystery. Vol. 7 of *Millennial Dawn* (later renamed *Studies in the Scriptures*), 1917. (Completed by Clayton J. Woodworth and George H. Fisher.)

The New Creation. Vol. 6 of *Millennial Dawn* (later renamed *Studies in the Scriptures*), 1904.

Object and Manner of Our Lord's Return. Rochester, N.Y.: Herald of the Morning, 1877.

Pastor Russell's Sermons, 1917.

Poems of Dawn, 1912.

Scenario of the Photo-Drama of Creation, 1914.

Tabernacle Shadows, 1911.

The Time Is at Hand. Vol. 2 of *Millennial Dawn* (later renamed *Studies in the Scriptures*), 1889.

Thy Kingdom Come. Vol. 3 of *Millennial Dawn* (later renamed *Studies in the Scriptures*), 1890.

B. Writings of J. F. Rutherford

1. Books

Can the Living Talk with the Dead? (Talking with the Dead), 1920.
Children, 1941.
Comfort for the Jews, 1925.
Creation, 1927.
Deliverance, 1926.
Enemies, 1937.

Government, 1928.
A Great Battle in the Ecclesiastical Heavens. New York: Self-published, 1915.
The Harp of God, 1921.
Jehovah, 1934.
Life, 1929.
Light, 2 vols., 1930.
Millions Now Living Will Never Die. Brooklyn, N.Y.: International Bible Students Association, 1920.
Preparation, 1933.
Preservation, 1932.
Prophecy, 1929.
Reconciliation, 1928.
Religion, 1940.
Riches, 1936.
Salvation, 1939.
Vindication (vol. 1), 1931.
Vindication (vols. 2 and 3), 1932.

2. Pamphlets

Advice for Kingdom Publishers, 1939.
Angels, 1934.
Armageddon, 1937.
Beyond the Grave, 1934.
Care, 1937.
Cause of Death, 1932.
Choosing, Riches or Ruin?, 1935.
Comfort All That Mourn, 1940.
Comfort for the People, 1925.
Conspiracy against Democracy, 1940.
Crimes and Calamities, the Cause, the Remedy, 1930.
The Crisis, 1933.
A Desirable Government, 1924.
Dividing the People, 1933.
End of Nazism, 1940.
Escape to the Kingdom, 1933.
Face the Facts, 1938.
Fascism or Freedom, 1939.
Favored People, 1934.
The Final War, 1932.
Freedom for the Peoples, 1927.

God and the State, 1941.
Good News, 1932.
Government and Peace, 1939.
Government: Hiding the Truth, Why?, 1935.
Health and Life, 1932.
Heaven and Purgatory, 1931.
Hell, 1924.
Hereafter, 1932.
His Vengeance, 1934.
His Works, 1934.
Home and Happiness, 1932.
Intolerance, 1933.
Jehovah's Servants Defended, 1941.
Judge Rutherford Uncovers Fifth Column, 1940.
Judgment, 1929.
Keys of Heaven, 1932.
The Kingdom, the Hope of the World, 1931.
The Last Days, 1928.
Liberty, 1932.
Liberty to Preach, 1939.
Loyalty, 1935.
Model Study No. 1, 1937.
Model Study No. 2, 1939.
Model Study No. 3, 1941.
Neutrality, 1939.
Oppression, When Will It End?, 1929.
Our Lord's Return, 1925.
The Peoples' Friend, 1928.
Prohibition and the League of Nations, 1930.
Prosperity Sure, 1928.
Protection, 1936.
Questions on Deliverance, 1927.
Refugees, 1940.
Restoration, 1927.
Righteous Ruler, 1934.
Safety, 1937.
Satisfied, 1940.
The Standard for the People, 1926.
Supremacy, 1934.
Theocracy, 1941.
Truth: Shall It Be Suppressed?, 1934.

Uncovered, 1937.
Universal War Near, 1935.
War or Peace, Which?, 1930.
Warning, 1938.
What Is Truth?, 1932.
What You Need, 1932.
Where Are the Dead?, 1927.
Who Is God?, 1932.
Who Shall Rule the World?, 1935.
Why Pray for Prosperity?, 1934.
World Distress: Why? The Remedy, 1923.
World Recovery, 1934.

C. Watch Tower Publications after Rutherford

All post-Rutherford publications are anonymous.

1. Books

Aid to Bible Understanding, 1971.
"All Scripture Is Inspired of God and Beneficial," 1963.
"All Scripture Is Inspired of God and Beneficial," 1990.
"Babylon the Great Has Fallen!" God's Kingdom Rules!, 1963.
Benefit from Theocratic Ministry School Education, 2002.
The Bible—God's Word or Man's?, 1989.
Branch Office Procedure of the Watch Tower Bible and Tract Society of Pennsylvania, 1958.
Choosing the Best Way of Life, 1979.
"Come Be My Follower," 2007.
Commentary on the Letter of James, 1979.
Comprehensive Concordance of the New World Translation of the Holy Scriptures, 1973.
Did Man Get Here by Evolution or by Creation?, 1967.
Draw Close to Jehovah, 2002.
Equipped for Every Good Work, 1946.
From Paradise Lost to Paradise Regained, 1958.
God's "Eternal Purpose" Now Triumphing for Man's Good, 1974.
God's Kingdom of a Thousand Years Has Approached, 1973.
Good News to Make You Happy, 1976.
The Greatest Man Who Ever Lived, 1991.

Holy Spirit the Force Behind the Coming New Order!, 1976.
Insight on the Scriptures, 2 vols., 1988.
Is the Bible Really the Word of God?, 1969.
Is There a Creator Who Cares about You?, 1998.
Is This Life All There Is?, 1974.
Isaiah's Prophecy—Light for All Mankind, 2 vols., 2000, 2001.
Jehovah's Witnesses in the Divine Purpose, 1959.
Jehovah's Witnesses—Proclaimers of God's Kingdom, 1993.
"The Kingdom Is at Hand," 1944.
Kingdom Ministry School Course, 1960.
Knowledge That Leads to Everlasting Life, 1995.
Learn from the Great Teacher, 2003.
"Let God Be True," 1946, rev. 1952.
"Let Your Kingdom Come," 1981.
"Let Your Name Be Sanctified," 1961.
Life Everlasting in Freedom of the Sons of God, 1966.
Life—How Did It Get Here? By Evolution or by Creation?, 1985.
Listening to the Great Teacher, 1971.
Live with Jehovah's Day in Mind, 2006.
"Make Sure of All Things," 1953.
"Make Sure of All Things: Hold Fast to What Is Fine," 1965.
Making Your Family Life Happy, 1978.
Mankind's Search for God, 1990.
Man's Salvation out of World Distress at Hand, 1975.
My Book of Bible Stories, 1978.
My Book of Bible Stories, 2004.
"The Nations Shall Know That I Am Jehovah" How?, 1971.
"New Heavens and a New Earth," 1953.
The New World, 1942.
Organization for Kingdom-Preaching and Disciple-Making, 1972.
Organized to Accomplish Our Ministry, 1983.
Paradise Restored to Mankind by Theocracy!, 1972.
Pay Attention to Daniel's Prophecy, 1999.
Qualified to Be Ministers, 1955, rev. 1967.
Questions Young People Ask—Answers That Work, 1989.
Reasoning from the Scriptures, 1989.
Revelation—Its Grand Climax at Hand!, 1988.
The Secret of Family Happiness, 1996.
Survival into a New Earth, 1984.
"Then Is Finished the Mystery of God," 1969.
Theocratic Aid to Kingdom Publishers, 1945.

Theocratic Ministry School Guidebook, 1971.
Theocratic Ministry School Guidebook, 1992.
"Things in Which It Is Impossible for God to Lie," 1965.
"This Means Everlasting Life," 1950.
True Peace and Security—From What Source?, 1973.
True Peace and Security—How Can You Find It?, 1986.
"The Truth Shall Make You Free," 1943.
The Truth That Leads to Eternal Life, 1968.
United in Worship of the Only True God, 1983.
Watch Tower Publications Index, 1961–1965, 1966.
What Does the Bible Really Teach?, 2005.
"What Has Religion Done for Mankind?," 1951.
Worldwide Security under the "Prince of Peace," 1986.
Worship the Only True God, 2002.
You Can Live Forever in Paradise on Earth, 1982, 1989.
You May Survive Armageddon into God's New World, 1955.
"Your Will Be Done on Earth," 1958.
"Your Word Is a Lamp to My Foot," 1967.
Your Youth—Getting the Best Out of It, 1976.

2. Brochures

After Armageddon—God's New World, 1953.
Basis for Belief in a New World, 1953.
"Be Glad Ye Nations," 1946.
Blood, Medicine, and the Law of God, 1961.
A Book for All People, 1997.
Can You Live Forever in Happiness on Earth?, 1950.
Centennial of the Watch Tower Bible and Tract Society of Pennsylvania, 1984.
Children Study Questions, 1942.
Christendom or Christianity—Which One Is "the Light of the World"?, 1955.
The Coming World Regeneration, 1944.
The "Commander to the Peoples," 1945.
Counsel on Theocratic Organization for Jehovah's Witnesses, 1949.
Counsel to Watch Tower Missionaries, 1954.
Course in Theocratic Ministry, 1943.
Defending and Legally Establishing the Good News, 1950.
The Divine Name That Will Endure Forever, 1984.
Divine Rulership—The Only Hope of All Mankind, 1974.
Does God Really Care about Us?, 2001.
Dwelling Together in Unity, 1952.

Enjoy Life on Earth Forever!, 1982.
Evolution versus the New World, 1950.
Fighting for Liberty on the Home Front, 1943.
Freedom in the New World, 1943.
Freedom of Worship, 1943.
God's Kingdom Rules—Is the World's End Near?, 1958.
God's Way Is Love, 1952.
The Government That Will Bring Paradise, 1993.
The Guidance of God—Our Way to Paradise, 1999.
Healing of the Nations Has Drawn Near, 1957.
Hope, 1942.
How Can Blood Save Your Life?, 1990.
Is There a God Who Cares?, 1975.
Jehovah's Witnesses and Education, 2002.
Jehovah's Witnesses and the Question of Blood, 1977.
Jehovah's Witnesses in the Twentieth Century, 1978, rev. 1989.
Jehovah's Witnesses—Unitedly Doing God's Will Worldwide, 1986.
Jehovah's Witnesses—Who Are They? What Do They Believe?, 2000.
The Joy of All the People, 1947.
Keep on the Watch!, 2004.
"The Kingdom Is at Hand" Study Questions, 1944.
"The Kingdom of God Is Nigh," 1944.
Lasting Peace and Happiness—How to Find Them, 1996.
Living in Hope of a Righteous New World, 1963.
"Look! I Am Making All Things New," 1959.
"Look! I Am Making All Things New," 1986.
Man's Rule about to Give Way to God's Rule, 1968.
The Meek Inherit the Earth, 1945.
"The New World" Study Questions, 1942.
One World, One Government, 1944.
Organization Instructions, 1942.
Our Problems—Who Will Help Us Solve Them?, 1990.
"Peace among Men of Good Will" or Armageddon—Which?, 1964.
Peace—Can It Last?, 1942.
The Permanent Governor of All Nations, 1948.
Preach the Word, 1953.
Preaching and Teaching in Peace and Unity, 1960.
Preaching Together in Unity, 1955.
The Prince of Peace, 1946.
Religion Reaps the Whirlwind, 1944.
Report on "Everlasting Good News" Assembly of Jehovah's Witnesses, 1963.

Rescuing a Great Crowd of Mankind out of Armageddon, 1967.
The Road to Everlasting Life—Have You Found It?, 2002.
A Satisfying Life—How to Attain It, 2001.
School and Jehovah's Witnesses, 1983.
A Secure Future—How You Can Find It, 1975.
Security during "War of the Great Day of God the Almighty," 1960.
"See the Good Land," 2003.
Sermon Outlines, 1961.
Should You Believe in the Trinity?, 1989.
Spirits of the Dead—Can They Help You or Harm You? Do They Really Exist?, 2005.
Take Courage—God's Kingdom Is at Hand!, 1962.
There Is Much More to Life, 1975.
"This Good News of the Kingdom," 1954.
"This Good News of the Kingdom," 1965.
Topics for Discussion, 1977.
"The Truth Shall Make You Free" Study Questions, 1943.
Unseen Spirits, 1978.
Watch Tower Publications Index, 1961.
What Do the Scriptures Say about "Survival after Death"?, 1955.
What Does God Require of Us?, 1996.
What Happens to Us When We Die?, 1998.
What Has God's Kingdom Been Doing since 1914?, 1965.
What Is the Purpose of Life? How Can You Find It?, 1993.
When All Nations Collide, Head on with God, 1971.
When All Nations Unite under God's Kingdom, 1961.
When God Is King over All the Earth, 1963.
When God Speaks Peace to All Nations, 1959.
When Someone You Love Dies, 2005.
Why Should We Worship God in Love and Truth?, 1993.
Will Religion Meet the World Crisis?, 1951.
Will There Ever Be a World without War?, 1992.
"The Word"—Who Is He? According to John, 1962.
World Conquest Soon—By God's Kingdom, 1955.
"World Government on the Shoulder of the Prince of Peace," 1965.
You Can Be God's Friend!, 2000.

D. Periodicals

Awake!, 1946– .
Consolation, 1937–1946.

Golden Age, 1919–1937.
Daily Heavenly Manna and Birthday Record. Brooklyn, N.Y.: International Bible Students Association (annual, 1907–1925).
The Watch Tower and Herald of Christ's Presence, 1907–1939.
The Watchtower and Herald of Christ's Kingdom, January–February, 1939.
The Watchtower Announcing Jehovah's Kingdom, 1939–.
Yearbook of Jehovah's Witnesses, 1927– .
Zion's Watch Tower and Herald of Christ's Presence, 1879–1906.

E. Song Books

Hymns of the Millennial Dawn, 1905.
Kingdom Hymns, 1925.
Kingdom Service Songbook, 1944.
Poems and Hymns of Millennial Dawn, 1890.
Sing Praises to Jehovah, 1984.
"Singing and Accompanying Yourselves with Music in Your Hearts," 1966.
Songs of the Bride, 1879.
Songs of Praise to Jehovah, 1928.
Songs to Jehovah's Praise, 1950.
Zion's Glad Songs, 1900.

F. Bibles

New World Bible Translation Committee. *New World Translation of the Holy Scriptures.* Brooklyn, N.Y.: Watch Tower Bible and Tract Society of Pennsylvania, 1961.
Wilson, Benjamin. *The Emphatic Diaglott: Containing the Greek Text of What is Commonly Styled the New Testament.* New York: Fowler & Wells, 1942.

III. WORKS BY EARLY ADVENTIST WRITERS AND EARLY INFLUENCES ON WATCH TOWER TEACHINGS

Edgar, John. *The Preservation of Identity in the Resurrection.* Glasgow, Scotland: Morton Edgar, 1918.
———. *Socialism and the Bible.* Glasgow, Scotland: Morton Edgar, 1918.
———. *A Tree Planted by the Rivers of Water.* Glasgow, Scotland: Morton Edgar, 1918.
———. *Where Are the Dead?* Glasgow, Scotland: Morton Edgar, 1918.

Edgar, John, and Morton Edgar. *Great Pyramid Passages.* 2 vols. Glasgow, Scotland: Morton Edgar, 1912.

Edgar, Morton. *The Great Pyramid and the Bible.* Glasgow, Scotland: Morton Edgar, 1918.

Redeker, Charles F. *Pastor C. T. Russell: Messenger of Millennial Hope.* 1918. Reprint, Pacific Palisades, Calif.: Pastoral Bible Institute, 2006.

Storrs, George. *An Inquiry: Are the Souls of the Wicked Immortal? In Six Sermons.* Philadelphia, Pa.: Self-published, 1847.

———. *An Inquiry: Are the Souls of the Wicked Immortal? In Three Letters.* Montpelier, Vt.: printed privately 1841.

———. *A Vindication of the Government of God over the Children of Men: Or "The Promise and Oath of God to Abraham."* New York: Self-published, 1871.

———. *The Wicked Dead: Or Statements, Explanations, Queries Answered, and Exposition of Texts Relating to the Destiny of Wicked Men.* New York: The Herald of Life, 1870.

IV. WRITINGS BY JEHOVAH'S WITNESSES (UNOFFICIAL)

Blackwell, Victor V. *O'er the Ramparts They Watched.* Aurora, Mo.: Stoops Publishing, 1976.

Byatt, Anthony. *Building a Theocratic Library.* Malvern, England: Golden Age Books, 1997.

———. *New Testament Metaphors.* Edinburgh, Scotland: Pentland Press, 1995.

Byatt, Anthony, and Hal Flemings. *"Your Word Is Truth": Essays in Celebration of the 50th Anniversary of the New World Translation of the Holy Scriptures, 1950, 1953.* Malvern, England: Golden Age Books, 2004.

Cole, Marley. *The Harvest of Our Lives.* Aurora, Mo.: Stoops Publishing, 1966.

———. *Jehovah's Witnesses: The Global Kingdom.* 1955. Reprint, Aurora, Mo.: Stoops Publishing, 1985.

———. *Living Destiny: The Man from MatthewMarkLukeJohn.* Aurora, Mo.: Stoops Publishing, 1984.

———. *Triumphant Kingdom.* New York: Criterion Books, 1957.

Furuli, Rolf. *Persian Chronology and the Length of the Babylonian Exile of the Jews.* Oslo, Norway: R. Furuli, 2003.

———. *The Role of Theology and Bias in Bible Translation: With a Special Look at the New World Translation of Jehovah's Witnesses.* Huntington Beach, Calif.: Elihu Books, 1999.

Henschel, Milton G. "Who Are Jehovah's Witnesses?" In *Religion in America*, edited by Leo Rosten. New York: Simon & Schuster, 1963, 96–102.

Leather, Albert E. *Seeking First the Kingdom.* San Diego, Calif.: Simon & Northrop, 2001.

Liebster, Simone, and Jolene Chu. "Jehovah's Witnesses: A Case of Spiritual Resistance" (unpublished manuscript, 1998).

Knorr, Nathan H. "Jehovah's Witnesses of Modern Times." In *Religion in the Twentieth Century*, edited by Virgilius Ferm. New York: Philosophical Library, 1948, 381.

Macmillan, A. H. *Faith on the March.* Englewood Cliffs: Prentice Hall, 1957.

Stafford, Greg. *Jehovah's Witnesses Defended: An Answer to Scholars and Critics.* 2nd ed. Huntington Beach, Calif.: Elihu Books, 2000.

———. *Three Dissertations on the Teachings of Jehovah's Witnesses.* Huntington Beach, Calif.: Elihu Books, 2002.

Woodward, Clayton J. *The Parable of the Penny.* Extracts from address to the IBSA's Convention, Boston, Massachusetts, 4 August 1917.

V. NON-WITNESS PUBLICATIONS RECOMMENDED BY WITNESSES

BeDuhn, J. D. *Truth in Translation: Accuracy and Bias in English Translations of the New Testament.* Lanham, Md.: University Press of America, 2003.

Gertoux, Gérard. *The Name of God Y.eH.oW.aH Which Is Pronounced as It Is Written I_Eh_oU_Ah.* Lanham, Md.: University Press of America, 2002.

Hislop, Alexander. *The Two Babylons: Romanism and Its Origins.* Edinburgh, Scotland: B. McCall Barbour, 1998. Originally published as *The Two Babylons: Papal Worship Revealed to Be the Worship of Nimrod and His Wife.* Edinburgh, Scotland: W. Whyte, 1858.

VI. SCHISM AND DISSENT WITHIN THE WATCH TOWER ORGANIZATION

Beverley, James A. *Crisis of Allegiance.* Burlington, Ontario: Welch Publishing, 1986.

Johnson, Paul S. L. *Another Harvest Siftings Reviewed.* Philadelphia, Pa.: Printed privately, 1918.

———. *Harvest Siftings Reviewed.* Brooklyn, N.Y.: Printed privately, 1917.

Magnani, Duane. *The Watch Tower under Oath: The Trial of Olin R. Moyle.* Clayton, Calif.: Witness, Inc., 1984.

Russell, Maria Frances. *This Gospel of the Kingdom.* Pittsburgh, Pa.: Printed privately, 1906. Available at http://www.heraldmag.org/olb/contents/bsllinks/ History.htm. Accessed 13 June 2007.

———. *The Twain One.* Pittsburgh, Pa.: Printed privately, 1906. Available at http://www.heraldmag.org/olb/contents/bsllinks/History.htm. Accessed 13 June 2007.

VII. SECONDARY SOURCES

A. Academic Studies

Beckford, J. A. *The Trumpet of Prophecy.* Oxford, U.K.: Blackwell, 1975.

Bergman, Jerry. *Jehovah's Witnesses and Kindred Groups: A Historical Compendium and Bibliography.* New York: Garland, 1985.

Burganger, Karl. *The Watch Tower Society and Absolute Chronology: A Critique.* Lethbridge, Canada: Christian Koinonia International, 1981.

Carr, F. W. *Jehovah's Witnesses: The African American Enigma.* Hawthorne, Calif.: Scholar Technology Institute of Research, 1993.

Crompton, R. *Counting the Days to Armageddon: The Jehovah's Witnesses and the Second Presence of Christ.* London: Lutterworth, 1996.

Czatt, Milton Stacey. *The International Bible Students: Jehovah's Witnesses.* Scottdale, Pa.: Mennonite Press, 1933.

Holden, Andrew. *Jehovah's Witnesses: Portrait of a Contemporary Religious Movement.* London: Routledge, 2002.

Horowitz, David. *Pastor Charles Taze Russell: An Early American Christian Zionist.* New York: Philosophical Library, 1986.

Penton, M. James. *Apocalypse Delayed: The Story of Jehovah's Witnesses.* Toronto: University of Toronto Press, 1985.

Peters, Shawn Francis. *Judging Jehovah's Witnesses: Religious Persecution and the Dawn of the Rights Revolution.* Lawrence: University Press of Kansas, 2000.

Pike, Royston. *Jehovah's Witnesses: Who They Are, What They Teach, What They Do.* London: Watts, 1954.

Reed, David A. *Jehovah's Witness Literature: A Critical Guide to Watchtower Publications.* Grand Rapids, Mich.: Baker Book House, 1993.

Rogerson, Alan. *Millions Now Living Will Never Die: A Study of Jehovah's Witnesses.* London: Constable, 1969.

Stroup, H. H. *The Jehovah's Witnesses.* New York: Columbia University Press, 1945.

Wills, Tony. *A People for His Name: A History of Jehovah's Witnesses and an Evaluation.* Morrisville, N.C.: Lulu Enterprises, 2006. Originally published under the pseudonym Timothy White. New York: Vantage Press, 1967.

B. Jehovah's Witnesses and the Holocaust

Buber-Neumann, Margarete. *Under Two Dictators.* New York: Dodd, Mead, 1950.

Hackett, David. *The Buchenwald Report.* Boulder, Colo.: Westminster Press, 1995.

Hesse, Hans, ed. *Persecution and Resistance of Jehovah's Witnesses during the Nazi Regime, 1933–1945.* Bremen, Germany: Edition Temmen, 2001.

Hoess, Rudolf. *Commandant of Auschwitz: The Autobiography of Rudolf Hoess.* Cleveland, Ohio: The World Publishing Company, 1959.

King, Christine E. *The Nazi State and the New Religions: Five Case Studies in Non-Conformity.* New York and Toronto: Edwin Mellen Press, 1982.

Kogon, Eugen. *Theory and Practice of Hell: The German Concentration Camps and the System behind Them.* London: Secker & Warburg, 1950.

Liebster, Max. *Crucible of Terror: A Story of Survival through the Nazi Storm.* New Orleans, La.: Grammaton Press, 2003.

Liebster, Simone A. *Facing the Lion: Memoirs of a Young Girl in Nazi Europe.* New Orleans, La.: Grammaton Press, 2000.

Pellechia, James H. *The Spirit and the Sword: Jehovah's Witnesses Expose the Third Reich.* (Slide lecture presented at the United States Holocaust Memorial Museum, Washington, D.C., 29 September 1994). Brooklyn, N.Y.: Watch Tower Bible and Tract Society of Pennsylvania, 1997.

Penton, M. James. *Jehovah's Witnesses and the Third Reich: Sectarian Politics under Persecution.* Toronto: University of Toronto Press, 2004.

Reynaud, Michel, and Sylvie Graffard. *The Jehovah's Witnesses and the Nazis: Persecution, Deportation, and Murder, 1933–1945.* New York: Cooper Square Press, 2001.

C. Accounts by Ex-Witnesses (Wholly or Partly Autobiographical)

Franz, Raymond. *Crisis of Conscience: The Struggle between Loyalty to God and Loyalty to One's Religion.* 3rd ed. Atlanta, Ga.: Commentary Press, 2000.

———. *In Search of Christian Freedom.* Atlanta, Ga.: Commentary Press, 1999.

Gruss, Edmond Charles, ed. *We Left Jehovah's Witnesses—A Non-Prophet Organization.* Phillipsburg, N.J.: Presbyterian and Reformed Publishing, 1974.

Harrison, Barbara Grizzuti. *Visions of Glory: A History and a Memory of Jehovah's Witnesses.* 1978. Repint, London: Robert Hale, 1980.

Schnell, William J. *Christians: Awake!* Grand Rapids, Mich.: Baker Book House, 1956.

———. *Into the Light of Christianity.* Grand Rapids, Mich.: Baker Book House, 1959.

———. *Thirty Years a Watch Tower Slave: The Confessions of a Converted Jehovah's Witness.* Grand Rapids, Mich.: Baker Book House, 1959.

Stevenson, W. C. *The Inside Story of Jehovah's Witnesses.* New York: Hart, 1967.

Wilson, Diane. *Awakening of a Jehovah's Witness: Escape from the Watchtower Society.* Amherst, N.Y.: Prometheus Books, 2002.

D. General Books on New Religions, Including Jehovah's Witnesses, and Book Chapters

Barrett, D. V. *The New Believers.* London: Continuum, 2000.

Beckford, James A. "The Embryonic Stage of a Religious Sect's Development: The Jehovah's Witnesses." In *A Sociological Yearbook of Religion in Britain,* vol. 5, edited by Michael Hill. London: SCM Press, 1972, 11–32.

———. "Two Contrasting Types of Sectarian Organization." In *Sectarianism,* edited by Roy Wallis. New York: John Wiley & Sons, 1975, 70–85.

Bergman, Jerry. "The Adventist and Jehovah's Witness Branch of Protestantism." In *America's Alternative Religions,* edited by Timothy Miller. Albany: State University of New York Press, 1995, 33–46.

Chryssides, George D. *Exploring New Religions.* London: Cassell, 1999.

———. *Historical Dictionary of New Religious Movements.* Lanham, Md.: Scarecrow Press, 2001.

Cooper, Lee R. "'Publish' or Perish: Negro Jehovah's Witnesses Adaptation in the Ghetto." In *Religious Movements in Contemporary America,* edited by Irving I. Zeretsky and Mark P. Leone. Princeton, N.J.: Princeton University Press, 1974, 700–21.

Festinger, Leon, Henry W. Riecken, and Stanley Schachter. *When Prophecy Fails.* Minneapolis: University of Minnesota Press, 1956.

Weddle, David L. "Jehovah's Witnesses." In *Introduction to New and Alternative Religions in America,* vol. 2, edited by Eugene V. Gallagher and W. Michael Ashcraft. Westport, Conn.: Greenwood Press, 2006, 62–88.

E. Journal Articles

Barclay, William. "An Ancient Heresy in Modern Dress." *Expository Times* 65 (October 1953): 31–32.

Beckford, James A. "The Watchtower Movement Worldwide." *Social Compass* 24 (1977): 5–31.

Bergman, Jerry. "The Jehovah's Witnesses' Experience in the Nazi Concentration Camps: A History of Their Conflicts with the Nazi State, Germany." *Journal of Church and State* 38, no. 1 (Winter 1996): 87–113.

Côté, Pauline, and James T. Richardson. "Disciplined Litigation, Vigilant Litigation, and Deformation: Dramatic Organization Change in Jehovah's Witnesses." *The Journal for the Scientific Study of Religion* 40, no. 1 (March 2001): 11–25.

Henderson, Jennifer Jacobs. "The Jehovah's Witnesses and Their Plan to Expand First Amendment Freedoms." *Journal of Church and State* 46, no. 4 (Autumn 2004): 811–32.

Holden, Andrew. "Witnessing the Future?" *Sociology* 36, no. 1 (February 2002): 28–31.

Lawson, Ronald. "Sect-State Relations: Accounting for the Differing Trajectories of Seventh-day Adventists and Jehovah's Witnesses." *Sociology of Religion* 56, no. 4 (Winter 1995): 351–76.

Malyon, David. "Transfusion-Free Treatment of Jehovah's Witnesses: Respecting the Autonomous Patient's Rights." *Journal of Medical Ethics* 24, no. 5 (October 1998): 302.

Metzger, Bruce M. "The Jehovah's Witnesses and Jesus Christ: A Biblical and Theological Appraisal." *Theology Today* 10 (9 April 1953): 65–85.

Montague, Havor. "The Pessimistic Sect's Influence on the Mental Health of Its Members: The Case of Jehovah's Witnesses." *Social Compass* 24 (1977): 135–37.

Munters, Q. T. "Recruitment as a Vocation: The Case of Jehovah's Witnesses." *Sociologica Nearlandica* 7 (1971): 88–100.

Muramoto, Osamu. "Recent Developments in Medical Care of Jehovah's Witnesses." *The Western Journal of Medicine* 170, no. 5 (May 1999): 297.

Schmalz, Mathew N. "When Festinger Fails: Prophecy and the Watch Tower (Leon Festinger, Jehovah's Witnesses)." *Religion* 24, no. 4 (October 1994): 293–308.

Singelenberg, Richard. "'It Separated the Wheat from the Chaff': The '1975' Prophecy and Its Impact among Dutch Jehovah's Witnesses." *Sociological Analysis* 50, no. 1 (Spring 1989): 23–40.

———. "The Blood Transfusion Taboo of Jehovah's Witnesses: Origin, Development, and Function of a Controversial Doctrine." *Social Science and Medicine* 31, no. 4 (1990): 515–23.

Stark, Rodney, and Laurence R. Iannaccone. "Why the Jehovah's Witnesses Grow So Rapidly: A Theoretical Application." *Journal of Contemporary Religion* 12, no. 2 (May 1997): 133–58.

Swift, J. M. "Jehovah's Witnesses." *Expository Times* 55 (February 1944): 117–20.

Viele, M. K., and R. B. Weiskopf. "What Can We Learn about the Need for Transfusion from Patients Who Refuse Blood? The Experience with Jehovah's Witnesses." *Transfusion* 34, no. 5 (1994): 396–401.

Wah, Carolyn R. "An Introduction to Research and Analysis of Jehovah's Witnesses: A View from the Watchtower." *Review of Religious Research* 43, no. 2 (2001): 161–74.

———. "Jehovah's Witnesses and the Empire of the Sun: A Clash of Faith and Religion during World War II." *Journal of Church and State* 44, no. 1 (Winter 2002): 45–72.

———. "Jehovah's Witnesses and the Responsibility of Religious Freedom: The European Experience." *Journal of Church and State* 43, no. 3 (Summer 2001): 579–604.

Woolley, S. "Children of Jehovah's Witnesses and Adolescent Jehovah's Witnesses: What Are Their Rights?" *Archives of Disease in Childhood* 90, no. 7 (July 2005): 715–19.

Zygmunt, Joseph. F. "Prophetic Failure and Chiliastic Identity: The Case of Jehovah's Witnesses." *The American Journal of Sociology* 75, no. 6 (May 1970): 926–48.

F. Critiques of Jehovah's Witnesses

Ankerberg, John, and John Weldon. *Fast Facts on Jehovah's Witnesses: Answers to the 20 Most Frequently Asked Questions about the Watchtower Society.* Chattanooga, Tenn.: Ankerberg Theological Research Institute, 1988.

Berry, Harold J. *Jehovah's Witnesses.* Lincoln, Nebr.: Back to the Bible, 1987.

Botting, Heather, and Botting, Gary. *The Orwellian World of Jehovah's Witnesses.* Toronto: University of Toronto Press, 1984.

Bowman, Robert M. *Understanding Jehovah's Witnesses: Why They Read the Bible the Way They Do.* Carlisle, England: OM Publishing, 1995.

Gruss, Edmond C. *Apostles of Denial.* Phillipsburg, N.J.: Presbyterian and Reformed Publishing, 1970.

———. *The Jehovah's Witnesses and Prophetic Speculation.* Phillipsburg, N.J.: Presbyterian and Reformed Publishing, 1972.

Harris, Doug. *Jehovah's Witnesses: Their Beliefs and Practices.* London: Gazelle, 1999.

Harris, Doug, and Bill Browning. *Awake! to the Watchtower.* Morden, London: Reachout Trust, 1993.

Hartmann, Helmut-Dieter. *Jehovah's Witnesses: A Challenge.* Melbeck, Germany: HDH Publications, 2001.

Hoekema, Anthony A. *The Four Major Cults: Christian Science, Jehovah's Witnesses, Mormonism, Seventh-Day Adventism.* Exeter, England: Paternoster, 1963.

———. *Jehovah's Witnesses.* Grand Rapids, Mich.: William B. Eerdmans, 1972.

Johnsson, Carl Olof. *The Gentile Times Reconsidered: Chronology and Christ's Return,* 3rd ed. Atlanta, Ga.: Commentary Press, 1998.

Magnani, Duane. *Bible Students? Do Jehovah's Witnesses Really Study the Bible? An Analysis.* Clayton, Calif.: Witness, Inc., 1983.

———. *Who Is the Faithful and Wise Servant? A Study of Authority over Jehovah's Witnesses.* Clayton, Calif.: Witness, Inc., 1979.

Martin, Walter R. *Jehovah's Witnesses.* Grand Rapids, Mich.: Zondervan Publishing House, 1957.

———. *The Kingdom of the Cults.* Minneapolis, Minn.: Bethany House, 1985.

Martin, Walter R., and Norman H. Klann. *Jehovah of the Watchtower.* Grand Rapids, Mich.: Zondervan, 1974.

Reed, David A. *Jehovah's Witnesses Answered Verse by Verse.* Grand Rapids, Mich.: Baker Book House, 1986.

Rhodes, Ron. *Reasoning from the Scriptures with the Jehovah's Witnesses.* Eugene, Ore.: Harvest House, 1993.

Roundhill, Jack. *Meeting Jehovah's Witnesses.* Guildford, England: Lutterworth, 1973.

Wijngaards, John N. M. *Jehovah's Witnesses.* London: Catholic Truth Society, 1998.

VIII. ELECTRONIC SOURCES

A. Videos and DVDs

The Bible—A Book of Fact and Prophecy, Volume I: Accurate History, Reliable Prophecy. 40 min. Watch Tower Bible and Tract Society of Pennsylvania, 1992. Videocassette.

The Bible—A Book of Fact and Prophecy, Volume II: Mankind's Oldest Modern Book. 40 min. Watch Tower Bible and Tract Society of Pennsylvania, 1993. Videocassette.

Engardio, Joel P., and Tom Shepard. *Knocking: The Untold Story of Jehovah's Witnessess.* 92 min. Harriman, New York, 2006. DVD.

Fear Not: Persecution and Resistance of Jehovah's Witnesses under the Nazi Regime. 64 min. Independent Television Service in association with PBS, Drei Linden Film, 1997. Videocassette.

Jehovah's Witnesses—The Organization Behind the Name. 55 min. Watch Tower Bible and Tract Society of Pennsylvania, 1990. Videocassette.

Jehovah's Witnesses: Organized to Share the Good News and *Our Whole Association of Brothers* (two discs). 30 & 44 mins. Watch Tower Bible and Tract Society of Pennsylvania, 2006. DVD.

The New World Society in Action. 76 min. Watch Tower Bible and Tract Society of Pennsylvania, 1954. Videocassette.

Purple Triangles. 25 min. Watch Tower Bible and Tract Society of Pennsylvania, 1991. Videocassette.

To the Ends of the Earth. Watch Tower Bible and Tract Society of Pennsylvania, 1995. Videocassette.

United by Divine Teaching. 54 min. Watch Tower Bible and Tract Society of Pennsylvania, 1994. Videocassette.

B. CD-ROMs

Kingdom News (1918–1946), Director (1935–1936), Informant (1936–1956). Research Applications International, 2006. CD-ROM.

The Pastor Russell Anthology. Research Applications International, 2003. CD-ROM.

Rutherford's Rainbow. Research Applications International, 1997. CD-ROM.

Selected Discourses by J. F. Rutherford. M. P. Technologies, 2000. CD-ROM.

The Story of the Photodrama of Creation. M. P. Technologies, 1999. CD-ROM.

The Watch Tower and Herald of Christ's Presence, 1920–1929. Research Applications International, 1996. CD-ROM.

The Watchtower and Herald of Christ's Presence, 1930–1939. Research Applications International, 1998. CD-ROM.

The Watchtower: Announcing Jehovah's Kingdom, 1940–1949. Research Applications International, 2002. CD-ROM.

Watchtower Library, 2006. Watchtower Bible and Tract Society, 2006. CD-ROM.

Yearbook, I.B.S.A. and Jehovah's Witnesses, 1927–1942. Research Applications International, 2003. CD-ROM.

Yearbook, I.B.S.A. and Jehovah's Witnesses, 1943–1959. Research Applications International, 2004. CD-ROM.

Zion's Watch Tower and Herald of Christ's Presence: Watchtower Reprints, 1879–1899. Research Applications International, 2000. CD-ROM.

Zion's Watch Tower and Herald of Christ's Presence: Watchtower Reprints, 1900–1909. Research Applications International, 2000. CD-ROM.

Zion's Watch Tower and Herald of Christ's Presence: Watchtower Reprints, 1910–1919. Research Applications International, 2001. CD-ROM.

C. Websites

1. Official Web Pages

Jehovah's Witnesses: Authorized Site of the Office of Public Information of Jehovah's Witnesses
www.jw-media.org

Watchtower: Official Website of Jehovah's Witnesses
www.watchtower.org

2. Unofficial Pages by Jehovah's Witnesses

Hyperglossary of American English Theocratese
http://www.tookyware.com/wordlists/e/eec/www/index.html

Jehovah's Witnesses: An On-line Community
http://e-jehovahs-witnesses.com

Jehovah's Witnesses United (scholarly, with useful hyperlinks)
http://www.jehovah.to

Stan Milosovic's Theocratic Library
http://www.theocraticlibrary.com

3. Archival Material

Bible Students' Library (includes original writings of Nelson Barbour, Alexander Hislop, J. H. Paton, C. T. Russell, Maria Russell, J. F. Rutherford, George Stetson, George Storrs, and Jonas Wendell).
http://www.heraldmag.org/olb/contents/bsllinks/history.htm

Bible Students On-Line: Bible Student History
http://www.biblestudents.net/history
http://www.biblestudents.net/history/light_after_darkness.htm

Bible Students On-Line: *Harvest Siftings*
http://www.biblestudents.net/history/harvest_siftings_1917.htm

Herald of Christ's Kingdom Index
http://www.heraldmag.org/archives/index1918.htm

Macmillan, A. H. *Faith on the March* (full text)
http://reactor-core.org/faith-on-the-march.html

Miller, William. *Evidence from Scripture and History of the Second Coming of Christ, About the Year 1843; Exhibited in a Course of Lectures*
http://www.earlysda.com/miller/evidence1.html

Russell, Charles Taze: Last Will and Testament
http://www.pastor-russell.com/legacy/will_doc.html

Storrs, George. "Six Sermons"
http://www.harvestherald.com/_scrips/toc_storrs.htm

Strictly Genteel Theocratic Library (writings of Russell and Rutherford; booklets and tracts)
http://www.strictlygenteel.co.uk

Zion's Watch Tower, 1879–1918
http://www.agsconsulting.com/htdbv5/links.htm

4. Schismatical Groups

Pastoral Bible Institute *Herald of Christ's Kingdom* (recent and archival material)
www.heraldmag.org/past.htm

Restoration Light Studies: Charles Taze Russell Resource Page
http://ctr.reslight.net

5. Secondary Source Material

Brief biographies of early Adventists
http://www.heraldmag.org/2006_history/06history_15.htm

Governing Body of Jehovah's Witnesses
http://www.freeminds.org/bethel/gov_body.htm
http://www.geocities.com/yedalianpages/Bible-Files/GB.pdf

Publications of the Watch Tower Bible and Tract Society
http://www.freeminds.org/sales/wtpubs.htm

Short History of the Watch Tower Organization
http://www.bible.ca/jw-history.htm

Wikipedia: Early Publications of Jehovah's Witnesses
http://en.wikipedia.org/wiki/Early_Publications_of_Jehovah's_Witnesses

6. Websites Critical of the Watch Tower Society

Associated Jehovah's Witnesses for Reform on Blood
www.ajwrb.org

e-Watchman
www.e-watchman.com

Free Minds, Inc.
http://www.exjws.net

Watchtower Information Service
www.watchtowerinformationservice.org

7. Related Sources

No Blood (blood management and avoidance)
www.noblood.org

About the Author

George D. Chryssides studied philosophy and religion at the University of Glasgow in Scotland and completed his doctorate at Oriel College in Oxford. He has taught philosophy and religious studies at several British universities and is head of religious studies at the University of Wolverhampton in England. He has acted as consultant on new religious movements to the United Reformed Church in England and served for several years as chair of the board for the Centre for the Study of New Religious Movements at Selly Oak Colleges in Birmingham, England.

Chryssides has studied new and minority religious movements extensively since the mid-1980s and has contributed to numerous academic journals and international conferences. His books include *The Path of Buddhism* (1988); *The Advent of Sun Myung Moon: The Origins, Beliefs, and Practices of the Unification Church* (1991); *The Elements of Unitarianism* (1998); *Exploring New Religions* (1999); *Historical Dictionary of New Religious Movements* (Scarecrow Press, 2001); *A Reader in New Religious Movements*, coedited with Margaret Z. Wilkins (2006); and *The Study of Religion: An Introduction to Key Ideas and Methods*, with Ron Geaves (2007).